Friends and Romans

Friends and Romans

On the Run in Wartime Italy

JOHN MILLER

ISIS
LARGE PRINT
Oxford

First published in Great Britain 1987
by
Fourth Estate Ltd

Published in Large Print 2006 by ISIS Publishing Ltd.,
7 Centremead, Osney Mead, Oxford OX2 0ES
by arrangement with
the Author's Estate

British Library Cataloguing in Publication Data
Miller, John, 1913–
    Friends and Romans: on the run in wartime Italy.
    – Large print ed. – (Isis reminiscence series)
    1. Miller, John, 1913– 2. World War,
    1939–1945 – Prisoners and prisons, Italian
    3. World War, 1939–1945 – Personal narratives,
    British 4. World War, 1939–1945 – Underground
    movements – Italy 5. Escapes – Italy – History
    6. Large type books
    I. Title
    940.5'47245'092

ISBN 0–7531–9342–6 (hb)
ISBN 0–7531–9343–4 (pb)

Printed and bound in Great Britain by
T. J. International Ltd., Padstow, Cornwall

Contents

To Florence, about 70 miles

N

GRAN SASSO

Pescara

CHIETI

NESPOLO

CARSOLI

AVEZZANO

SULMONA

Tiber

TIVOLI

ROME

ANZIO

CASSINO

Garigliano

CENTRAL ITALY

NAPLES

SCALE 0   10   20
        miles

PART ONE

Escape

A burst of gunfire echoed through the dust towards a distant line of rolling stock and echoed round the vaults of the station. It strangled the words on our lips as we stood chattering together on the platform and left in its wake a silence broken only by the clatter of boots on the railway line and the bellow of raucous German voices. I stepped forward from my place in the queue and stared into the dark recesses of the station from which the noise had come. But I could make out little in the dying light — only the silhouette of a German guard running across the track with his rifle at the ready.

I sensed a tremor of fear run down our ranks and the spittle in my mouth turned sour. I was one of six hundred prisoners of war assembled in the station of Sulmona, the old capital of the mountainous region of the Abruzzi in central Italy. We looked more like tramps than British officers, perhaps because each of us was dragging behind him a sack, made of blankets, in which we carried the possessions lovingly assembled during our captivity. Yet there was about us a regimented uniformity, both in the dejection of our bearing and in the shabbiness of the clothes which covered our lean bodies. Only the little eccentricities of dress — the bush shirt, the faded corduroys, the American flying jacket, the spotted scarf which had started life in Cairo — gave a clue to the personality of the owner.

Our voices were not silenced for long. An angry murmur rose from the far end of the platform and gathered momentum like the chords of an orchestral movement. The rumour passed from mouth to mouth along the length of the queue and reached the point where I was standing beside Michael Ardizzone, a tall lieutenant wearing the black beret of the Royal Tank Corps. Apparently three officers had made a dash across the lines towards the cover of a stationary carriage. The German guards had opened fire. Their shots had halted two men, hit and killed the third.

Confirmation came a few minutes later when two guards carried his corpse past us on a stretcher. They walked with a studied deliberation, as though determined to ensure that the implication of attempting escape should not be lost on us. The head and body of the corpse were covered with a blanket. Only the upraised feet were visible.

"The bloody bastards!" said Michael.

"Who was it?" I asked. "Any idea?"

"No — but a big man, judging by the size of his boots."

I could see that, like myself, Michael was feeling sick. I hoped that the incident would not weaken his resolve to escape, for I feared that my own would crumble without his moral support. We both knew that, if we were not to spend the rest of the war in Germany, we must make a break in the course of the journey on which we were now embarking. Under my battle-dress I was wearing civilian clothes which I had obtained from a friendly Italian guard in exchange for cigarettes and a packet of tea. Michael carried a crowbar secured inside his trouser leg. I tapped his thigh and it emitted a reassuring twang.

It was the last day of September, 1943. When, on the 8th September, the armistice with Italy had been announced to coincide with Allied landings on the southern coast, we had been prisoners of the Italians. We had thought our troubles were over. But the Germans had taken over our camp from their ex-Allies and moved us into the mountains to another camp at Sulmona. Now we were on the move again. And this time our destination was Germany.

All afternoon we had been kept standing on the sandy parade ground of Sulmona while our German guards, a detachment of tough young parachutists armed with grenades and machine-guns, had combed the barracks in search of the fifty or so officers who, as the Germans rightly guessed, had concealed themselves above the ceilings and under the floors of the wooden huts. The rest of us had sweated in the blazing sunshine, our eyes glued on the unconstrained spaces beyond the prison wire. We had watched the shadows creep up the grassy lower slopes of Mount Morrone, where the peasants still pastured their sheep in much the same way as they did when Ovid was a boy amongst them, till only the rocky summit glowed pink in the setting sun. And we had cursed the ill fortune which it seemed was to condemn us to Germany when our troops were only 150 miles away to the south.

When the German Commandant was satisfied that our numbers were complete, he had called the parade to attention and told us that we were going to Germany. He had warned us that his guards had orders to shoot to kill and stressed the futility of attempting to escape. This advice had been greeted with derisive cheers, though when these guards had loaded us into trucks and driven us through a brilliant sunset to the station, it had become increasingly evident that they were both ruthless and vigilant.

They had herded us on to the platform and made us hump our heavy baggage down its long length. By this time we were already physically exhausted and, from the point of view of our guards, psychologically ripe for the sight of a corpse on a stretcher.

"I wish to Christ they'd get a move on," said Michael. "Apart from everything else, I'm bloody cold."

The heat had gone out of the day with the setting sun. Dried sweat now stiffened our limbs.

"The sooner we get into the train, the sooner we'll get out."

We were trying to bolster our waning confidence. As though in answer to our wishes, a long line of cattle wagons drew towards us into the siding. We were near the head of the queue and able to count them as they rumbled past us.

"I made it nineteen," said Michael.

"That means about thirty a wagon."

"The LCC wouldn't approve."

"You mean the RSPCA."

We might be bullocks on the way to the slaughterhouse, I thought, as I climbed into one of the wagons. We crowded down on the floor astride our rolls of baggage. The guards slid fast the heavy door and bolted it with an iron bar.

There are occasions in life when time slips out of gear. A minute may seem an eternity, an hour may pass in the blink of an eye. I have never been able to decide for how long the train remained stationary in the siding at Sulmona. For three hours, perhaps? Or nearer five? Apart from Michael, my companions were unknown to me, and their anonymous voices, issuing from the intense darkness around me, gave to the passage of time the quality of a dream. I was amazed to learn from their conversations that many of them could still make-believe that the train would never get to Germany; that the German line of retreat had been cut; that the railways to the north had been bombed to smithereens. Without the barbs of Michael's wit to sustain me, I could have fallen for their wishful thinking.

A quick search of our surroundings told us all that we wished to know. High up on one side of the cattle truck were two horizontal ventilators, narrow, but large enough to allow passage of a man's body. They had been boarded over. Even so, we were sure that, as soon as the train started, we would be able to force them open with Michael's crowbar.

Meanwhile we could only try to rest and pray that the train would start before we had all suffocated. The atmosphere quickly became fetid, but we dared not touch the ventilators for fear of drawing them to the attention of the guards. They were making a show of force, stamping up and down the platform and shouting orders in their guttural voices. I wondered to what extent this was designed to intimidate us and how many would in reality board the train.

One by one my companions dropped off to sleep and I felt my resolve slipping out of me like grain from a torn sack. Was I really going to throw myself out of that ventilator into the night? The idea seemed faintly ludicrous. Perhaps the optimists were right and the train would never start. I would sleep for a little and see how the night developed.

A violent jolting of the truck shook me out of my torpor. The couplings clanked together, the wheels creaked into action. For perhaps ten minutes the train shunted up and down the platform. Then it steamed out of the station in the direction of Germany.

No sooner had the train gathered speed than I felt the pressure of Michael's hand upon my knee. He crawled towards me, manoeuvred himself upright and pulled the crowbar from his trousers. In a matter of moments we had forced down the flap from the ventilator above me, causing a rush of cold air to blow into our faces. To reach the second ventilator, we had to pick our way between heads and backsides. Their owners turned in their sleep and grumbled, all except a fair young man who sat up and announced that he meant to follow us into the night. We opened the second ventilator and made a practice climb up to it. We found that it was easy to swing oneself up on to a short bar immediately below the slit, though it would not be easy to hold one's footing there for any length of time. From a squatting position on the bar it appeared possible to bound through the ventilator in a sideways crouch.

An alternative method of exit, namely to lower oneself gently over the edge of the ventilator and hang momentarily on the outside of the truck, did not appeal to me, partly because I had a fear of being sucked under the train when I let go, but chiefly because I was afraid of being shot at. We had no idea how many guards there were on the train nor whether they were positioned to fire at us from observation cars or even from the roof.

We knew that the train was likely to take one of two routes, either north-west towards Florence or west towards Rome. If it was the latter we would be travelling in a direction parallel to rather than away from the Front. In this case there would be no hurry to jump. There would indeed be something to be said for waiting till we were well clear of the Sulmona area with its German garrison.

For perhaps an hour we went through bare, mountainous country, though it was only when the moonlight momentarily pierced the clouds that we could see much of the landscape. Every few minutes we climbed up on to our perches to scan the terrain and wait for the train to slacken its speed, perhaps on the rise of a hill. We planned to jump through our respective ventilators at the same time, preferably at a spot which offered both cover and a soft landing.

We must have been some forty miles from Sulmona when the train started to slow down as it passed through a tree-lined embankment. I was balanced precariously on the bar beneath my ventilator and saw that Michael was similarly poised on his. This is it, I said to myself. I eased my head and shoulders through the slit — and saw to my dismay the outlines of buildings ahead of us.

"Station coming up," I whispered, drawing back my head and swinging myself down on to the floor.

As I did so, Michael's body hurtled past my ventilator like a tumbling pheasant. Immediately I swung myself back on to my perch. But already the train had slowed to a crawl. A moment later it drew into a station.

I knew that there were many coaches behind us and I visualized Michael lying beside the rear of the train, an easy target for a German bullet. But no shots broke the silence, only the stamp of guards walking along the platform. I cursed my good eyesight which had warned me that we were approaching a station. The split second had cost me Michael's company and, possibly, his respect; for he might never realize why I had not jumped behind him.

As soon as we were on our way again, the fair young officer took up Michael's position. I wondered if other men were jumping from other coaches. Michael's success had made me desperate — with envy of his boldness and scorn for my own caution. I knew that if I did not follow his example my life would be unbearable. It was just a question of choosing the right moment in time and space. That moment came as we drew out of the next station. I let the train gather speed for as long as I dared. Then, facing the engine, I kicked myself through the narrow slit.

I landed on my hands and knees, close up against the train. I lay prone where I fell, my face pressed on the ground, listening to the rhythm of the wheels as they clanked and jangled beside my head and steeling myself for the sound of a shot. Suddenly the last coach had passed me by and I was no longer an escaping prisoner, a target for a German bullet. I was just a man lying, for no apparent reason, beside a railway line.

I picked myself up and looked around me. A dog was barking and I fancied I could see the outline of a building in the vague distance from where the sounds were coming. I turned the other way, crossed the line and began to climb up a steep embankment covered with vines. It was hard to see where I was going in the darkness and it took me some time to negotiate the vineyard and reach the top of the little hillock above and beyond it. Here I paused to listen and to get back my breath. I could hear nothing but the pounding of my own heart.

I became conscious, for the first time, that my left knee was aching. I massaged it with my hands and decided that the damage was nothing more serious than a bruise. But I noticed that both my hands were cut and bleeding. I wiped them on a tuft of grass and sucked at the pieces of grit, invisible in the darkness,

11

which were embedded in the palms. The realization that these minor cuts and bruises were the full extent of my injuries filled me with wonder.

I sat down on the top of the hillock and stared at the distant horizon. Had my eyes grown accustomed to the darkness, I wondered? Or was the sky indeed lightening above the rim of distant mountains? I could not be sure. I decided that in any case I would stay where I was until the dawn had revealed what lay in the valley beneath me. The fresh air, so cool and clean compared with the fug of the cattle truck, refreshed me. The grass beneath me was damp to my touch, but I did not mind. I was spellbound by the silence and emptiness of the night. In the crowded community of a PoW camp to be alone, even in the latrine, was an impossibility. I had to dig my nails into the earth to reassure myself that I was not dreaming.

I had given little thought to what I would do once I was free, perhaps because I had contemplated escape as an act of defiance rather than as a means to an end. Certainly I had never expected to find myself free and alone. I believed that the Allies would reach this part of Italy in a few weeks' time. I could either lie up and await their arrival or walk south to meet them. The latter scheme seemed the more enterprising.

In either case I was determined to base my plans on my conviction that I could expect to receive help from the Italian peasants. I lit a cigarette and settled down to await the break of dawn. Not for the first time, I reviewed in my mind the grounds for my belief that the ordinary Italian had welcomed the armistice, and that he resented the continued presence in his country of his German ex-Allies.

I had been a prisoner of war in *Campo di Concentramento* PG 21 for almost exactly a year when the news had broken, on 25th July, 1943, that the ageing King Victor Emmanuel II, supported by the majority of the Fascist Grand Council, had arrested Mussolini and appointed Field Marshal Pietro Badoglio as Prime Minister in his place. The camp was on the same latitude as Rome. It lay at the foot of a rounded hill on the crest of which stood the medieval town of Chieti, a few miles inland from the Adriatic sea. At this time we numbered about a thousand British and five hundred American officers. Most of the British amongst us had been captured in the Western Desert of Libya, at the fall of Tobruk in June, 1942.

We prisoners had not been altogether surprised by the overthrow of Mussolini, for our camp oracles had been detailing the rift between the Italians and the Germans ever since the last Axis soldier had been driven from Tunisia in mid-May. And we had certainly realized the significance of the King's action, which had summarily ended twenty-two years of Fascist dictatorship, because we had personally witnessed the resultant celebrations among both our guards and the citizens of Chieti.

That July evening some of us had shaken hands with those of our Italian guards who, despite the disapproval of their Commandant, an ardent Fascist, had been unable to contain their delight; and all of us had

13

watched the festive bonfires blaze on the hillside above the camp. Thereafter our Italian contacts made it clear that the King's move had been interpreted by the people as the prelude to an armistice. We learnt that hatred of Mussolini and his German allies was being openly expressed in cafés and factories, and in Italian barracks, aerodromes and naval bases both at home and abroad.

As the hot, dusty summer had run its course, the feeling that we were standing on the brink of momentous events had mounted daily. The completion of the capture of Sicily in mid-August had further strengthened Italian suspicions that the war was lost. And when, on 3rd September, spearheads of the Eighth Army had crossed the Straits of Messina, our guards had echoed our own surprise that no armistice had been declared. By this time most of the activities which we prisoners had devised as a substitute for normal living had been disrupted. Attendances at the classes and lectures, which had at one time given the camp the air of a university, had dwindled away. Debates and gramophone recitals had lost their appeal, cards and dice their compulsive hold. Only our theatre and softball games retained some of their magnetism. We spent our days dissecting the news bulletins compiled by our star journalist Michael Ardizzone from the Italian press and from broadcasts received on our secret radio; and we speculated endlessly as to whether our captors would move us to camps in north Italy before we had been set free by the long-anticipated arrival of peace.

I had had more opportunity than most PoWs at Chieti to assess the strength of anti-German feeling amongst the Italians. Throughout the summer, I had been acting as Camp Liaison Officer with the Italian canteen from which we were able to buy a few luxuries such as musical instruments, paints, dried figs and cake. This job had brought me into contact with an Italian officer and his corporal for about fifteen minutes at a time several days a week. I had obtained it only because all our fluent Italian speakers had been moved to a camp in the north, probably as a precaution against escape. I had never been to Italy before the war and, indeed, had seen it for the first time from the windows of the Savoia troop-carrier in which I had been flown from North Africa.

Apart from giving me the opportunity to practise the little Italian which I had learnt in the classrooms of Chieti, my contact with the Italian canteen had led me to think that the mass of the Italian people felt no hatred for the English and greatly preferred us to the Germans, their traditional enemies. This conviction was shared by most PoWs who were connected with the camp escape organization. Consequently, it had come as no surprise to hear many of our guards join in the storm of cheering with which, on the late afternoon of 8th September, we had greeted the long-awaited news of the signing of an armistice between Italy and the Allies.

On the next day we heard the details on Italian radio of the successful Allied landings on the coast near Salerno. We also listened to — and sometimes believed

15

— many wild rumours of Allied successes, such as a story that we had landed troops, both by sea and air, in more northerly parts of Italy. Most of us, including our Senior British Officer, had taken the view that the Germans would withdraw to a line far to the north of Chieti, and that our own troops would reach us in a matter of days; he had given orders that no one was to leave the camp and had encouraged us to live in a fool's paradise of premature celebration.

This point of view, defensible perhaps at the onset, had been discredited when most of our Italian guards, showing more enterprise than their charges, had decided to make their escape before the Germans entered the camp. Before so doing, many of them had advised us that we would be wise to follow their example. Unfortunately our SBO had chosen to ignore this advice, preferring to listen instead to the Camp Commandant, a wily and unscrupulous Fascist, who assured him that the Germans were on the run. So it had happened that, on the fifth day after the announcement of the armistice, we had woken to find the sentry boxes manned by German parachutists, the same men who had just rescued Mussolini from the ski-hut on the top of the nearby Gran Sasso mountain, where he had been imprisoned by King Victor Emmanuel.

These Germans promptly scooped us up from the Adriatic plain and drove us westwards, into the mountains of the Abruzzi, to a huge, hutted camp on the outskirts of Sulmona. Here we languished for a week, thinking of nothing but escape. Each day our hopes had risen that the Germans might be too preoccupied with the defensive battle which they were waging near Naples to be able to move us to Germany. But on the last day of September those slender hopes had been crushed by the order to parade with all our kit. Most of us then knew that only a miracle or our own initiative could save us from spending the rest of the war in a German *Oflag*.

By the time I had relived the three weeks which had passed since the armistice, the sun had crept up over the rim of mountains behind the bank on which I was sitting. I deduced, correctly, that these mountains were the high peaks of the Abruzzi. Below me to my left I could see the red roofs of a town, evidently the place where the train had halted. To my right the railway ran northwards along a valley. As the morning light flooded the eastern horizon, I could see that an escarpment sheered down to a distant plain across which, I guessed, lay the city of Rome. I spied out the lie of the land, and decided that the important thing was to move off the open hillside and withdraw into the cover of the forest, which rose up behind the hill on which I was sitting, into the high mountains. I must quickly put some distance between me and the town which, for all I knew, might contain a German garrison. Before nightfall I would put myself at the mercy of some peasant by asking for food and shelter.

But first I had one task to perform; again I blessed the Italian corporal at Chieti who had got me the rough blue slacks and grey flannel shirt which I was now wearing beneath my battle-dress. I took out the contents of my pockets — a little map which I had torn from a book at Chieti, a pocket dictionary, a handkerchief, cigarettes and matches — and transferred them into those of a waterproof jacket which I had concealed in my rucksack at Sulmona. Then I crawled into a patch of scrub and slid my battle-dress trousers down over the slacks. Feeling like a murderer disposing of the evidence of his crime, I stuffed my battle-dress into a hole and covered it with earth and rotting leaves. I went back to the open hillside, slipped on my waterproof jacket and took a last look at the railway line which stretched below me in the direction of Germany.

"I have buried the Army captain," I said to myself, and then, in Italian, "*È morto il capitano inglese.*" From now on, I decided, I must not only look and act like an Italian peasant, I must *be* an Italian peasant.

I walked up the hill towards the chestnut woods, into the rising sun.

PART TWO

A Mountain Village

CHAPTER
ONE

Sensations commonplace in ordinary circumstances, but invested with overwhelming novelty to someone who had been a PoW for fifteen months, filled me with delight as I climbed a fence and entered the woods. It took me some minutes to accustom myself to the idea that I was at liberty to move in any direction for as far as I wished. I was excited, too, by the discovery that I was now part of the landscape rather than a pair of eyes which looked at it from behind a prison wall. I had forgotten that nature was something to experience physically and not just visualize from memory or from the pages of a book.

Soon I was in the depths of the forest and climbing with each step as I followed the twists and turns of a mule path. The sun was creeping up in the sky and casting shadows through the branches of the huge trees, already heavy with ripening chestnuts. I realized that it was the first day of October, a happy augury, it seemed to me, for the start of my adventure. My walking warmed me and eased the stiffness in my cramped limbs. The tang of a light breeze blowing on my face, the spring of the turf beneath my feet and the smell of autumn leaves, all intoxicated me, making me forget where and why I was going, so that I would cross a stream for the pleasure of the jump and climb a stile for the feel of wood beneath my hand.

Nothing, save the hum of a lone aircraft circling high above the treetops, disturbed my solitude until I came across a woodcutter chopping logs beside his donkey on the side of the mule path. As I passed him, he straightened up from his labours and bade me good day, apparently noticing nothing strange in my appearance. I wished him *buon giorno* and continued on my way. The time had not yet come, I felt, to break the spell of the morning.

I must have covered several miles in this state of euphoria, for the sun had risen high in the sky when I at last emerged from the edge of the forest. A ravine stretched before me. Across it I could see a village perched on a hilltop level with my own height. The twin towers of the church beckoned me. Shall I go there? I deliberated, as I sat down on a bank and started to eat the bread which I had hidden in my rucksack. Lazily I gazed at a big white house in the centre of the village. A nice place to spend a honeymoon, I mused, shifting my eyes to a car parked alongside it. My God, it was a Volkswagen! Furthermore, two men in uniform were standing on the balcony of the house and one of them — or was it only in my imagination? — was staring at me through a pair of binoculars.

With what I hoped was an air of nonchalance, I got up and strolled back into the woods. Once under cover I quickened my pace and hurried along a small path which led uphill into thick forest. Soon I had lost my bearings, for the sun had vanished behind a bank of clouds and I was already deep in a tangle of thorn and scrub before I realized that the path had vanished. I was halfway up the side of a steep outcrop. Grasping the branches of stunted trees with my lacerated hands, I pulled myself up to the top, from where I could again see the twin towers of the village church. They were still uncomfortably close. I slithered down the other side into a ravine and, driven now by panic, crashed my way through the undergrowth and fell into the bed of a stream.

The stream led me to a small bridge, from which a rough road twisted up the hill in the general direction of the village. I sat at the side of the road and rested. I picked burrs off my trousers and scraped down my boots, which were caked with mud from the bed of the stream.

These little acts, reminiscent of everyday chores, composed me and made me realize that I was in danger of losing my head. I lit a cigarette and tried to weld my fractured thoughts into a coherent plan. The sight of the man with binoculars had sobered me up and made me conscious of my predicament. My knee was aching and I felt desperately tired. The time had come to seek the help of some friendly peasant.

I did not know that in this part of Italy the peasants live mostly in villages from which they walk each day to their work in the fields. Consequently I was surprised that during the morning I had seen no isolated farmhouses and was already regretting that I had not stopped to talk with the woodcutter. If I was to find someone to help me, there seemed no alternative but to follow the road beside which I was sitting. Fearing that downhill it would lead back to the railway, I decided to walk uphill, in the general direction of the village where I thought I had seen the Germans, hoping to find a track or side road leading off to the right towards the high mountains.

I had not been walking for more than five minutes when a German staff car swept round the corner towards me. My instinct urged me to dive into the cover of the scrub, yet I found myself walking on with no apparent concern. As the car passed me, I could see the steely eyes of a German officer as he sat with a map on his knee beside the driver. The presence of the enemy, at once so close and remote, gave me a pleasant twinge of excitement and a welcome boost to my confidence in my appearance. I blessed my Celtic ancestors for bequeathing me dark hair and features which could pass for Mediterranean.

A little further on I found what I was looking for: a cart road forking right, up into the high hills. "A Nespolo, 5 Chilometri", I read on a battered signpost. I liked the name, which as I chanced to know meant a medlar tree, and also the inference of the signpost that the village lay at the end of a cul-de-sac.

In the mountains of the Abruzzi the autumn storms gather quickly and break with a fury which transforms in a moment that sunny pastoral landscape which so delighted Ovid into a gaunt fortress dominated by rock and sky. As I walked up the road to Nespolo, the dark shadows of clouds raced up the valley towards me, until

I and the whole mountainside were engulfed in a false twilight. I was still some way from my destination when the storm broke on my shoulders with such force that I was wet to the skin before I could reach the cover of a twisted oak tree.

When the downpour had slackened, I continued up the zig-zag road, down which now ran two rivulets of muddy water. On rounding the next corner I came across two figures standing on the grass verge. They huddled beneath a tattered umbrella. At their feet was a large suitcase, its bursting sides roped together, and a plump sack which reminded me of an army kit-bag. The man was small and thin. The woman tubby. They had about them the misplaced air of chickens in a duck-pond.

As I approached them, the man shouted something to me which I interpreted as "Hey there!". I stopped beside them. The man wore a woollen jacket and grey trousers beneath the cuffs of which I could see the pointed toes of his shoes, the thin black shoes of a townsman. Traces of make-up showed through the rain running down the woman's face.

"*Buon giorno*," I said. "What ugly weather!"

"*Brutto tempo*," the man agreed.

He made some demand of me which I could not understand and which later transpired to be a suggestion that I should carry his baggage. I shrugged my shoulders and brought out an Italian sentence which I had carefully rehearsed and which I hoped would tell me whether his sympathies lay with the Allies or with the Germans.

"Are you *Badogliani* or *Fascisti?*"

"And you, who are you?"

At the time it surprised me that the tone of his voice should echo animosity, for it did not then cross my mind that he might think I was German. We stared at each other like sparring cats. I studied his pale, sad face and noticed that the eyes were kind and alert. I will tell him the truth, I thought. If he turns nasty, I can always run for it.

"I am a British officer, a prisoner of war. I escaped this morning from a train which was taking me to Germany."

"*Scappato!*" His voice mirrored the esteem in which most Italians hold the notion of escape, believing, rightly, that running away can represent the assertion of an individual's rights. "We, too, are fugitives, fugitives from Rome. So we are friends." He held out his hand.

"I am called Arturo Platano and this is my sister, Ida."

"And I am Giovanni, Giovanni Miller."

"*Bravo, Gianni!* Where are you going?"

"Towards the Front, I suppose, but I don't even know where I am!"

"You'd better come with us, then. We are on our way to Nespolo, to join my wife. She was born there."

I expressed my thanks as best I could.

"It's only a peasant's house which we have," he went on, injecting the word *contadino* with a townsman's scorn for the peasantry. "But you are welcome to stay there. Just think of it! An Englishman in Nespolo!"

I slung his sack over my shoulder and together we walked on up the road. Soon I could see above me the village perched on the top of a rocky spine which jutted from the wooded hillside.

"*Ecco Nespolo!*" said Arturo, as though proud of his discovery. "You see what a squalid village it is! Poor people, the Nespolini."

In my eyes the grey stone houses, clinging like barnacles to the rocky hill face, seemed beautiful in their architectural uniformity. A shaft of sunlight pierced the black clouds and lit up the façade of the church which crowned the village. It was protection, not beauty, which I then desired, though doubtless closer scrutiny would reveal the squalor. "To me it looks *bello*," I said.

"*Non è bello, è un brutto paese.*" He gave a wry smile which hinted that he and I were used to better things. "You will see, Gianni. The Nespolini live like their animals, they *are* animals."

There seemed to be no answer to this, certainly not in my limited Italian. We walked on in silence until we came upon an old peasant astride a donkey the colour of his master's whiskers. The man agreed to load the baggage on the back of his beast, behind which the four of us now walked, waving sticks and shouting words of encouragement.

As we entered the village, the tempo of the storm increased, driving all the Nespolini into the shelter of their dark houses. No curious eyes witnessed our arrival before the little wineshop which formed the focal point of a village too poor to have a proper *piazza*. Outside it we halted and unloaded the baggage.

"Come under my umbrella," said the woman, Ida, leading the way up a narrow, cobbled alley, down the steps of which streamed a cascade of rain, urine and dung. We halted before the third house on the left. Stone steps led up from the lane to a doorway above a manger, in the dark depths of which I could glimpse the outline of some goats.

"This is my country castle," joked Arturo. "Inside are my wife and family." He paused on the top step and turned to me. "*Sono tutte femmine*," he added, with a smile of masculine superiority. "But now that you have joined me, we will be two cocks among the hens."

As I stood on the threshold of Arturo's house, I did not realize that this door was for me the gateway to Italy. It is true that I had been in the country for fifteen months, but they were months lived in a limbo behind the wire and walls which had formed a curtain between me and the Italian people on the other side. Although an occasional glimpse through the curtain had encouraged me to believe that many of them preferred the English to their German ex-Allies, I was ignorant of both the delights and the irritations of the Italian way of life.

Arturo had already assumed that I had come to stay for some time and was inventing, with evident relish, an alibi suited to my person.

"Leave everything to me and don't talk more than is necessary," he counselled as he opened the door. "I shall tell my family that you are a Swiss clerk from the bank in which I work in Rome."

I followed him into the single room which formed the ground floor of the house, a long, dark room scantily furnished with a wooden table and chairs, a dresser and an improvised bed. Sticks crackled in the open fireplace, on the chimneypiece of which hung a medley of copper pots and pans. Bunches of onions and tomatoes and a long roll of salami were nailed on the opposite wall.

Three women rose to their feet. From the cries of surprise it was obvious that our arrival was unexpected; nor could I discern from their tears and laughter whether it heralded success or catastrophe. I stood awkwardly in a corner until the pandemonium had subsided. Then Arturo drew me forward and introduced me to everyone as a colleague from his bank. First to his mother, an old lady with hunched shoulders and a fine, aquiline face framed in a black shawl which gave her skin the texture and colour of scarred ivory. Then to Maria, his eldest sister, a tall brunette with dark, flashing eyes and the proud bearing of a self-confident woman of the land.

"And this is my wife, Rina," Arturo concluded, shoving forward a younger woman, a pretty blonde with high cheekbones and a surly mouth. She had a leggish, colty look, despite the baby which she carried in her arms. Another little girl, aged about four, clung to her skirt.

I mumbled a few words as the women drew us up to the fire and removed our sodden jackets. Arturo, I could see, was about thirty, my own age. He looked tired and sickly but his manner was cocky and his eyes were bright with humour. Divested of her coat, Ida revealed herself as a plump brown partridge. On the road she had rarely opened her mouth, making me wonder whether she was annoyed with Arturo for asking me to stay. Now, in the warmth of the fire, she began to relax, and I realized that her silence had been due to reasons other than unfriendliness.

She pulled off her shoes, revealing a large hole in the toe of one of her stockings.

"*Dio mio*! I'm tired and hungry," she said. "But you must be too. *Un po' di pazienza* and we will eat."

As Ida spoke, Maria dropped fistfuls of *pasta* into the cauldron of boiling water which swung above the roaring brushwood fire. Meanwhile, the old lady, *La Nonna* — the grandmother — had filled a jug with red wine from the demijohn which stood beside a heap of apples and potatoes in a corner of the room. I asked what time it was and was told to my surprise that it was only four o'clock; I had been on the road for more than ten hours.

When the *pasta* had cooked, Maria drained off the water and poured the contents into a large bowl to which she added olive oil and grated goat's cheese. She placed it beside the jug of wine on the long table. I sat down between Ida and Arturo. I was dazed by my good fortune and too exhausted to make any sense of the passionate discussion raging around me. In silence I wolfed down a heap of spaghetti and slaked my thirst with draughts of the rich rough wine. I could not understand for what reason Arturo was, like me, a *scappato*, a man on the run. But I was ready to trust him as a child trusts a magician at a Christmas party, and admit myself into the care of his crooked smile and nimble, bird-like gestures.

After I had rounded off my meal with a huge scarlet apple, I followed Arturo and Maria up the stairs which led up from one end of the room to the upper floor. We stopped in the first of two small intercommunicating bedrooms with whitewashed walls and shuttered, paneless windows. I sat on a chair, while Arturo told my story to Maria, who had commented on the cuts on my hands. She fetched a basin and washed off the dirt and caked blood. Then she pointed at the large bed, above which hung a crucifix.

"Sleep, Gianni," she said. "I can see that's what you need."

It was the first real bed I had seen since I had been in Cairo two years previously. I threw off my rainsoaked clothes and climbed between the rough sheets of homespun hemp. I fell asleep immediately.

"*Svegliati! Svegliati!*"

The pressure of hands shaking my body confirmed the meaning of the words and I opened my eyes to find Arturo and Maria standing beside my bed. "Quick, Gianni, wake up! The *tedeschi*, the Germans, are in the lane below."

I tumbled out of bed, unaware that I had been asleep for only twenty minutes and too dazed to notice my nakedness. I could hear the guttural Teutonic words

31

beneath my window and the clatter of boots on stone. I slipped into the trousers which Arturo was waving at me and watched him place a chair on the table in the corner of the room.

"Get up," he told me, pointing to a trapdoor in the ceiling, "and I will follow you."

I scrambled on to the chair, hoisted myself through the narrow hole and pulled Arturo up after me. Maria replaced the chair and went downstairs.

A few minutes later we heard the Germans enter the house. Lying in the darkness of the attic, our ears close against the boarded floor, we tried to make out what was happening beneath us. I could hear the wail of a woman — was it La Nonna? — and the bark of a command terminated with the word *schnell*. Two pairs of heavy boots thumped towards us up the stairs. Who could have given me away, I wondered. The old man with the donkey? Surely not.

"You see there is no one else here." Maria's words were now clearly audible. "We are all women in this house."

Her manner was evidently convincing, for the Germans withdrew downstairs and out into the lane, slamming the door behind them.

A few minutes later Maria came to the trapdoor and explained to us that they were making a house-to-house search. I failed to understand for whom they were looking but learnt with relief that it was not for me. She advised us to stay in the attic until they had left the village.

Arturo and I lay in the dark for another hour during which he tried to tell me about some drama which had happened in Nespolo on the previous day. The word *morti* recurred with sinister frequency. But who was dead or why was more than I could assimilate.

At last we heard German voices shouting orders in the parking place two houses down the lane from our front door. We heard an engine start and the noise of a truck receding in the distance. A moment later Maria returned to the trapdoor and helped us down. My head ached abominably, my knee throbbed and my hands shook as I lifted to my mouth the glass of wine handed to me by Maria.

I crawled back into bed and slept for fourteen hours.

CHAPTER
TWO

When I awoke, I could tell from the relaxed state of my limbs that my sleep had been both long and deep. I lay for some seconds with my eyes shut and listened for the noises which I associated with the awakening in a prison dormitory of twenty captive men: the spluttered coughs, the muttered curses and the creaking of the tiered wooden bunks on which we had slept, all noises presaging the imminent blast of the bugle that summoned us each morning to rollcall. Instead I heard only the clatter of cartwheels on a cobbled lane, the crow of a cock and, from a distance, the querulous bray of a donkey. My heart leapt in happiness as I opened my eyes. Though the room was in darkness, I could judge from the white brilliance of the vertical line which cleaved the shutters of the window that the sun was already high in the sky. I rolled over on to my back, the better to savour the softness of the straw mattress on which I lay, and let myself enjoy the unfamiliar sensation of being free to lie in bed for as long as I cared.

My thoughts travelled back through the three Italian PoW camps and two Libyan prisons in which I had been confined for a total of fifteen months; to the hot

June day in 1942 when I had been captured in Tobruk. I remembered how the battle had burst on us so unexpectedly at dawn with the crash of falling shells as the Axis guns unleashed their attack along the perimeter of the fortress, and had ended so ignominiously with the surrender of the garrison by its South African Commander. The affront to the name of Tobruk had wounded those few of us present who had lived through the great siege of 1941. And it was only now, with the recovery of my freedom, that I felt able to contemplate the disaster without acrimony.

Outside my window the birds were singing. When, I wondered, had I last listened to their song? Certainly not in the fortress of Tobruk nor in the Libyan desert. My thoughts drifted back through an uneventful year of soldiering in Scotland to the first weekend of the war, which I had spent filling sandbags on a gun site near Woolwich; and then to peacetime London, where I had worked in the City in a job which meant little to me because I felt sure it would soon be interrupted by war.

I peeled off two more skins of memory and passed through the golden, carefree days of Cambridge in the early thirties and four long years at Marlborough to the first morning of my first holiday from my prep school. At the memory of this I halted. I had pinned down the moment in time for which I had been subconsciously searching, the moment with which I associated my present wellbeing.

I was back in my bedroom in my country home in Scotland. I could see again the blue and orange curtains which hung at the window and, on the washstand beside it, the brass jug of hot water over which the maid had placed a towel. I was nine years old. Then, as now, I was exhilarated by the momentous discovery that I was no longer one of a herd and that I was free to decide how I should spend my day.

Such was the intensity of association of past and present that several minutes elapsed before I realized that the two situations were far from similar, if only in terms of the length of time for which they might be expected to continue. This morning I could lie undisturbed in the huge and comfortable peasant bed. But what of tomorrow? For that matter, what of this afternoon? Even at this moment the Germans might be returning to the village. I thought of the minutes which I had spent in the attic listening to their voices in the room beneath me and decided that I must get Arturo to explain to me again why they had come and for whom they were searching.

I climbed out of bed, noticing as I did so that my left leg was painfully stiff, crossed to the window and prised open the shutters a little way. My eyes were level with the brown roof of the house across the narrow lane. Beyond the roof the ground sheered down into a long, open valley, behind which the high peaks of the Apennines pierced the blue distances. Beneath me to the right, I could see the lower half of the village which clustered round the church. Turning my head to the left, I followed the gradient of the rocky spur as it ran up into the chestnut woods. The whole scene was bathed in brilliant autumn sunshine.

I slipped on shirt and trousers and walked to the head of the stairs. A voice, Arturo's, shouted up to me from the dark confines of the room beneath me.

"*Gianni! Tu prendi il caffè?*"

"*Sì, con piacere.*"

"*Te lo porto.*"

I went back into my room and waited for him to bring me my breakfast, a cup of *ersatz* coffee made from roasted barley grains.

Arturo's first act, after he had placed my cup on the table, was to close the shutters.

"To trust is good, not to trust is better," he quoted. "We don't want anyone to know that there is an *inglese* in the house."

He gave me a conspiratorial wink. I was glad to see that he was in high spirits and that a night's rest had brought a new precision to his rapid gestures.

He told me that it was already ten o'clock. He had been for a walk in the village, to pick up the gossip. Everyone was full of fear, wondering what the Germans would do next.

"Please," I said, "explain to me again what is going on here in Nespolo? Speak slowly, because yesterday I only understood half of what you told me. For whom are the *tedeschi* searching? You mentioned *morti*, dead men. Who has been killed?"

"The two men I spoke of were *tedeschi*. They were shot by two *contadini*, two men of the village."

"When?"

"The day before yesterday. So you see, Gianni, we have arrived here at a *brutto momento*. The *tedeschi* are out for revenge."

Arturo drew his fingers across his throat, a gesture more eloquent than words.

"How did it happen? The shooting, I mean."

"If what I am told is true, a *tedesco* sergeant drove up to Nespolo the day before yesterday and demanded to see the *podestà*."

Each commune of Italy had its *podestà*, a sort of village mayor.

"It was the first time that a *tedesco* had set foot in the village since the armistice," Arturo went on.

"Do you know where he came from?"

"They say that there is a *tedesco* command at Poggio Cinolfo, a few miles down in the valley. Anyway, this sergeant told the mayor that he had orders to take away food and wine. And he wanted to know how many *bestie* there were in the village — cows, sheep and goats."

"What did the *podestà* do?"

"What could he do, Gianni? He gave him food and wine. Most of the men of the village were at work in the fields. Those who weren't were made to load the *tedesco* truck, while the sergeant and his driver swaggered round the village."

"And then?"

"They drove off down the valley. But two Nespolini were waiting for them at a corner just outside the village. They ambushed the truck and shot dead the two *tedeschi*."

★ ★ ★

Later I was to learn more details of the Germans' behaviour on that afternoon which had led to the grim climax on the roadside. I heard how the two Germans had drunk a lot of wine and then strutted round the village with the odious effrontery typical of soldiers in occupied territory who have drunk too much. The villagers had watched their progress in sullen rage, their anger mounting. Two of them, braver and more politically aware than the rest, slipped out of the crowd to get their guns and prepare an ambush.

"And where are they now, the two who shot the *tedeschi*?" I asked Arturo.

"Certainly not in Nespolo. *Si dice* that they are already many miles away in the mountains."

Gossip in Nespolo, I was soon to learn, was always preceded by this phrase *si dice*, which means literally "it says itself."

"Who are they? Do you know them?"

"They are called Paolo and Riccardo. I know Paolo a bit. He's an old friend of Rina's family. *Si dice che è comunista.*"

Whether or not Paolo was a Communist, I could see that I had walked straight into a hornet's nest; yet it was a relief to know that the Germans had not been searching for escaped PoWs on the previous afternoon.

"What will happen next?" I asked Arturo.

"Who can tell, Gianni? If what people say is true, the *tedeschi* will never find the two whom they call the murderers. So they are taking away hostages — they arrested several men and women yesterday, while we

39

were in the attic. They will be back for more, I expect, for they want twenty. They say that for each *tedesco* killed, ten Italians must die. That is their rule."

"Then I must move on south immediately. I have had a good rest, thanks to your kindness, and my leg is much better."

"*Per carità!* Are you mad?" said Arturo. "Don't you understand that the *tedeschi* are patrolling the hills round the village looking for the two? They would pick you up immediately. Then they would find out that you had stayed here with us and we would all be in trouble. To leave now would be *cosa di pazzo* — crazy. Stay with us, at any rate until the hubbub has died down. We can always hide in the attic again."

I could see the sense in what he was saying and that, for good or ill, I had already involved him and his family in my escapade, a complication which impinged on my freedom of action. Perhaps I was less of a danger to Arturo in his house than I would be wandering in the woods and courting the danger of arrest and interrogation. And I had other, less disinterested, reasons for staying. My leg was more painful than I pretended. I was lonely. I liked Arturo.

"All right, I'll stay if you really want me to. For another day, anyway."

"*Benissimo!*"

He really does want it this way, I thought, nor is he thinking just of his own safety. Or have I missed some clue to his behaviour? Here is a man who looks like a lizard and is talking to me histrionically in a language of which I understand very little, and who yet is behaving like a hero out of the *Boy's Own Paper*.

"You are very kind," I said. "What about the rest of your family? Shall we tell them that I am English?"

"We will tell my mother and sisters. Maria and Ida know already. But we won't tell Rina, my wife. She is a terrible chatterbox and is related to half the village. We'll let her think that you are a Swiss clerk from my bank in Rome — and the same goes for Signorina Greta. You didn't meet her yesterday, did you? She's a bit mad, that one. Her old father, who is a retired officer in the *Carabinieri*, sends her to board with us from time to time."

"*Capito*," I agreed, "I understand. And tell me another thing: this house we are in, to whom does it belong? I gather that you all live in Rome . . ."

"Yes, our home is in Rome. This house belongs to Rina's widowed mother. The family are *contadini*. They own a few fields and three houses in the village. This one was empty, so I leased it for a month. It makes a holiday for Rina and the children — and for my mother. They had meant to go back to Rome this week. But now that I have joined them, we will stay for a bit longer."

I asked Arturo why he had left Rome so suddenly (for his arrival in Nespolo had obviously been unexpected), and what he had meant when he had said that he was, like me, a *scappato*, a man on the run. He explained that Rome was a dangerous place for young men at present because the Germans were rounding them up and enrolling them in labour gangs to build

41

defences. A few days previously Arturo had been picked up in what he called a *rastrellamento* (literally a "raking-up") when he was coming out of the local cinema. He had found the *piazza* cordoned off by German and Fascist police. In the confusion he had managed to make his escape. But the incident had frightened him and he had decided to make a bolt for Nespolo. Before leaving Rome he had got Ida to telephone the manager of the bank where he worked and tell him that he had been caught in the *caccia d'uomo*, the manhunt.

"He believes that I'm now digging trenches for the *tedeschi!*" Arturo concluded with a broad smile. "Let him think so! I only hope that the bank will pay for my holiday. Soon the *anglo-americani* will arrive. Then I shall go back to Rome."

When will that be, I wondered. Three weeks? Six at the most.

"And now," said Arturo, "Maria will bring you some water to wash in. And she has some clothes for you, I believe."

He gave Maria a shout. A few minutes later she brought me a jug of hot water, a dark brown jersey and a pair of woollen socks. My own had been torn to shreds by my walk of the previous day.

"Don't bother to shave," said Arturo as they left me. "Twice a week is good enough for Nespolo."

After I had bathed the cuts on my hands and knees and dressed myself with unaccustomed pleasure, I joined Arturo in the kitchen. He led me outside to a little shed at the back of the house, low-roofed and malodorous. Into this I crawled. The height was just sufficient to allow me to crouch on my haunches. And there, in the company of two scratching hens, one of which I later discovered to be blind, I completed the final act of my morning toilet.

It was now time for lunch, for which the whole family had assembled in the kitchen living-room. I counted them up and wondered where the eight of them could possibly have passed the night. Maria explained that Arturo had slept in the kitchen with his wife and two little daughters, and that, due to my monopoly of the second bedroom, she herself had shared a bed, admittedly a large one, with her mother, her sister Ida and the Signorina Greta.

The thought of sharing anything with the Signorina, to whom I was now introduced, was distasteful. In appearance about forty, though she may have been younger, she weighed at least fifteen stone. She had a huge head, which lolled from side to side as she talked, greasy black hair and a large, masculine nose. She moved with the ponderous gait of a bear. The overall effect was not unlike a certain portrait of Samuel Johnson with which I was familiar.

I sat myself down well away from her, between Maria and La Nonna. Behind me a large pot of *polenta* simmered above the fire, the bubbles emitting a series of wonderfully odoriferous plops as they rose to the surface and burst. Maize porridge was one of the staple foods of the Italian peasant. In northern Italy it was allowed to cool after cooking until the texture was firm, when it was cut up into slabs. But in the south it was eaten liquid with a tomato sauce and grated cheese. Its taste, alas, like those of ground coffee and freshly baked bread, never quite lived up to the promise of its smell. But to me, accustomed to the lean diet of a prison-camp, it was ambrosia. After two large helpings, followed by a sour but pleasant goat's cheese and an apple the size of a croquet ball, my shrunken stomach was stretched to its limits.

"You eat well, Gianni," said Rina, smiling at me from her place across the table.

"*Sì, ho buon' appetito.*"

"*Bravo, Gianni!*"

I thought how pretty she was, with her light brown hair, transparent skin and delicate, tip-tilted nose, which made so fascinating a contrast to the sluttish curve of her mouth. It seemed a pity that I could not confide in her that I was English. The last time I had spoken to a pretty girl had been in Alexandria, nearly two years previously, and I felt a sudden twinge of sexual curiosity. Arturo had warned me that she was a chatterbox. Now I guessed that she was also a flirt and that she was bored with Arturo and her children. I must watch my step with Rina if I wished to avoid trouble. My thoughts were diverted by the Signorina Greta.

"What do you eat in Switzerland?" she asked me. She talked in a high, singsong voice which had nothing of the gruff bearishness of her appearance.

"Everything," I said. "Like in Italy."

"Not *polenta*, surely?"

"No, not *polenta*."

"And spaghetti? Do you eat spaghetti?"

"Sometimes."

"Then it's not like Italy."

"Not altogether."

The woman had the persistence which often goes with mental deficiency. I could guess that Rina was laughing at my discomfort, though she could not guess that I knew little of Swiss eating habits. Arturo came to my rescue.

"Come, Gianni. You and I have work to do. I want to brick up the window in the attic. We may have to hide in it again and I don't want the *tedeschi* to see that it is there."

Had my Italian been more fluent, I would have argued with Arturo that the sight of freshly laid bricks would draw attention to its existence, rather than the converse. In view of my later experiences, I doubt whether such an argument would have caused him to change his mind. Arturo liked to preconceive his ideas and then twist logic to support them. It was a habit which disconcerted me, but it usually won the day.

We spent an hour together in the attic. I am not practical with my hands and I was impressed with the efficiency with which Arturo worked. No sooner had he laid the last brick than Maria came up to tell us that a German truck was driving up the hill towards the village. By the time it had drawn to a halt at the end of our lane, we had removed all exterior traces of our work and were safely ensconced in our hide-out, which was now totally dark.

We lay there for more than an hour, smoking the last of my cigarettes and wondering what fresh calamity was striking the village. From time to time we could hear the clatter of boots on the cobbles beneath us, the rough German voices and once the sobs of a woman in distress. When Maria had told us that the truck had driven off and that it was safe to come down, we were met with a mass of conflicting rumours. It appeared certain that the two whom the Germans called the murderers had not been found. Opinions differed as to whether the Germans knew their names, the affirmative school using the fact that they had just arrested Paolo's mistress as evidence that they did know. They had arrested others as well and the number of hostages now held in the German prison at Poggio was estimated at somewhere around fifteen. I did not know whether or not to believe a story that a German patrol had picked up five escaped American airmen in the woods.

Rina went off to see her mother who lived at the other end of the village. The *podestà* was one of their many cousins and she hoped that her mother might know the truth about what the Germans were doing. While Maria and La Nonna prepared our supper, I sat at the kitchen table with Arturo and showed him my little map; I discovered that I was about fifty miles east and slightly north of Rome, and that the small town near which I had jumped from the train was called Carsoli. There were a lot of Germans in Carsoli, Arturo told me. After their sudden flight from Rome two days previously, he and Ida had spent the night there on a bench in the station, waiting for the morning bus to take them up the valley. The bus had dropped them where the side road forked right to Nespolo. From there they had had to walk, and it was during this walk that they had met me.

My map showed me that Carsoli lay on the extreme western fringe of the Abruzzi. Nespolo was about six miles away as the crow flies. After supper, in the cover of darkness, Arturo walked me round the village, along the spur of hill on which it sprawled, up and down the narrow, cobbled lanes which linked the upper with the lower confines. The night was clear and still. A suspicion of frost in the air made me thankful that I would not be sleeping in the open. He showed me first the small *dopolavoro*, the "afterwork", where some of the peasants would collect each evening to drink a glass of wine and play cards. It was close to our house, unpleasantly so, for it was here that the Germans liked to do their business with the *podestà*. We walked uphill to the church, then down to the bridge at the lower end of the village. Arturo pointed out the houses of interest: the house of the village priest, Don Giuseppe, the house of Rina's mother, and that of the one man known to own a wireless set. Before returning home we drew two buckets of water from one of the village wells.

CHAPTER
THREE

Memory plays many tricks. When I try to reconstruct in my mind the happenings of my first few days in Nespolo, I tend to do so in the light of knowledge which I could not at that time have possessed. I see myself as the polished actor in a role which I was then only rehearsing: the role of a man whose mother was a peasant and whose brother was a Roman bank clerk. Yet there is little doubt in my mind that, from the moment of my arrival in Nespolo, I began subconsciously to model my behaviour on that of Arturo. I copied his gestures and the way he wore his clothes. I adopted with the women of the family those highhanded ways which are the norm in a country where male dignity is sacrosanct. I began to appreciate that *furberia* was considered to be a virtue, a quality lacking in the literal English translation of "slyness". Evidently the symbolic significance of burying my battle-dress on the hillside had been more effective than I might have supposed.

That I should have been able to Italianize myself so rapidly was due to the immediacy with which the Platanos accepted me as one of the family. We were linked together by a bond of fear. The lives of everyone in Nespolo at that time revolved round the affair of the two dead Germans and my identification on this score with the communal worries of the village helped to diminish my sense of isolation. The climax of each day came with the arrival, usually in the late afternoon, of a German sergeant, or more rarely an officer, from the Command at Poggio, accompanied by a section of soldiers. Always they would park their transport outside the *dopolavoro*, and there the sergeant would remain for half an hour or so in conference with the *podestà*. Meanwhile, his men would storm round the village, collecting men and women for interrogation or sometimes for removal to the gaol at Poggio. I imagined that they were the equivalent of a Field Security Section, but of this I could not be sure, as military distinctions of this kind meant nothing to Arturo, who was my sole source of information.

During their visits, Arturo always hid with me in the attic. His experience in Rome had made him fearful of being conscripted into a labour gang. Apart from this, he was frightened of Rina's close friendship with Paolo's family. The Germans had already removed to Poggio several of this "murderer's" close friends, as well as his mistress who, I now discovered, was the mother of his five children.

After the Germans had left, we would discuss the new rumours which their visit precipitated. Usually the discussion ended with my suggestion that I should leave Nespolo and walk south towards the Front. Why didn't Arturo come with me?

"It would be mad to leave, Gianni," he would answer. "The hills are full of *tedeschi*. Have a little *pazienza.* The affair will die down soon or the Allies will arrive. If not, then we can go to the *macchie.*"

The word *macchie* was a continual puzzle to me. I looked it up in the tiny pocket dictionary which, together with my map and toothbrush, had comprised my escaping kit. "*Macchia,* a stain", I read. My dictionary failed to give the word its secondary meaning of "rough woodland", from which the French Resistance fighters — the Maquis — took their name.

As I felt it unwise to show myself in the village during daylight, I spent my days dozing, eating and gossiping with Arturo and Maria. Each meal was a pleasure. After initial opposition on the grounds that it was an affront to my masculinity, I was allowed to help in their preparation — in the role of scullery maid rather than cook. I also chopped up the firewood and, in the evenings, helped Maria and Ida fetch the next day's supply of water from one of the two village wells. But I never tried to emulate Maria's skill in carrying on her head one of the large copper pitchers, known as a *conca,* which we used for this purpose.

My command of Italian, laced with dialect, improved rapidly and with it my knowledge of the lives of the *contadini.* I learnt how, long before I had awakened from a sleep sounder than any I had known for many months, another day of toil had started. How an hour before dawn the peasants would have risen from their beds and after a spartan breakfast the men of the village, accompanied by some of the stronger women, would set off to the fields, vineyards and chestnut plantations from the produce of which Nespolo scraped its scanty living. Each man carried with him, wrapped in a coloured handkerchief, the hunk of home-made bread, with perhaps an onion, a slice of sausage or a piece of cheese, which was to provide his midday meal. Some of them would have to walk as much as three miles before they reached the scene of their labours. The lucky ones rode, or led behind them, a donkey or a mule.

This long, timewasting walk before the work of the day could start resulted from a crazy system of landownership. It is true that the peasants of Nespolo were luckier than some, for most of them owned at least part of the land which they cultivated. But their individual plots, consisting of narrow strips of field or groups of chestnut trees, were of such diminutive size and often so distant both from each other and from the central village that much of their time and energy was wasted in getting to and from their work.

Back in the village there was plenty to do for the women, old men and children left behind. There were the goats to feed and milk, the water to fetch from the well, the homegrown hemp to beat and stitch into sheets, the fruit and nuts to store, the bread to bake and, every day of the year, the evening meal to prepare before the menfolk returned home at dusk. These activities filled their days to the exclusion of everything else, leaving no time for diversion — not even for romantic love. For most Nespolini the act of love was little more than the satisfaction of sexual hunger allied to a wish for sons.

Arturo told me that about five hundred people lived in Nespolo. I doubt if there were as many as that at the time of which I write, for a good proportion of the young men had been conscripted into the armed forces. Life there can have changed little since medieval times. Like their forefathers, the peasants lived and slept above their animals in the squat, stone houses which flank Nespolo's narrow lanes, which were graded with steps and paved with cobbles. They were basically a self-supporting community, subsisting on their own flour, maize, oil and wine. They slept on sheets bleached and woven from their own hemp and they cooked their meals on fires of charcoal made from their own trees. Their most important crop, and the only one which in a good year provided a surplus for export, was chestnuts. There was a post office in the village but neither school nor shop, and the nearest thing to a pub was the *dopolavoro*.

I asked Arturo if there were other Communists in the village besides Paolo, one of the two men who had shot the Germans. He told me that Paolo was the only one, that he was an eccentric, *brav' uomo ma un po' matto*. Politics played no part in the lives of the peasants. They were the business of the *pezzi grossi*, the "big pieces" (important men) of the world beyond the village. The government and its administrators were symbols of authority to be avoided or, whenever possible, cheated. The only respected authority was the Church, represented by Don Giuseppe, the village priest, who was also the largest landowner in the village.

To the Nespolini, war was a calamity which occurred spasmodically, more disastrous but of the same nature as a severe drought or a particularly wicked government. It was instigated, presumably, by the *pezzi grossi* for their benefit. The alliance with Hitler was unpopular because the *tedeschi* were the traditional enemy. Consequently the Nespolini had delighted in the news of the September armistice. At this time they had never seen a German soldier nor heard a bomb drop. And, in their misguidedness, they believed that they never would.

After the armistice a few sons of the village had deserted from the army and made their way home, bringing with them the same wild rumours of Allied landings and German retreats which had swept through the camp at Chieti. These rumours, together with the peasants' ignorance of the procedure of war, made it impossible to find out what was happening on the battle front. When I had escaped I had estimated that the nearest Allied troops were within a hundred miles of Nespolo, but after a few days I did not know what to think. Maria and Arturo would feed me with the wildest scraps of news gathered around the village well. One day I would be told that the Americans had reached Avezzano, only twenty-five miles away. Someone had even heard the noise of Allied guns. A denial would come the next day. The Front had not moved at all, had perhaps receded. In my frustration, I resigned myself to staying a little longer in Nespolo. My leg was getting better each day. I concentrated on eating hugely and building up my strength. And I urged

Arturo to listen in person to a news broadcast from *Radio Londra*. There must, I felt, be more than one wireless set in the village.

Although I was confining my walks in the village to the hours of darkness, I would quite often come face to face with neighbouring peasants who would drop in from time to time for a gossip with Maria or La Nonna. On such occasions my tactics would be to talk as little as possible and withdraw to my bedroom at the first opportunity. Usually our visitors were women, for most of the men spent the hours of daylight working in the fields and woods. Among them were Palmira, a cheery, red-faced sister of Rina, who lived close to us with her small son and two uncles, for her husband was a PoW in Russia, and Berendina, a toothless old hag who lived in a hovel across the lane from us and was forever trying to borrow food or cooking utensils from La Nonna.

It was thanks to Berendina that I first broke down La Nonna's shyness with me. There was a classical fineness in the old lady's features which was emphasized by the black shawl in which her head was always draped. It took me a few days to realize that behind them lurked a lively and devastating sense of humour. One morning I was helping Maria peel potatoes when La Nonna suddenly burst in at the front door. She had been having an argument outside with Berendina.

"*Madonna mia! Sono porchi cretini, questi Nespolini!*" she exploded.

I asked her why the Nespolini were cretinous pigs.

"You've seen Berendina, haven't you? You know she sleeps with her sheep!"

"With her sheep?"

"*Si, si, proprio colla pecora*. It lies on her bed day and night. And its long hair is all matted with mud and muck! I don't know which of them stinks the most!"

"Really, *mamma*!" laughed Maria.

I had to admit that neither Berendina nor the hovel in which she lived was appetizing. Her bed stood in the centre of the earthen floor, surrounded by rotting potatoes, chestnuts and apples. The smell from the doorway, which was as far as I had ventured, was asphyxiating.

"And now," continued La Nonna, "the ignorant old woman is asking questions about you. She has got it into her head that you are Ida's *giovanotto*."

"Her boyfriend? Why should she think that?"

"Because Ida won't have anything to do with Domenico. Berendina has made up her mind that you are the reason."

Domenico was Berendina's only son, a coarse-featured but handsome youth. He had met Ida during the previous summer and had fallen for her ample charms. He was one of those who had deserted from the army after the armistice and made his way back to Nespolo.

"How did you answer that?" I asked La Nonna.

"I told her not to say *stupidaggini*. I said that Domenico didn't please Ida, that he was *brutto*."

"But he's not ugly, he's *bello*." I realized suddenly that La Nonna enjoyed being teased, "taken in a circle" as the Italians say.

"For me he is *brutto*. He is also a cretin!"

"You told her that?"

"*Si, certo.*"

"And she was angry?"

"*Si, arrabbiatissima!*"

At the recollection of Berendina's rage, La Nonna threw back her head, clicked her tongue and let out a whoop of delight.

"Poor Berendina." I pretended to be shocked.

"Poor nothing! She's a wicked old woman with a nasty tongue.

"But seriously, Gianni," she went on, "the Nespolini are cretinous pigs, most of them. Not at all like the peasants of my home in Apulia."

"You and your Apulia," laughed Maria. She turned to me. "*Mamma* is always talking about the happy days when she was young and beautiful!"

"*Eh, beh!*" A seraphic smile lit up La Nonna's face. "This evening I will tell you about Apulia, Gianni, about the village where I was born. We will be alone, for the others are having supper with Rina's mother."

So it happened that it was from La Nonna that I heard the details of the family history. We sat by the fire on wooden chairs with glasses of good red wine in our hands. A paraffin lamp glimmered in the far corner of the room where Arturo's baby Marilanda was sleeping peacefully in her cot; his elder daughter, Stellina, noisy and spoilt in the way of Italian toddlers, had been taken out to supper.

I knew that the region of Apulia, which covers the heel of Southern Italy, had been in ancient times a Greek colony. In the flickering light of the crackling brushwood fire it was easy for me to discern the Hellenic influence in the cast of La Nonna's features. She was born, she told me, in a village which cannot have been many miles from the airport to which I had been flown from North Africa in a Savoia troop-carrier. I could well recall the harsh beauty of the landscape in which her forebears had tilled the soil.

After her marriage to a peasant whom she had known since childhood ("I was eighteen, Gianni, and he was twenty-three, a fine figure of a man then, tall and fair"), the young couple had moved to Lecce where her husband had found work as a cobbler. They had four daughters in a row.

This coincidence called for an interjection.

"Imagine!" I said. "Four in a row!"

"*Si, quattro figlie*! I can laugh now, Gianni, but at the time it was not a joke. Maria was the first to come, then Ida, Iolanda and finally Lucia."

I could picture the dismay which the sex of Lucia, the fourth daughter, must have provoked in a country where masculinity is venerated.

"*Finalmente ho avuto un maschio.*" The old lady's voice echoed the pleasure with which she must have welcomed the birth of Arturo, her fifth and last child. "And what a beautiful baby he was! *Poveretto*, he was still small when we left Lecce. My husband decided to take a job in the State Railways at Rome. There was not much money to be made as a cobbler in Lecce."

"When would that have been?" I asked.

"Let me see. Arturo is now twenty-eight, he was about seven when we moved. It must have been soon after the first war. There was already Mussolini. And how old are you, Gianni?"

"I am exactly thirty."

"And have you brothers and sisters?"

"Two sisters — and a mother. My father is dead."

"And how is it that you are so dark? I thought all *inglesi* were fair."

"Not all," I said. "Anyway, I come from Scotland."

"*La Scozia!* And where is that?"

"Next door to England."

"Is it far away? Over the sea?"

"Yes, over the sea."

"You look like an Italian, Gianni. Only you are too tall. Berendina thinks you are *bello*!"

"But you told me that she is a liar and a cretin!"

"Now you are teasing me!"

I felt completely at my ease. The soft intimacy of conversation by the fireside was something which I had forgotten during my four years of soldiering. La Nonna had brought my family very near to me, made me think of my youth. It seemed strange and wonderful that I, the product of a public school and Cambridge, should be drinking wine with an old Italian peasant woman.

She filled up our glasses.

"Go on with your story," I said. "Tell me about your two daughters whom I have not met, Iolanda and Lucia."

"Iolanda is a midwife and nurse. She is living now with a noble Roman family — very rich they are. Lucia works with one of the Ministries. She lives with us in our flat in Via Famagosta. She's there now, looking after my husband. *Poveretto quello, è tanto vecchio.* Too old to come here with us. He doesn't like Nespolo. You must meet him one day."

"I've always wanted to see Rome."

"*È tanto bella, Roma.*"

"Not at all like Apulia, I'm sure. How did you like it when you first went to live there?"

Back in 1932, I thought, La Nonna must have been already middle-aged. But as she described her life in Rome, it became clear to me how easily she had adapted herself to its ways. In the poorer quarters of the great cities of central and southern Italy, so much time is spent in the streets that there is less difference than one might imagine between urban and village life. The Platanos had lived for a few years in an apartment on the top floor of a decayed *palazzo* in the Piazza Navona and La Nonna had readily immersed herself in the bustling, communal life of the old square, which provided an arena for gossip not unlike the village *piazza* to which she had been born. Later they had moved into a modern block of apartments north of the Vatican. La Nonna's life centred round St Peter's and a day rarely passed without her spending a few minutes within the great church. Cynical of all other emblems of authority, she believed implicitly in the infallibility of the Pope.

It was through La Nonna's friendship with a priest of St Peter's that Arturo had become an acolyte in the Vatican. La Nonna had hoped that he would himself become a priest, but it became evident by the time he was sixteen that he had no religious vocation. Instead he had found work in a Roman branch of the *Banco di Santo Spirito*, first as an office boy, then as a junior clerk. Perhaps it was a small consolation to his mother that he should be employed by the Bank of the Holy Ghost, founded in 1605 and so christened because its founders, a family of Portuguese Jews, had adopted the name of Santo Spirito after their conversion to Christianity.

From what La Nonna told me I understood that, at this time, Arturo had had enough money in his pockets to enjoy the normal pastimes of a young Roman *piccolo borghese*; expeditions to the beach at Ostia, carefree evenings in cafés and cinemas. He had owned a motor bicycle, played the guitar. Listening to La Nonna describe his youthful life, I decided that she was exaggerating the charms of a much-loved only son. It was not until later, when I saw the family scrapbook, that I realized to what extent Arturo had aged in so short a time. Photographs showed him to have been bright-eyed and lithe, his clear complexion framed by a mass of carefully groomed curly hair. Now his figure had thickened, his hair thinned, his skin wrinkled in such a way as to emphasize the reptilian aspect of his features. Only his eyes retained the fire and dash of the earlier photographs.

La Nonna inferred that his troubles had begun when he met Rina. Born and bred in Nespolo, Rina had been staying in Rome with a married sister when she met Arturo for the first time. The country girl was dazzled by his magpie sophistication, while he was captivated by her pretty face and flattered by her admiration. Before he had time to realize the shallowness of their relationship and the implications of her love for extravagance, he had been trapped into marriage just in time to legitimize the birth of Stellina.

At this moment in my conversation with La Nonna, we were interrupted by the return of the rest of the family from their supper with Rina's mother. I noticed Arturo's eyes were blazing.

"Do you know that there are two *tedeschi* in the village!" he exclaimed. "They must have stayed behind after their afternoon talk with the *podestà*. They have been drinking in somebody's house, down by the post office. Now they are stumbling around in the dark, singing songs. *Criminali!*"

We listened. We could hear in the distance the sound of laughter, a snatch of song, then a stream of curses.

"It's women they are after tonight, not men," I said. "Perhaps the girls should go to the attic for a change!"

Everyone laughed.

"Let's all go to bed," said La Nonna.

Next morning we heard that the two Germans had broken into the house of a *muto*. The old man, intending to show that he was dumb, had unadvisedly waved his arms above his head, whereupon one of the Germans had shot and killed him. In his defence the German had later stated that he had feared that the *muto* was about to throw a bomb at him. The Command at Poggio expressed their "profound regret" at the incident.

Arturo liked to joke with me about the dirtiness and stupidity of the Nespolini. He did this, I think, partly to impress me with the higher standard of living to which he was accustomed in Rome. But much of his scorn was genuine and probably stemmed from his disillusionment with his marriage to Rina. Maria viewed the failings of the Nespolini with greater tolerance. She had been twenty-two when the family had moved from Apulia to Rome, for she was fifteen years older than Arturo. And she understood the peasants in a way which he could not.

Tall and strong, with luxuriant black hair which she parted in the middle and wore in a bun, Maria looked much younger than her forty-three years. She was the only one of the four sisters to have married. Her husband had been killed in the early stages of the war and she now earned her living by teaching sewing and dressmaking at a children's school in Rome.

Maria had a quick temper but a big heart. She enveloped me with kindness and was forever plying me with food and drink.

"Eat, eat, Gianni," she would urge me, picking out the best apple and putting it on my plate. "You are far too thin. I thought that in England you had five meals a day."

Maria also liked to tease me. A favourite ploy was to encourage the Signorina Greta to embarrass me with an endless stream of questions.

The Signorina (the family always addressed her thus, in deference to the fact that her father was an officer in the *Carabinieri*, a *pezzo grosso* in their eyes) was in some ways very sly. She fancied herself to be much better educated than the rest of us. Correctly so, for her deranged mind had absorbed many scraps of factual learning. Unlike the Platano women, who had no idea where Switzerland even was, the Signorina had once spent a holiday there. As she believed me to be Swiss, she was determined to pick my brains. Did I know Geneva, Zürich, Lausanne? Why had I come to Italy?

She was also curious about my family. What was my father's business? How many brothers had I? And sisters? I used to answer in curt monosyllables and go on with what I was doing. Meanwhile Maria would giggle at my discomfort.

"He is not good company, that *giovanotto*," the Signorina complained one evening to the others after the severity of her inquisition had driven me early to bed.

La Nonna silenced her by explaining that my mother had just died and that consequently I did not feel like conversation. Thereafter the Signorina and I would sometimes sit together in silent communion, peeling potatoes for our dinner. From time to time she would put down her scraping knife on the table beside me and start to grab with her hands at imaginary flies which, in her delusion, she saw swarming round her large, beaky nose.

CHAPTER
FOUR

By the end of my first week in Nespolo I was feeling healthier than I had for many a month. Plenty of food and sleep had built up my strength. My leg was no longer stiff and the cuts on my hands had healed. But my spirits did not match my health. I was depressed by the negligible advance which the Allies had made since my escape. Arturo had by now actually heard a *Radio Londra* broadcast which confirmed our worst fears. The Allied troops were still some distance south of Cassino and nearly a hundred miles away from Nespolo and Rome.

Nor was there any sign of the Germans at Poggio relaxing their war of nerves against our village. On the contrary. It was now established that they held twenty hostages in gaol and that they were threatening to kill them unless the two "murderers" gave themselves up. And how could this happen if, as was generally believed, Paolo and Riccardo were miles away in the mountains, perhaps already behind the Allied lines? Some people maintained that the hostages were already dead.

An atmosphere of fear, such as now pervaded Nespolo, is a breeding-ground for treachery. And I blessed Arturo's wisdom in keeping my identity a secret to all but a few.

I was ripe for action. Only my involvement with the Platano family deterred me from taking risks. I disliked the knowledge that my recapture could fall more heavily on their shoulders than on mine, that while I could claim prisoner-of-war status and demand to be returned to a prison-camp, they would have to face a firing squad, should their association with me be discovered.

I was considering this moral dilemma during an afternoon siesta when Arturo burst into my bedroom. I could tell from his agitation that some crisis had developed. His voice had lost its customary calm.

"Come, Gianni, quick! The *tedeschi* are down by the church. They have surrounded the village and are taking away all the young men. Berendina is down below in the kitchen, crying her head off — they've arrested Domenico."

There was no time to argue the merits of the plan which he now outlined. "We must leave immediately," he said, "and make for the farm of one of Rina's cousins."

He explained that it lay in the forest about five miles from the village, in the *macchie*. Rina and Maria would come with us to give our flight the air of a normal excursion.

I slipped on my waterproof jacket and shoved my few possessions into its pockets. Arturo kissed Ida and La Nonna goodbye and, to my surprise, the old lady hugged me to her breast. It was easy to slip unnoticed into the cover of the chestnut woods, which climbed steeply up behind our cottage into the mountain face, and in a matter of moments the four of us were walking up the steep path deep into the forest.

With each step my spirits rose. The sun was shining and a light wind, blowing down from the open slopes above the tree-line, rustled the leaves of the giant chestnut trees. Why, I thought, had we not left the village days ago? It was only now, as the tension slid from my shoulders, that I realized to how taut a pitch my nerves had been strung. Arturo had regained his composure. I could not understand (and to this day I have never known) what made Arturo flee so precipitously from Nespolo and, in doing so, act in direct contradiction of all the arguments which he had used to persuade me to remain there. Was he holding back some piece of information from me? Had La Nonna persuaded him to go? Or had he simply lost his head? Most likely the latter, I thought. The important thing was that I welcomed his decision.

As we walked, Arturo explained that Rina and Maria would come with us to the farm and then retrace their steps to Nespolo. Arturo and I would spend the night at the farm and decide tomorrow whether to remain there or continue to move south through the mountains to meet the advancing army. He had a little money in his pocket, he confided. But I felt sure that he had no idea of the hardships of walking in the mountains at this time of year, still less of the hazards, such as guns and mines, which we might expect to encounter should we ever reach the front line. He was a townsman through and through.

It took us nearly two hours to reach the stone hut which lay in a scrub-covered hollow among the woods. The owner, Angelo de'Angelis, was sitting crosslegged on a bench outside his dwelling, puffing at his clay pipe. With his cropped white hair and bristly beard, he resembled a wizened squirrel rather than the angel that his name implied. Arturo introduced me as a colleague from his bank, recounted what was happening in Nespolo and explained that we were on our way south. This appeared to please the old man. He shook my hand and uttered a long sentence of which, owing to the breadth of his dialect and his complete lack of teeth, I could understand only the one word. Surprisingly, the word was "America". Arturo explained that in his youth Angelo had worked in the abattoirs of Chicago, where he had saved enough money to return home and buy his farm. He was one of the few peasants in this part of the Abruzzi who lived on his own plot of land and not in the central village.

Angelo produced a carafe of wine, then a wife, considerably younger than himself, and finally a daughter aged about seven. It seemed impossible to me that he could have been potent so recently. We drank a glass together, then said our farewells to Rina and Maria and waved them goodbye down the path to Nespolo along which we had come. The old man showed Arturo and me where we were to sleep, then took us out to his vineyard. The sky was promising a wonderful sunset. I picked a bunch of purple grapes, moist and covered with powdery bloom. They seemed to symbolize the peace and beauty of the autumn evening.

"*Hände hoch!*"

The words burst on us like a spray of bullets. Simultaneously several Germans, tommy-guns at their hips, ran out from the woods on all sides of us. Still clutching the grapes, I raised my hands slowly above my head. Arturo did likewise. A tall, fair sergeant — a *Feldwebel* — stepped forward. He pointed his gun at us.

"*Documenti,*" he commanded.

I stood, aghast, listening to the whirring of my brain. Arturo produced his identity card from his wallet. I caught his eye, hoping to glean from it some inspiration.

He handed his card to the *Feldwebel*, then pointed in my direction.

"He is my brother," he announced in a level voice. "He is not well, he is *muto*. And just now he is suffering from shock."

I remembered that two days before, the Germans had shot a dumb man in error. Perhaps Arturo's words would touch a raw spot in their consciences.

"He is suffering from shock," Arturo continued, the fury mounting in his voice, "because of the bloody English. They have bombed his home in Rome and destroyed all his possessions, including his *carta d'identità*. *Poveretto!* And he was always the weak one of the family."

Arturo tapped his head with his fingers. I dropped my jaw and grinned oafishly in confirmation.

The *Feldwebel* seemed, not unnaturally, to be rather astonished at this improbable story. Or was it just that he could not understand much Italian? For whatever reason, he paid little attention to me but continued to question Arturo.

I was thinking, It won't wash, it's a crazy story, when my thoughts were interrupted by a piercing scream. Turning round I saw two more Germans dragging Maria from the woods. Rina walked behind. The patrol must have seen us arrive together at the farm, and watched the women leave. Events happened so quickly that they could not have gone more than a few hundred yards.

"My brother," wailed Maria. "What are you doing to my brother?" Or did she say "brothers"? I could not be sure.

She slumped to the ground at our feet. Angelo and I helped one of the Germans to carry her into the farmhouse. She put her arms round my neck. Catching her eye, I realized that she was acting, that her faint was a pretence. We laid her on the floor of the kitchen. I made use of the diversion to drop my map, together with some diary notes written in abbreviated Italian, behind the dresser. Days later I was disturbed by the remembrance that Angelo's little daughter had seen me doing this.

Meanwhile Arturo was pleading with the *Feldwebel*, elaborating his fiction of how my documents had been destroyed. He spoke slowly, as the *Feldwebel*'s knowledge of Italian was clearly less than mine. So that I was easily able to follow Arturo's argument and act the part of the dumb, bomb-happy halfwit whom I was supposed to be.

"Your brother must come with us to our Command at Poggio," said the *Feldwebel*. "We must check his identity. You others, you are free to go."

I tried to will Arturo to go off with the women while he was free to do so; go to Rome, go anywhere. But he refused to take the easy course.

"If you take my brother, you take us all," he told the *Feldwebel*.

My heart sank. These Germans were clearly not Field Security men. They made no attempt to search me, nor to trick me into speech. I presumed that they had been told to find two named Italians who had killed two of their comrades, that they were not interested in anyone else. But at Poggio there would surely be a German trained in Intelligence work or else a Fascist Liaison Officer. It would be child's play for either to discover that I was neither Italian nor dumb.

The sun was dropping behind the mountain top as we started back along the path in the woods towards Nespolo where the patrol had evidently left their transport. The *Feldwebel* walked in front with, alongside him, Rina and Maria. I could see that both of them were doing their best to win his good favour. Arturo followed with a German on either side of him. I came next, walking unevenly under the weight of the ammunition box which I had been ordered to carry. The remaining four men of the patrol brought up the rear, thereby decreasing my chance of making a successful dash for freedom.

My first thought as I started back to Nespolo was one of amazement at the courage which Arturo had shown on my behalf. Was it entirely disinterested, I wondered cynically? Or did he feel that I would give the show away immediately if my identity was established and that this would lead to the arrest and assassination of all his family? Whatever his motive, he had acted with great presence of mind. So had Maria.

Throughout the long walk I seemed to be able to see and observe myself from outside my person, a fantasy which I have since learnt to be common enough in moments of extreme emotion or danger. I was weighing up the physical chances of making a successful break (it would soon be dark, I noted with pleasure) and at the same time trying to decide whether or not I had the moral right to make the attempt. I was appalled at the prospect of having to bear the responsibility for the deaths of people who had been so kind to me and of whom I had grown so fond. For the first time the realization that a civil war, such as that which now encompassed Italy, provoked a more cruel dilemma than did a national war struck forcibly home. That La Nonna and the other women of Arturo's household should find themselves in extreme danger solely because they had behaved towards me with a natural humanity appeared to be a monstrous injustice, an evil of a different order to the dropping of a bomb on a civilian whose country was at war.

Yet should I fail to escape and be taken to Poggio, I could see little prospect of bluffing through with Arturo's story for any length of time. Sooner or later someone would guess that I was English. Because of my dark hair and generally Latin appearance, and because I was wearing the right clothes and had three days' growth of stubble on my chin, there was no visible reason why I should not be Arturo's brother, especially in the eyes of a platoon of ordinary soldiers who were searching for two particular men. But, even allowing for the fact that Germans tend to have one-track minds and to discount the possibility of the unexpected, I knew enough about Intelligence methods to guess that at Poggio they would quickly expose my alibi.

Whichever way I looked at the problem, death seemed close, either to me or to the Platano family. My code of ethics urged that it was I who must die. Perhaps the best solution was that I should make a suicidal dash for freedom.

As I trudged through the dark, floundering under the weight of the ammunition box, harried by the occasional dig of a machine-gun muzzle and irritated by the taunts of my escort (for I was playing the part of the village idiot with a talent which surprised me), my dominant emotions, apart from fear, were regret for all the things in life which I had not experienced and surprise that the ladder of life should have led me to my present predicament. For some reason I had always assumed that I would survive the war. Now I felt less certain. I cursed the impulse which had made me jump from the train; or to be more exact I cursed the fact that my life had become entwined with those of the Platanos. I knew that I would leap at the chance of being once more a PoW, provided that the Platanos could go free.

My introspective gloom vanished as soon as we came to the outskirts of Nespolo. News of our imminent arrival under escort had evidently preceded us, for we found a sympathetic crowd gathered to greet us.

"*Poveretto, è muto!*" someone shouted, or so it seemed to my ears. The sight of Berendina and her sheep among the crowd shook me out of my fatalistic mood. I could see no sign of La Nonna and wondered whether anyone had told the old lady what was afoot.

We halted in front of the *dopolavoro*, outside which two German trucks were parked. It now became evident that Rina and Maria had not been wasting their time with the *Feldwebel* during the long walk and had persuaded him to take up the matter of my identity with Rina's cousin, the *podestà*. While she went to fetch him from his house, the Germans hustled me and Arturo into the *dopolavoro*, wherein they conducted all their business with the village. It was the first time that I had been inside. It was a dingy little place, empty save for two old men playing cards. Arturo and I were made to sit down at a wooden table with a German on either side of us. In conformity with village custom, Maria stayed outside.

We had not long to wait before the *podestà* arrived. I had never seen him before. He was a man of about fifty with sad, worried eyes and a drooping moustache. He wore a jacket but no tie, and a hat which he had put on,

I suspect, so that he could now doff it before the *Feldwebel*, a gesture which he made with a certain flourish. He nodded at Arturo and eyed me with an air of perplexity. I wondered what Rina had told him about me. He must have known that I was not Arturo's brother but, like Rina herself, he had no reason to believe that I was English.

While he and Arturo talked excitedly with the *Feldwebel*, I contorted my face into what I hoped was an idiot's mask of happy indifference to his fate, a task made more difficult by the fact that I was trying to take in every word of the conversation. I was glad to see that the *Feldwebel* was gulping down the rough red village wine as fast as the *podestà* could fill up his glass, and I could sense the sentimental juices of his nature seep through the hard Nazi crust. The *podestà*, accustomed as he was to dealing only with the day-to-day administration of village matters, appeared ill at ease in confrontation with both the German and with someone as nimble-witted as Arturo. Indeed, it was the latter, or so it appeared to me, who had taken charge of the conversation.

From what I understood, the *Feldwebel* was interested in one thing only: whether or not I was one of the two "murderers" who had killed his comrades. My hopes soared as I realized that Arturo was bringing to bear all his powers of persuasion to prove that this was not the case. Having first called for pen, ink and paper, he let forth a torrent of words into the *podestà*'s ear at a rate which made their comprehension utterly

75

impossible for the *Feldwebel*, at the same time thrusting the pen into the *podestà*'s horny hand. The latter gripped it as though it were a stave and, after wiping his hand on his walrus moustache, proceeded to write with careful deliberation.

"The *muto* is called Giovanni Platano," he wrote. "He is the brother of Arturo whom I have known for many years and who is married to my cousin Rina. He had nothing to do with the murders on 30th September."

The *Feldwebel* now turned to me. Up till now he had paid me no attention whatsoever, which made me hope that he knew about the accidental killing of the *muto* and was consequently sensitive regarding my supposed affliction. He now gave me another piece of paper and the pen. The *podestà*, he ordered, would ask me some questions at his dictation and I must write down the answers. I grinned feebly and nodded my consent.

"What are you called?" asked the *podestà*.

"Giovanni Platano," I wrote. Luckily I had been able to read the *podestà*'s statement.

He then asked my age.

"*Trenta*," I wrote.

"*Dov'eri?*"

This meant, literally, "where wert thou", but I had not yet mastered the imperfect tense of the Italian verb "to be", and the question meant nothing to me. To cover my dismay I rolled my eyes in Arturo's direction and cupped my hand to my ear.

"*Poveretto*, he is also a little deaf," said Arturo and bawled into my ear "*Da dove vieni?*" meaning "From where do you come?"

"*Vengo da Roma*," I come from Rome, I wrote.

A question about my identity card followed and, prompted again by Arturo, I managed to write down that it had been destroyed in an air-raid on Rome. I signed my statement with all the flourish I could muster.

The *Feldwebel* seemed satisfied. He took my written statement and that of the *podestà* and put them carefully in his wallet. He called for more wine and signalled to the rest of his patrol, who had been drinking quietly in a corner of the room, to join his table. I got tentatively to my feet, for I understood that I was free to go. But the *Feldwebel* waved me down with his hand. I was innocent, Arturo and I must drink with him. Never had I wanted liquor more, or company less.

We sat in a circle, seven Germans, two Italians and one Englishman. The wine circulated freely. The Germans started to sing songs rich for me in nostalgic memory: "*Du kanst nicht treu sein*" and "*Trink, trink, Bruderlein trink*". I remembered happy evenings drinking in the Hofbräuhaus in Munich during a Cambridge vacation. They are not bad fellows, these Germans, I began to think, and realized with horror that I was getting tight. Another glass of wine and I, the *muto*, might join in the chorus of "*Lili Marlene*".

Eventually Arturo managed to extricate us from the party.

"*Schlafen Sie wohl*," said the *Feldwebel*, bidding me goodnight and shoving a packet of cigarettes into my shaking hand. I screwed up my face into a final oafish grin and, with Arturo, stepped out into the sanctuary of the silent darkness.

When I came down to breakfast next morning, the German truck was already parked outside the *dopolavoro*. Each time I heard the tread of boots approaching our house, I feared that they would stop outside our door, the door would open, and the *Feldwebel* would enter and order me to accompany him to Poggio.

I was nervous on two counts. First, that some brighteyed boy at Poggio, either a Fascist Liaison Officer or a German trained in Intelligence work, would read the notes which I had written out for the *Feldwebel* and notice some alien features in my supposedly Italian calligraphy. Secondly, that the Germans would come to hear that I was no more dumb than anyone else. Too many people in the village had heard me talk; for instance, Rina's sister, Palmira, old Berendina, and the peasant with a donkey who had witnessed my arrival in Nespolo with Arturo and Ida. I was particularly worried about Berendina because Domenico had been arrested on the previous day and was now in the gaol at Poggio. Who could blame her if she informed the Germans that I was not a *muto*, in order to save her son?

All my instincts urged me to flee. But I knew that, if discovered, my flight must appear as evidence of guilt.

Nor was I confident that I could slip unseen through the German net which surrounded the village. Had it just been bad luck that the Germans had spotted our arrival at Angelo's farm? Or was there a German with binoculars on the hill-top, as rumour maintained?

Unlike me, Arturo was in high spirits. I had to concede that he had cause for self-congratulation. The coolness with which he had handled the *Feldwebel* and the agility with which he had invented my alibi had astonished me and killed for ever my English prejudice that a boastful man was never brave. I told him my fears that the Germans would return to interrogate me.

"Then we will fool them again. They're stupid, these *tedeschi!*" He emphasized his judgement by tapping his forehead with all four fingers and thumb.

"Not so stupid as all that. And what if Berendina tells them that I am no more dumb than she is?"

"Don't worry, Gianni. She's an old mad woman. Who will listen to her?"

Nevertheless he suggested that together we should write out a detailed account of my history in readiness for further questioning.

Once having decided that I should stay in Nespolo and brazen out my story, we realized that the affair of my arrest had some advantageous consequences. There was no longer any point in hiding in the attic when the Germans paid their daily visit. Nor was there any reason why I should not walk openly round the village, provided I kept up the pretence of being dumb. Consequently, on the evening of the day after my arrest, I was able to go with Arturo to the churchyard to which the men of Nespolo had been summoned by the village priest. In spite of his air of rotund jocularity, Don Giuseppe was not a popular figure, having a reputation of being servile to his superiors and autocratic with the peasants whom he employed to work his land. It was said, too, that he was pro-German.

The churchyard was crowded, mostly with old men wearing hats and sucking at their pipes. Arturo and I pressed as close as we could to the church steps on which Don Giuseppe stood silhouetted in the thin moonlight. The priest told us that he had received an ultimatum from the Command at Poggio. This stated that, unless the two "murderers" were handed over to the Germans within the next four days, the twenty hostages would be shot and the village of Nespolo burnt to the ground. He went on to tell us what steps we must take in order to prevent this calamity.

He spoke with an unctuousness which reminded me of a lecture by my late commanding officer on the steps which the troops must take to avoid contracting VD. Though, in justice to the priest, I must admit that he had been saddled with a difficult task.

For the next four days, he said, all the able-bodied villagers must spend the hours of daylight beating and combing the woods round Nespolo for the two "murderers". The Germans had made it quite clear what would be the price of failure.

A murmur of protest rose from his audience. But only a murmur. This, I was beginning to realize, was the sort of thing Abruzzesi peasants expected of life. To them existence had always been a struggle against insuperable odds. They had grown up to expect injustice, and the only variance from the norm was that, on this occasion, injustice was being meted out, not by government or landlord, but by the *tedeschi*. The fact that every one of them knew that they would never find the "two" made little impact. It was typical of the way authority wasted their — the peasants' — time. What everyone wondered was whether the *tedeschi* would carry out their threat to burn down the village.

As to this, there was really nothing on which we could base our judgement, neither I nor anyone else. I walked home with Arturo and three *contadini* who were arguing the pros and cons of whether the German threat was a bluff. One of them was old Zio Zompa, an uncle of Rina's. He put forward an ingenious theory which was later to gain much publicity. He maintained that as those in authority always told lies, the village would not be burnt.

Back in our kitchen we found the women of the family anxiously awaiting the news. Arturo told them of the German ultimatum and of the farcical search which was to begin at dawn next day.

"*Madonna mia!*" said La Nonna. "What cretins, these *tedeschi*! What do they think they'll find? And you and Gianni, have you got to beat the woods?"

"No," said Arturo. "Only the natives of the village must go."

"That's something, anyway."

I went to bed conscious that my own predicament had been cut to measure by the sword of Damocles which now hung suspended above every hearth in Nespolo.

Next morning, before I had risen, the men of Nespolo set off in groups of a dozen or so into the woods which surrounded three sides of the village. Some of them carried guns, the others had armed themselves with sticks with which they could beat out the undergrowth. I saw many of them arrive back that evening at dusk. They might have been retainers of a medieval baron returning from a boar hunt. Their bag consisted of two Indian escaped PoWs, who were promptly despatched to the gaol at Poggio.

I could feel the tension mounting in the village. As it rose my fears increased that someone would inform the Germans that I was not a *muto*. It surprised me that they were prepared to spend so much time and energy in trying to avenge the death of their two comrades. Their actions were not those of an army fighting a battle for survival only a hundred miles away. The implication was not lost on me.

I was consumed by a feeling of impotence. Even though I was beginning to believe that I had got away with the pretence of being Arturo's dumb brother, the incident had left its mark on me. During my walk at gunpoint back through the woods from Angelo's farm, I had tasted despair. The realization that I had been so nearly responsible for the deaths of the Platano family had altered my outlook in such a way that I could no longer view my escape as a game of chance in which the penalty for defeat was return to a PoW camp. I am a gambler by nature, but I had no appetite for gambling with the lives of my friends.

To escape from my depression my thoughts kept returning to Chieti. Owing to the necessity of always pretending to Rina and the Signorina that I was Swiss, it was only at night that I could completely relax. I would lie in the comfort of my warm bed and remember with envy the companionship and security of the many months which I had spent behind those walls. It was easy then, as it is now, to forget the unpleasant aspects of prison life: to forget the hunger and cold, and all the many frustrations of physical confinement, and to remember only the pleasant things: the warmth of friendships and the wealth of the world in microcosm which we had created round us. My public school education at Marlborough had at least equipped me to endure the miseries and enjoy the pleasures of a PoW camp, if only because it had already made them both familiar. Most of us at Chieti had readily found congenial occupations. We attended classes and lectures on subjects which ranged from philosophy to business management. We formed our own theatre, orchestra and jazz bands. We wrote, painted and debated. We played cricket and softball, poker and bridge. We read voraciously. We conversed endlessly. We dug tunnels.

But the important thing which Chieti gave to me and many others was time — time without responsibility. The necessity to earn a living and the restrictions normally imposed on behaviour by convention simply did not exist. For the first, and probably the only, time in our lives we were living in a kind of limbo in which anything we might do need have no connection with either past or future. This had a wonderfully liberating effect, providing us with an opportunity to widen outlooks, review values, experiment with new personalities and develop previously unrealized potential. Despite our physical enslavement, prison life became for some of us an exercise in freedom, and for this reason it made a good springboard from which to launch myself into the world of Nespolo.

I cannot be sure to what extent I was conscious of this as I pulled the sheets of my bed over my head and pretended to myself that I was back in the crowded community of Chieti, for there is always a temptation to reconstruct past thoughts in the light of present beliefs. Certainly I realized that a break in my life had occurred when I had escaped and that my experiences as a PoW had in some way prepared me for the adventure which I was now living. Previous to my arrival at Chieti, the course of my life had resembled a railway line built on the sleepers of my birth and upbringing. When I escaped, I had left the rails for the first time and had launched myself into untracked country. In so doing, I had stripped myself of all the privileges of nationality, class and wealth which I had previously taken for granted.

My thoughts often revolved round the destination of the real train after I had left it at Carsoli. I speculated, too, on the present whereabouts of those of my friends whom I knew to have also escaped. In particular I thought of Michael Ardizzone. I guessed that the station at which he had jumped was Avezzano, only twenty-five miles away from Nespolo. Where was he now, I wondered? I longed for his company, but at the same time I was conscious of the advantages of being on my own. Even Arturo, I thought, could not have convinced the *Feldwebel* that he had two dumb brothers.

For four successive days, while I dreamed of Chieti by night and gossiped with Arturo throughout the long, anxiety-ridden days, the men of Nespolo searched the woods for Paolo and Riccardo, whom everyone, except the Germans, knew to be many miles away. At dusk on the fourth day we watched the beaters return, empty-handed as before. We joined the crowd gathered outside the *dopolavoro*, inside which a German officer and sergeant were in conference with the *podestà*. We watched the Germans stride out, silent and poker-faced, get into their truck, slam the door and drive away.

Now everyone was asking the same question. Would the Germans set fire to the village or was their threat a monstrous piece of bluff? The *podestà* did not know. Nor did Don Giuseppe. Nobody knew. We went home and slept. What else could we do?

Next day the rumour spread through the village that the matter had been referred to the German Command at Rome and, with it, the tension eased perceptibly. Then came a piece of news which kindled hope in every heart. The Command at Poggio had moved to Riafreddo, several miles further down the valley from Nespolo.

From that day on, the German visits to the village ceased. It seemed that the Command had finally accepted that they would never find the "two". Had they ever intended to burn the village? Or had Rome forbidden them to carry out their intention? We would never know. Whatever the reason, Zio Zompa's hunch had proved correct.

CHAPTER
FIVE

It was only gradually that life in Nespolo resumed its normal rhythm. We could not be sure that the Germans did not have some other punishment in mind for the village, nor that their daily visits would not shortly recommence. The uncertain future of the twenty hostages, now known to be in the gaol at Riafreddo, haunted their friends and relatives. Poor Berendina spent many hours in our kitchen with La Nonna, weeping over the fate of Domenico. We tried to convince her that, at the worst, he would be sent to Germany. In our hearts we believed that he would be shot.

Nevertheless we knew that a crisis had been reached and surmounted. And we drew much consolation from the fact that the German Command was now several miles further away.

As each day passed without a visit from the Germans, my hopes rose that they had put away their files on the Nespolo affair and with them the particulars of my own interrogation. And one morning I woke feeling sure that the nightmare had ended. A future existed for us all, and it was a future which I could influence by making plans. My thoughts began to concentrate again on the safest and quickest method of crossing the line.

It seemed a good moment to take mental stock of my situation. Three weeks had passed since the morning of my escape from the train, and during them I had progressed only a few kilometres — in the wrong direction — from my point of departure. Nor had the Front, if our news was correct, moved appreciably nearer to me. Looked at like this, there was little cause for satisfaction. On the credit side, however, I was at least still at liberty, I was in good health and I had made firm friends with the Platano family. Practice at speaking had given my basic Italian a reasonable fluency and I had become adept at playing the part of an Italian peasant.

Now that I could leave Nespolo without jeopardizing the safety of the Platanos there was no reason why I should not revert to my original intention of walking south towards the Front. But one morning I opened the shutters of my bedroom window to find that the first snow of winter had fallen; lightly on the hill behind the village, more heavily on the high range of mountains which flanked one side of the valley. The whole countryside sparkled in the morning sunshine. So clear was the atmosphere that I felt that I could stretch my hand over the roof-tops and run my palm along the ridge of deep snow on top of the most distant range.

The prospect of walking through this snow along the spine of the Apennines did not appeal and influenced me in favour of an alternative plan, which was to go to Rome. Two days previously Ida and Rina, together with baby Marilanda, had hitched a lift there in a lorry belonging to the Red Cross. We were waiting impatiently for their return as we wanted an accurate picture of conditions in the capital; we had heard all kind of tales and were counting on learning the truth from Arturo's youngest sister, Lucia.

"Tell me about Lucia," I asked Arturo.

"*È intelligente e bella.*"

Intelligent and beautiful! I had already guessed that she was Arturo's favourite sister.

"She lives in the family flat in Via Famagosta," he went on. "Now only my father is with her, but usually of course *Mamma* lives there, also Maria and Ida. Rina and I have a separate flat."

"And what does she do, Lucia?"

"She has a good job — with the Ministry of Culture. But now she is thinking of leaving it. The Fascists want her to go with them to Verona, where Mussolini has set up his new capital. But she hates the Germans, does Lucia. She will be excited to hear about you."

That evening, Ida and Rina returned. The news which they brought back with them was, on the whole, encouraging. Though the centre was full of Germans, Rome was outwardly quiet. The *caccia d'uomo* — the manhunt — had abated, but the respite was probably only temporary. For Rome was crowded with people who were in hiding for one reason or another — with Jews, with refugees from the north who had hoped to reach the Allied lines, and with deserters from the armed forces, the police, and the Civil Service. All the men in these categories, and indeed all able-bodied men, were wanted by the Germans and Fascists for the building of defensive works. Some of them, such as senior officers and well-known anti-Fascist politicians, were wanted for more sinister reasons.

From the Platanos' point of view, the chief deterrent to a return to Rome was the food shortage, which was already a problem and was likely to grow worse. Plenty of food was available for those who could afford black market prices, but these were rising at an alarming rate, and most of the Platanos were out of work. October was drawing to a close, and if they were to return to Rome, it was absolutely essential that they should take with them a sufficient quantity of basic food to see them through the next two months. We had all lost faith in the imminent arrival of the Allies but we still felt confident that they would be in Rome around Christmas time.

Both La Nonna and Arturo were insistent that I should go with them, should they decide to return to Rome. The dangers which we had shared together had made me one of the family, that keystone of Italian life.

Before our move would be possible we would first have to acquire in Nespolo sufficient food for our needs in Rome and then find a way of transport adequate for both our persons and our provisions. Trains to Rome were running very intermittently as the lines were being bombed several times a week. And whether I travelled by rail or road, it would be necessary to devise some means of negotiating the control posts which guarded the entrances to the capital.

Lucia, who had heard all about me from Ida, had already got busy on my behalf. Having decided to leave her job at the Ministry, she had not wasted her time on her last day in the office. Taking with her a photograph, chosen from the family scrapbook by Ida on the grounds that it resembled me, she had stuck it on a *Gruppo Giovani Fascisti* identity card — conveniently to hand in the Ministry — and stamped it with the official seal. Although not the normal identity card which every Italian had by law to carry, my new document showed that I had been a member of the GGF (a Fascist youth league) since 1937.

My new name was Antonio Maggi. The original Maggi was a callow, bespectacled youth with a long nose, and I thought that Ida might have chosen a more prepossessing photograph. But when I had parted my hair in the middle and put on a pair of spectacles, also provided by Lucia, I had to admit that it bore a certain resemblance to my thin face.

Lucia had also faked for Arturo a pass from the German Command which stated that he was exempt from conscription to a labour gang.

Our chief problem was therefore to find suitable transport to take us to Rome, and we hoped that Rina's pretty face had already solved it for us. On the return journey from Rome, she had scored a hit with a German corporal who had given her and Ida a lift to Nespolo in his truck. Furthermore he had told Rina that he would be returning to Rome in about ten days' time and that he would be happy to take us with him.

There was ample room in his truck for all of us and for the provisions which we hoped, by then, to have acquired.

The ordinary German soldier was always very kind about giving lifts to people in country districts.

All this news, so uniformly excellent, deserved celebration. That evening we sat round the fire roasting the first of the year's chestnut crop. The nuts hissed and popped in the glowing ashes, the carbide lamp purred. Four-year-old Stellina cried for attention until bribed into silence with a glass of wine. For once the Signorina was driven off the conversational stage and sat silent in the wings, stuffing nuts and husks into her great mouth with indiscriminate abandon.

The wine had stimulated Arturo's volatile imagination.

"You'll see, Gianni, what a fine time we will have in Rome. We'll go to the cinema, to the cafés! Perhaps I can take you into the Vatican — I have friends there, you know. Or we can go south to Frosinone, to a monastery where my cousin is."

"Better than the mountains," I agreed. I couldn't really imagine Arturo walking through the snow, picking his way through a minefield at the Front.

"Far better. Rome is a big city, you know. Like America! Huge shops, skyscrapers even! Our block of flats has seven storeys! Not like this piggery." He smiled his man-of-the-world smile.

"You will see St Peter's," said La Nonna, "such a beautiful church! And I will teach you to play our card games, *briscola*, and *scopa*."

Maria smiled indulgently at the old lady and gave me a wink.

"*Certo*, we will play cards together," I said.

"Yes, we will enjoy ourselves in Rome," La Nonna continued. "How long will it be, Gianni, before your friends arrive?"

"Who knows! Before Christmas, I hope."

"But why do they make this war, the *tedeschi*? I don't understand. When it started, Lucia told me it was all about a *corridoio*. Where is this corridor and why does anyone want it?"

"It's at Danzig," I said.

To tell the truth, I had forgotten all about the Danzig corridor, but I could see that the image of a long, dark passage had captured her imagination. Perhaps it symbolized for her the misery of war.

"Promise me, Gianni," she went on, "that when you get back home you will not fight any more."

"I may have to."

"But why?"

"We have got to finish this war."

"Let someone else do it!"

"Why not me?"

"But you might get killed!"

"It could be."

"*E la tua mamma, poveretta!* What of her?"

"My mother will understand."

"But if you get killed, all the help we have given you will be wasted!"

There was no answer to this, so I shrugged my shoulders and threw my hands out sideways with the palms upward.

The passion rose in La Nonna's voice.

"Why can't everyone go to their homes? *Ognuno a casa sua*, I say. *Italiani, tedeschi, inglesi, americani, russi.* They are all stupid."

"Life is stupid."

"It is *you* that is stupid. Why don't you stay with us till the war is ended?"

"Perhaps I will." I caught Maria's eye and smiled. La Nonna noticed.

"You are laughing at me! Mascalzone! Give the rascal some more wine, Maria. Give me some too."

Like me, Maria delighted in her mother's love of ridicule. She could be equally gay but, unlike La Nonna, she was subject to moods of depression. Ever since the day of my arrest she had complained of headaches and had maintained that her hair was coming out in handfuls.

But now she was laughing loudly as she put more chestnuts on the fire. She filled up our glasses. "Drink, *Mamma*," she said, "it will do you good."

Sitting over the fire and rubbing her hands in pleasure, the old lady looked like a cross between a witch and a Giotto saint. The more wine she drank, the richer her dialect became. The conversation had turned to Berendina and her despair over Domenico.

"Poor thing," said La Nonna. "Now she has only her *pecoredra*."

"Her what?" laughed Arturo. "*Arcipicchia!* She means her *pecora*, her sheep. Don't listen to her, Gianni, or you will never learn to speak Italian. She is talking in the dialect of Apulia."

"*Bravo, Mamma*," said Maria, "and a *gallina*, a hen, how do you say that?"

"*La gadinedra*."

More laughter.

"*Il porco?*"

"*Lu porcicedru!*"

"And the donkey, *il ciuco*?"

We could see that La Nonna was fishing in the depths of her memory. She smiled in triumph as she finally hooked and landed the archaic word.

"*Lu ciuceriedru!*" she exclaimed.

I was pleasantly drunk when I got to bed that night, and very happy. The Platanos were the kindest people in the world, La Nonna the most entertaining old lady. I realized that I was no longer acting a part but had assumed many of their habits and manners, not with deliberate intent but because it was natural to me to copy people whom I liked and admired.

The prospect of going to Rome excited me and I prayed that the German corporal would not let us down. I could visualize myself recounting the story of my escape in later years and saying, "Well, actually a German drove me fifty miles of the way." In my cups, this seemed uproariously funny.

I looked forward to being in a big city again, particularly one which was linked in my imagination with so much splendour. It was nearly two years since I had been in Cairo and tasted any of the pleasures of urbanity. I was intrigued, too, by the prospect of meeting Lucia.

On the next day Arturo, Rina, their daughters and I moved to the house of Rina's widowed mother, Italia. Her son and daughter were away for a week or so, leaving two empty bedrooms for us. By making the move we would release my old bedroom for La Nonna to share with Maria, whose nerves had never recovered from her brush with the Germans.

Italia was tall and her youthful carriage belied her leathery wrinkled face. She lived across the stream, on the lower slopes of the village. We carried our belongings down past the *dopolavoro* and over the bridge which bisected the village. A cobbled lane led us to her house, one of a group clinging to the lower slopes of the gentle hill beneath the church. I could see immediately that it was one of Nespolo's better houses. Several goats were tethered in the partially underground *cantina*, the cellar above which rested the thick, stone walls of the two-storeyed house. A strong but not unpleasant smell of dung, cheese and apples met us as we walked up the steps into a large kitchen/living-room, in the corner of which a huge triangular oven filled the space from floor to ceiling.

Italia greeted me politely, if a trifle coldly, and told us to sit down at the long table, on which she now placed a carafe of wine and a roll of salami. Her formidable bearing gave me an impression of capability and dourness. She had none of the soft, southern charm that rippled from Maria and La Nonna. I felt that the wine was being offered to me not from a desire to please but rather because custom ordained that hospitality should be offered to a stranger. In her presence Arturo lost much of his customary bounce, and I guessed that there was no more love lost between her and Arturo than between La Nonna and Rina.

Italia spoke in broad dialect and I found much of her speech incomprehensible. Previously I had thought that Rina had a hard, somewhat grating voice. Now I realized that it was her Abruzzesi accent, so harsh in comparison with the soft volubility of La Nonna's Apulian words and gestures, that had given me this impression. Italia's ignorance of pure Italian made it easy for me to convince her that my own brand of that language was a northern dialect, whether of Piedmont or Switzerland made no difference to her. Nevertheless it irked me to have to act in her presence. Should Rina guess that I was English, Arturo could frighten her into silence, but it was important that Italia should not guess; with her we were treading on more dangerous ground.

When we had eaten and drunk, Italia went off to work in her fields from which she did not return till dusk. She was a tremendous worker, and if at the time I found her manner to Arturo and me both cold and forbidding, I now understand that she was by nature a person who liked others to mind their own business. Her toughness was also an understandable product of the hard climate, both physical and social, in which she had struggled all her life. As Arturo once said to me, in a voice which echoed the plaintiveness of his observations, "*A Nespolo non ci sono divertimenti.*" At Nespolo there were no diversions, no pleasures, because there was no time for a peasant to divert himself from his work.

Arturo took me on a tour of the house as soon as Italia had left us. Her own bedroom was on the same floor as the kitchen. Above were two rooms, one for Arturo and family, the other for me. The house was warm and dry, altogether more spacious than my previous home. We had a look inside the *cantina*, which in addition to stabling her goats was used to store the produce of Italia's fields: potatoes, apples, maize and the first of the year's chestnut crop.

This crop was now ripening and, for the next few days, its harvesting became our urgent preoccupation. If we were to go to Rome with Rina's German corporal friend, we had not much time in which to assemble our stock of food. We were buying as much flour and potatoes as we could afford. Chestnuts we intended to purloin. Like the rest of the land, the chestnut woods were divided into small holdings, each strip of trees being owned by a different peasant. The harvesting of another's chestnuts was just as much a crime as digging up his potatoes or picking his grapes. The legality or otherwise of picking from the ground a nut which has fallen was a point which I was never able to clarify.

Since my arrival in Nespolo there had been a lot of rain and wind, interspersed by the occasional fine day such as that on which I had been arrested. Now the skies cleared, the winds dropped and with them the temperature. The weather settled into a succession of cold, calm days, marked by early morning frost and brilliant midday sunshine. Each morning, after Italia had set off to harvest her own chestnuts, Arturo and I, with empty sacks slung on our shoulders, would walk up into the heart of the forest. We would choose a deserted strip of wood which had not, like some of the larger, richer strips, been fenced around, and would furtively collect together as many full burrs as we could find beneath the trees. Then, more daringly, we would shake the low branches within our reach and watch the golden-green burrs, so reminiscent of sea-urchins, bounce down among the leaves on to the brown earth.

Despite the stealth with which we worked, we were each rewarded on our first morning with a sack heavy enough to make the walk home a suitable penance for our pillage. We weighed our haul and found that it amounted to thirty kilograms. By the end of the week we had accumulated five times this amount; we stored them, having first sprayed them with water to keep them fresh.

The grapes were now ripe for picking and I wanted to help Italia with her *vendemmia* as Arturo was doing. But he dissuaded me because he distrusted one of Italia's labourers whose son was among the hostages at Riafreddo. Rina was occupied with her children and spent most of her time either supervising Italia's huge oven, to which many villagers brought their home-made bread for baking, or gossiping in the homes of her various relations. For a day or two I was left very much on my own.

I preferred not to walk around the village unless accompanied by Arturo, for there was no point in courting disaster. Several peasants, Italia and Berendina for example, had heard me talk and believed that I came from either Switzerland or Piedmont. Others, who had witnessed or heard an account of my arrest, thought that I was dumb. Or did nobody really believe this? I just could not tell. Arturo was evasive on the point. When I complained about the confusion of my aliases and asked him whether or not I was to open my mouth should we meet a friend of his in the street, he would shrug his shoulders and say *vediamo*, meaning let's wait and see. I had no alternative but to accept his tactic of playing everything by ear, though it seemed to me that it would lead to trouble. In trying to assess why it worked, I can only suppose that the Nespolo peasant's innate distrust of active interference had taught him to muzzle his curiosity, and that he preferred to keep his eyes and ears shut rather than invite disaster by learning too much. Many Nespolini probably suspected that I had committed some act against the law, for which misdemeanour they would, in the way of their tradition, feel only sympathy and respect.

While Arturo was helping Italia with her *vendemmia*, I would spend much of the day sitting in the sunshine on the balcony at the back of the house and reading. There were four books in Italia's library.

These were, firstly, Manzoni's *I Promessi Sposi*, the pages of which were, and remained, uncut; secondly, a romantic extravagance entitled *Quilla, Figlia del Sole*, from which I learnt something of the sexual habits of the Aztecs; then there was a child's elementary grammar containing many phrases ("*Il gallo canta*", "*La ragazza sta a casa*", "*E arrivata la Zia Maria*") which were later to become familiar to me when broadcast as coded messages to partisans by *Radio Londra*.

The fourth book was the one which I found particularly absorbing. Called *Il Primo Libro del Fascista* it was an instructive manual for young members of the *Gioventù Italiana del Littoria*, and took the form of questions and answers.

As I, or rather Antonio Maggi, was now a member of the GGF, I felt I ought to study this "simple guide to the development of Fascist spirit and behaviour". I read:

Question: What is the ever-present duty of the Fascist?

Answer: Fascism understands life to be a moral obligation, a means of elevation and conquest, and a continuous effort to fulfil the command of *Il Duce*: To believe, to obey, to fight!

And again I read:

Question: What results, in the spiritual field, from the practice of all the duties of a Fascist?

Answer: There results that which one can call the Fascist Mystique, which is a totalitarian conception of duty carried to the ultimate point of sacrifice.

The manual concluded with a section headed "The defence of the race" and explained the regulations taken to maintain its purity. It defined who, in Italy, was legally a Jew and listed the special laws applying to them, and also the professions and activities from which they were barred by their blood.

I had to give up studying Italian on the balcony after noticing one day that I was being watched from the windows of the adjoining house by a woman who was noting with amazement the motion of my lips as I repeated the conjugations of an irregular verb.

"Come with me, Gianni," said Arturo one fine morning, about a week after our arrival in Italia's house. "I have had a brainwave. I can see no reason why Antonio Maggi should not have a ration card like everyone else. We will pretend that you are registered in Rome and that your old card has expired."

"Why not?" I answered. "But first tell me who I am pretending to be today. Where do I live? Am I or am I not dumb?"

Not so very long ago, the *podestà* had signed a statement to the effect that I was called Giovanni

Platano and that I was a *muto*. One would presume that his assistant would know the story and be surprised by my reappearance under another identity.

Such inconsistencies did not seem to worry Arturo.

"*Beh!*" he exclaimed. "Your name is Maggi, of course, and you come from Rome. But whether it will be necessary for you to speak, *vediamo*, we will see. Just leave it for me to decide."

I knew by now that it was a waste of time to try and commit Arturo to a pre-arranged plan. When it came to the point he would follow his instinct, whatever we had decided previously. So why worry? If the assistant could believe that my name was now Maggi and not Platano, he could equally well believe that I had miraculously recovered my power of speech. I fetched the identity card which Lucia had forged for me and put on my Antonio Maggi spectacles.

We walked across the village to the little office where the assistant conducted his business. He had evidently expected us and greeted us affably. While he and Arturo talked together, I filled in the particulars from Antonio Maggi's identity card on to a form which had been designed for people who had changed their domicile. Everything was proceeding smoothly when I noticed a mischievous glint in Arturo's eyes.

"Maggi has a wife and two children," he announced. "Tomorrow they will be arriving from Rome. Be a good chap and give us their ration cards too."

"*Non è possibile.* They must come round themselves."

"*Per carità*," Arturo pleaded. "Don't make difficulties. Besides, his wife is not well."

"Then she must wait until she is better."

"How can she wait? She's expecting another *bambino*."

"Then get Maggi to bring round her card."

"But why? He's here now, isn't he?"

"Of course he's here! But the card of his wife is not here!"

"What matter! Do you think she has no card?"

(My God! I thought, hearing the indignation in Arturo's voice, he actually believes not only in the existence of my wife but of her card as well!)

"I never said that she has no card! Only that I ought to see it." He threw his arms into the air in a gesture of despair, and turned to me.

"Is it really true that your wife and children are arriving tomorrow?"

"*Si, si,*" I said. "*Proprio domani.*"

He cast an admiring glance at Arturo in recognition that he had been beaten by a better man and handed me four ration cards.

Arturo was very pleased with himself as we walked back to Italia's for our lunch. I was still angry with him because for a few moments I had been very frightened indeed.

"You're mad!" I complained. "You took a quite unjustifiable risk. It's lucky you didn't land us both in prison!"

"But Gianni, you don't understand," he said. "These Nespolini, they are not like us. They are stupid people, stupid."

Later, when we had used my four ration cards to buy a considerable quantity of flour and potatoes, I began to understand that the increase to our larder had more than justified my minute of panic.

CHAPTER
SIX

On the day after Arturo's successful deception of the *podestà*'s assistant our plans received a severe setback. The German corporal who had befriended Rina drove up from Riafreddo to tell her that he had been posted to Verona and would consequently be unable to take us to Rome in his truck. I again suggested that we should go by train, but here we were up against many difficulties. One problem was to find a method of getting the stock of food which we had accumulated to the station at Carsoli ten miles away. There was the further difficulty of getting these provisions through the control post on the railway line at the gates of Rome, without paying the high duty which the Germans had imposed in their attempt to prevent refugees from entering the already overcrowded capital. Nor were we at all confident that my identity card would survive close scrutiny.

We must be patient and wait for the chance of a lift, said Arturo. He had several ideas of how to get us one: with the Red Cross, perhaps, or with the Italian police who came from Rome periodically to buy food.

This was not very satisfactory and caused me to toy with the idea of walking south again. I had at last succeeded in listening to *Radio Londra* and knew that the Fifth Army had made a slight advance to the south bank of the Garigliano river, eighty miles away. However, at this moment I heard a discouraging account of conditions near the Front.

I heard it at second hand from the two "murderers", Paolo and Riccardo, who had returned to Nespolo during the previous night to hear what was happening in the village. They had been completely out of touch since the day when they had killed the two Germans and were horrified to hear of the events which had stemmed from their action. They took flight back into the hills at the break of dawn, but not before they had recounted their adventures during the past weeks.

Apparently they had reached the Front without much difficulty but there their troubles had started. The area had been evacuated of civilians and was swarming with Germans; and their several attempts to cross the line had been defeated by German patrols and minefields. The German defences, they said, were being strengthened each day, and heavy falls of snow were making movement in the high passes increasingly difficult.

These two were tough men. It seemed unlikely that I could succeed where they had failed.

Paolo's *amante* was one of the hostages in the gaol at Riafreddo, but four of his illegitimate daughters were at liberty in the village and it was from the eldest of these that Arturo heard the story. At the same time he arranged that his youngest daughter, a precocious brunette of eleven years called Pina, should come and live with us in Italia's house. The arrangement suited everyone. Pina was a great help to Rina, both as cook and children's help, and received in return free board and lodging. She was pretty, tough as nails and forever smiling.

Although official visits from the Command at Riafreddo had ceased, a few Germans would sometimes drive up in the evening to dance and drink in Nespolo. The attraction was a painted blonde from Trieste, one of the few Fascists in the village, which had christened her *la spia* — "the spy". She had staying with her two Nespolo girls who, according to local gossip, now earned their living on the streets of Rome. One evening, while I was returning home with Arturo from the village well, a group of Germans crashed into us at the corner leading up to the house of *la spia*, and in doing so knocked from my hand one of the buckets of water which I was carrying. Seeing that he had bruised his knee on the rim of the pail, I apologized profusely. To my surprise, he was extremely polite, admitted that the fault was his and bade me goodnight.

Rumour had it that the unit to which he belonged was enjoying its final fling of pleasure before being posted to the Front.

It was not unusual for us to wake in the middle of the night to the heartening throb of huge formations of Allied bombers as they passed overhead on their way, presumably, to raid the heavy industry of northern Italy. Their passage always stimulated my imagination, providing as it did a link in space, not only with aerodromes now in Allied hands, but also with my friends of Chieti, though I considered it probable that the latter were now in Germany and out of range of the air armada. The Nespolini welcomed the roar of their engines as much as I did. But on the following morning they would be disappointed at not being able to see any concrete results of their flight. Arturo's comments illustrated his total ignorance of strategy. "Where can they have been going to?" he would ask me. "Why can't they drop their bombs on the *tedeschi* at Riafreddo?"

One afternoon six Spitfires flew over Nespolo. They were the first Allied planes which had come over in daylight. Arturo and I stood on the balcony in Italia's house and admired the pencilled lines of their parabolas as they dived down in the valley beneath us to shoot up the transport on the road. That evening the news reached Nespolo that the village lorry, returning from Rieti with the week's rations, had been among the transport attacked. The driver and another villager had been killed, two others wounded and the lorry with its precious cargo set on fire.

I explained to Arturo that it was difficult for our pilots to know whether a lorry was Fascist or anti-Fascist, and whether it was carrying war material or food for peaceful civilians. To my amazement I discovered that he, the quick-witted, cynical Roman, had accepted the local interpretation of the tragedy: namely that the Spitfires, though bearing the red, white and blue roundels of the RAF, had been piloted by Germans. I did not try and convince him of his error.

Lying in bed that night, I mused on the gullibility of the human species. Reason is an acquired and not an intuitive faculty. All of us tend to believe what we wish to believe. It took a Galileo to convince people that the world was not flat, and it would have needed such a man to convince the Nespolini that the Spitfires were not German. At any rate, they argued, the men inside them were German. It was typical of the *maledetti tedeschi* that they should use planes with British markings for their nefarious purpose, and without doubt the pilots had attacked the Nespolo lorry because they knew that its driver was a good anti-Fascist.

Three days later I attended the funeral. We joined the chief mourners at the house of one of the dead men. It lay outside the village, about a kilometre down the valley. Half the population of Nespolo had assembled to honour the dead, for they had died in the service of the community. The coffins were loaded on a cart drawn by two donkeys. We formed up in a long queue behind this simple hearse, which headed up the road towards the village. I walked between La Nonna and Ida, neither of whom knew the dead men. Yet the tears came streaming from their eyes, as from those of all the other mourners; wails and lamentations filled the air. I watched a horny old peasant lift his head and howl to the heavens, and realized that my own dry eyes were making me conspicuous. I was interested, too, to see if I could succumb to the mass hysteria which surrounded me. Deliberately I let slip that control under which an Englishman is trained to keep his

110

emotions, unlocked the floodgates and let the tears stream forth. "*Ahimè!*" I wailed with the others. "*Ahimè!*"

At the doors of the church the procession halted. Only the relatives and close friends of the dead men were expected to do further homage. Instead, we went home to lunch. The catharsis had given a fine edge to our appetites.

About this time Arturo made contact with an officer of the *Polizia Africana Italiana* who had come from Rome in a large lorry to buy flour, potatoes and chestnuts for the Mess of his Command. The *PAI* was a security police force which had moved to southern Italy after the Italian defeats in Libya. At the time of the September armistice, many of the *PAI* were prepared to co-operate with the Germans and in Rome they had taken over certain duties of the *Carabinieri* who, being pro-Allied, had deserted almost to a man. Arturo took great trouble with this *PAI* officer, exuding friendship and offers of assistance. He was rewarded with a promise that on his next trip to Nespolo, the officer would take all of us, and our provisions, back to Rome in his lorry.

This was excellent news and helped me to withstand the depressive effect of a subsequent conversation with Arturo. We were sitting in Italia's kitchen, rolling dried tobacco leaves into cigarettes. The week's supply had gone up in flames with the ration lorry.

"It looks as though the peace which we have enjoyed during these past few weeks is over," he began. "A

111

tedesco officer came here today from Riafreddo to see the *podestà*; he wanted to know how many troops the village could accommodate."

"And what did the *podestà* answer?"

"He said there was no room anywhere."

"I wonder why they want to come to Nespolo?" I said. "Perhaps they are withdrawing and plan to hold a new line here."

"Who knows?"

"Or perhaps they are bringing up more reserves," I continued, reason overcoming my natural optimism.

Arturo showed little interest in my speculations.

"And that's not all the bad news, Gianni."

"Oh?"

"Today the *tedeschi* bought five sheep from Zio Zompa — or rather they stole them. They forced him to sell them for five hundred lire the lot. They are worth more like five thousand! And the *tedeschi* took away a load of potatoes and flour. It is said that they are coming back for more — more sheep, cattle, everything."

"What will the peasants do?"

"Hide their beasts, I imagine. That is what *Radio Londra* advises."

"The sooner we go to Rome the better," I said. "When will the *PAI* lorry be back?"

"Not for another ten days. I believe that the trains from Carsoli to Rome are running again. I think that I will go to Rome tomorrow. I want to make sure that it will be safe for you and me to live there, also that Lucia has got everything ready for your arrival."

I suggested that he should take me with him but he insisted that the journey would be too dangerous. There was a stringent document check on the train. Nor did he want me with him in Rome at present. He had too much to do there; he wanted, for instance, to check up with a friend at his bank whether or not he would be able to get his job back.

The implications consequent on the requisition of Zio Zompa's pigs were not lost on Italia and that afternoon she killed a lamb. We ate it for dinner, a young, succulent lamb, roasted on the embers of a wood fire. Only once before in Nespolo had I eaten meat.

"You like lamb, I see," Rina said to me as she watched me suck the tender meat from a bone. We had all decided that our fingers did the work better than knives and forks.

"*Si, mi piace molto.*"

"*Bravo,* Gianni. So do I. I like also veal and pork."

"Also I."

"Life at Nespolo is good when there is meat to eat and no *tedeschi* to frighten us, *non è vero?*"

"Very good."

"*Bravo,* Gianni!"

This was a fair sample of Rina's conversational powers with me or anyone else. Otherwise she opened her mouth only to scold her children or argue with Arturo. She started to nag at him as soon as we had finished dinner and were sitting drinking wine round the heap of bones which was all that remained of the baby lamb. She wanted to go to Rome with him on the

113

morrow and Arturo was digging in his toes. Usually I felt some sympathy for Rina in these domestic quarrels. For Arturo could always count on La Nonna and Maria, neither of whom ever had a good word to say for Rina, to take his side. On this occasion the boot was on the other foot. The sight alone of Italia, straight-backed and unsmiling, would have been enough to daunt most sons-in-law.

Arturo was white with anger, or tiredness, or both. If Rina went with him to Rome, it would mean taking baby Marilanda too. I knew that he was already worried about the journey and that he had many things to sort out in Rome. Rina only wanted to go because she was bored with Nespolo. Or had she a boyfriend there, I wondered?

From time to time both Rina and Arturo turned to me for support. It was hell not being able to talk freely in front of Rina. As always, I was hamstrung by my fear of giving away the fact that I was English. She must have found me very wet.

When we went upstairs to bed, Arturo was still holding out. He came into my bedroom with me.

"Lucky you," he said, "not to be married. There are too many women in the world, Gianni. *Le donne, sempre le donne!*"

I saw what he meant. Arturo had a mother, four sisters, a wife, two daughters and a mother-in-law.

Later, as I lay in bed, I could hear Rina shouting abuse at him in the room next door. What she needed, I thought, was a man who would slap her and then

114

make love to her. I didn't believe Arturo could be much good in bed. That was probably half the trouble.

I thought of Rina's slim body lying between the rough hemp sheets on the other side of the wall from my head. Of her delicate nose, wide mouth and small un-Italian breasts. So close to my own body in space, yet so inaccessible to me. "*Sempre le donne,*" Arturo had complained. Always women. Nearly two years had passed since I had held one in my arms, and I felt a sudden surge of sexual desire.

I solved my problem in the only way possible. Then I started to think how little sex, or rather the absence of it, had bothered most of us at Chieti, and it struck me what a lot of nonsense had been written about the sex life of convicts — of how, deprived of women and driven half-mad with frustration, they had lain on their bunks with sweat pouring off them, totally obsessed with longing. Perhaps Devil's Island, unlike Chieti, had given its prisoners ample nourishment — in my opinion, the sexual urge was largely dependent on diet, and although in Chieti we were not starved, we were certainly preoccupied with food to the exclusion of all other appetites.

In Chieti, our need for sex was also lessened by the absence of erotic stimulation. We never saw a woman, nor even a picture of one, and although half the camp was a little in love with our star "actress" — a cheerful female impersonator of considerable acting talent — homosexuality was very rare.

Whether or not my theory was valid, I can remember the effect on me of a month of good feeding, culminating in a feast of baby lamb. Or was it due entirely to the tantalizing presence on the other side of my bedroom wall of a pretty, angry and frustrated girl?

We were all up at dawn. In the course of the night Rina had won her argument. It had been decided that she and Marilanda were to go to Rome together with Arturo, Ida and the Signorina, who, I was thankful to hear, was to be returned to her father's care. I was to move back to the other house to stay with La Nonna, Maria and Arturo's elder daughter, Stellina.

To catch their train, Arturo's party had first to walk five kilometres and then take the bus to the station at Carsoli. Just as they were about to leave, Maria burst into hysterics. Arturo would get arrested at the control post at the entrance to Rome, she wailed; or else he would get picked up in a *rastrellamento* in the city. Had he not heard of Marshal Graziani's new manifesto which ordered all young men to report for national work?

I knew that there was some sense behind Maria's outburst because, by this time, Arturo had described to me the three weeks which he had spent in Rome between the Italian armistice on 8th September and his flight to Nespolo at the end of the month.

He had heard the news of the armistice on the radio in a café where he was drinking a glass of *carpano* with a fellow bank clerk. Rina and the children had just gone to Nespolo for a month and he was making the most of the break in his domestic life to enjoy the pleasures of his bachelor days.

Like everyone else in the café, Arturo had been expecting the announcement ever since the King had dismissed Mussolini back in July and he had welcomed it as a victory for common sense. He was fed up with the war and with the presence of the Germans in Rome. He had imagined, as we had at Chieti, that Italy's defection would force the *tedeschi* to withdraw to the north. Then the *anglo-americani* would enter Rome, and the war would end.

At that moment there had been about ten thousand Germans in Rome, but few of them were fighting troops. Many were SS men, disguised in civilian clothes and dispersed in hotels, boarding houses and private homes. But on the next day a German Division had moved on the capital. It had met with a measure of resistance from units of the Italian army, alongside which had rallied a number of civilians who had armed themselves with weapons discarded by deserting soldiers. After three days of sporadic fighting both inside and outside the city's perimeter, days during which the King and Marshal Badoglio had fled south to join the Allies, the Germans had gained control — to such an extent that Field Marshal Kesselring was able to announce from his headquarters in the Alban hills that Rome was under German martial law.

Despite his disappointment at the turn of events, Arturo had still imagined that it was only a matter of weeks before the Allies would drive the Germans out. He had gone to work in the bank as usual, happy to know that his wife, children and mother were safe in Nespolo. He was not, like men in the armed forces,

117

faced with the choice of either continuing to fight alongside the Germans or of being classified by them as a deserter, because thanks to a tubercular chest he had been exempted from military service. He had appeared to be in no immediate danger.

Consequently, his seizure towards the end of September by the Germans in a manhunt had shattered him. He knew that it was only by a combination of luck and his own quick wits that he was not now digging defences as his bank manager believed him to be doing.

Remembering his narrow escape, Arturo must have wondered if Maria was not right. The tears cascaded down her cheeks as she implored him not to leave. It was my first sight of the southern temperament *in extremis*.

"*Madonna mia*, you're mad!" she screamed. "You are putting your head on the block. The *tedeschi* will arrest you again for sure."

We calmed her down as best we could, telling her that Rome was quieter now, that there were dangers in Nespolo too. La Nonna was speaking with her hands. She had clasped them together in an attitude of prayer and was shaking them first at Maria, then at Arturo. She was crying gently, but I fancied that a part of her was enjoying the emotional excitement.

"We can't stay in Nespolo for ever," Arturo argued. "This house is not ours, for one thing. Besides, I must go back to work."

"*Mamma mia!*" wailed Maria, who was not even listening. "What will become of us!"

118

"Besides," Arturo went on, "Lucia says that Rome will be quite safe for me. Also for Gianni."

The mention of her clever young sister provoked a further outburst from Maria.

"Lucia! You always listen to Lucia!"

"And I have my card, signed by the *tedeschi*. The one Lucia forged for me."

"*Già*," said La Nonna. "Arturo has his card. Run, run, all of you. If not, you will miss the bus."

Within ten minutes of their leaving Maria was her normal, happy self. She made me an extra mug of barley coffee and produced a couple of cigarettes which she had hidden away. I spent a pleasant morning, gossiping and joking with her. I decided that in Arturo's absence it would be wise to stay indoors. Nor did the weather encourage exercise. Icy winds from the snow-clad peaks were sweeping down the spine of hill to which the village clung. The pools of urine outside our front door froze hard each morning, and ice covered the ponds where, in the summer, the peasants soaked their hemp.

The house seemed strangely empty, but there were consolations to be appreciated. With the departure of Rina and the Signorina, all the household knew that I was English. It was a relief to be able to drop all pretence. I was tired of my many alibis. Only Stellina, full of the curiosity of her four years, could plague me with awkward questions, and it maddened me that she should be able to express them in an Italian so much more grammatical than my own. One day, exasperated

119

beyond measure, I lost my temper with her, put her over my knee and smacked her on the bottom. Maria was furious with me but La Nonna could hardly disguise her delight.

La Nonna and Maria competed in trying to spoil me with food and wine. In anticipation of German requisitioning, the peasants were slaughtering some of their stock, so that lamb and kid were comparatively cheap to buy. After immense suppers, we would sit round the fire and talk. The room, dark and dismal in daytime, glowed in the light of fire and lamp. One evening the conversation turned to religion.

"*Non sei Cristiano*," said La Nonna.

"But yes. I am a Christian."

"But how can you be? You don't go to Mass, you don't worship the Pope."

"I am a Christian but not a Catholic."

"It's not possible. *O Cristiano o no!*"

"I am a Protestant."

"*Protestante!* I too make the protest, sometimes. Against the King, against the *porco* Mussolini! What has that got to do with *Gesù*, or with the Madonna? You're not an Arab, are you?"

"What on earth have the Arabs to do with it?" said Maria.

"Don't you know *gli arabi*, Maria? They live in Africa, they have a black god, what's he called? *Maometto*, something like that."

"No, I am not a Mohammedan! Come to England," I went on, "and I will show you thousands of people like me, Christians who don't worship the Pope."

"I don't believe you, Gianni. But I will come to England."

"Any time you like," I said.

"*Vengo, vengo*. Of course I'll come to England. Is it far from here? You can come and fetch me in an aeroplane."

Next day La Nonna took the children to visit some friends and I was left alone with Maria. At lunchtime her black eyes were bright with excitement.

"I have a surprise for you, Gianni."

"Good, I like surprises. What is it?"

"*Momento*." She took a large pot off the hook hanging above the fire. "Shut your eyes, Gianni."

I obeyed. I heard her walk across to the table and put a plate down in front of me.

"*Va bene*. You can open your eyes."

I did so. On the table before me was the head of a sheep, its pinkish tongue lolling forward between two rows of pointed, glistening teeth. Its glutinous eyes looked bashful, even shy. The hair stood up straight from its low brow.

"*Guarda, com'è bella!* See how beautiful it is!"

I made a suitable comment in praise of its *bellezza*.

Smiling with pleasure, Maria took a small hatchet and split the head neatly down the middle. One profile she handed to me.

"You mustn't tell *Mamma*," she confided. "I thought that, if we ate it today when she was out, we could have half each."

I mustered a smile, hoping she would mistake my trepidation for excitement. Summoning all my

121

manhood, I took up my knife and fork and started to scrape the hairy skin from the left temple. The eye, which was of a bluish tinge, seemed to criticize my clumsy surgery.

"Take out the eye and put it aside," she said. "It is the best bit of all and should be kept for last."

I tried to copy the neat movement with which she had scooped the eye from the half head on her own plate.

Wishing that the sight of the eye and molars had not upset my stomach, I struggled on until my profile had been reduced to a heap of bones. Maria did likewise and soon there was nothing edible left on either plate except for the two lonely eyes.

"Now, Gianni!"

I forced myself to concentrate on the succulence of oysters, then gulped. The eye slid down in a single swallow. I took a long swig of wine and smacked my lips.

"How good, Maria! Thank you for the lovely surprise."

"You liked the eye? Then you must have mine too."

"No, no," I implored, appalled at the result of my feigned enthusiasm. "It would be too greedy of me to have both the eyes."

I am glad to say that she did not protest.

CHAPTER
SEVEN

Arturo had gone to Rome on the 3rd November with the intention of staying there for three days. By the morning of the 9th we were beginning to fret a little at his continued absence. Had Maria's premonition been right and was Arturo now helping to dig the defences which the Germans were said to be constructing south of the city limits? Though trying to maintain the phlegmatic Englishman's façade of confidence, I was secretly more than a little worried. My anxiety was increased by a rumour that the *tedeschi*, having heard that Paolo and Riccardo had been back to Nespolo, were snooping round the village in the evenings, dressed in civilian clothes, in the hope of surprising them.

Late on the evening of the 9th, Arturo, Rina, Ida and baby Marilanda arrived back in Nespolo. The journey had been a nightmare. The railway junction at Tivoli had been bombed again, causing the cancellation of trains from Rome. When they had eventually reached Carsoli more than a day later than they had intended, they found that they had missed the last bus up the valley. They had walked for a mile or so before being given a lift by a German, who took them as far as the

Nespolo turning. And they had walked the final five kilometres up the hill to the village.

Arturo reported that he had now satisfactorily completed all his plans and that he was ready to move as soon as the *Polizia Africana Italiana* officer — whose friendship he had been so assiduously cultivating — could send a lorry. Although Rome had been declared an open city, there were many Germans about and *rastrellamenti* were taking place from time to time. The Allied air forces were respecting the centre of the city and were confining their raids to the perimeter and marshalling yards, if one discounted the mysterious lone plane which, a few days previously, had dropped a stick of four bombs straight across the centre of the Vatican. (At the time no one knew the nationality of this unidentified plane, but history has since disclosed that the pilot was a Fascist sergeant of the Italian air force who aimed by his actions to make believe that the Allies were disregarding Vatican neutrality.) Identity cards were carefully scrutinized on the train, but Arturo hoped that, by travelling in a *PAI* lorry, we would escape with a more cursory check.

Lucia had made arrangements for me to stay at the family flat in Via Famagosta with herself, her old father, La Nonna and Ida. This would be a much safer place for me than Arturo's flat on the south-western outskirts of the city; apart from which, Arturo hoped to be soon back at work while Lucia, now without a job, was free to look after me.

All now depended on the arrival of the *PAI* officer at the end of the week and the fulfilment of his promise to take us to Rome, together with our stock of food.

Next morning, snow, which had previously only lain on the ridges of the Apennines, fell on the village. We spent most of the day tying up the provisions which we had accumulated: two huge sacks each of chestnuts, flour and potatoes, smaller bags of apples and charcoal. On the 12th La Nonna, Ida and Stellina left for Rome in the back of a Red Cross lorry. On the same day Maria moved to the nearby village of Colle Giove where she had arranged to spend the winter teaching sewing and dressmaking to the village children. Now our numbers were reduced to four: Arturo, Rina, little Marilanda and myself. The next day the officer of the *PAI* arrived from Rome with his sergeant and driver.

Their lorry, I was glad to see, was huge. It might well have been a furniture van. We borrowed a barrow and wheeled our seven sacks down to the lower end of the village to a piece of open ground where the driver had parked his lorry, and we stacked them under a stunted tree which did little to protect them from the rain, now falling steadily. A crowd of peasants hoping for a lift had already assembled. The *PAI* officer was supervising the loading of the provisions which he had bought for his Mess at Rome. He was an arrogant little man, full of bounce and bombast, and he was ordering the peasants around as though they were slaves, a habit perhaps acquired during his service in Somaliland or Abyssinia. I took an intense dislike to him.

125

As we watched the level of the load creep up towards the roof, we wondered whether there would be any space left for us. The officer confirmed his promise to Arturo that we would get preference over other would-be passengers. He hoped to leave at 4p.m.

By 4p.m. the last of the *PAI*'s purchases had been loaded. We would leave at 6p.m.

By 6p.m. our own sacks had been loaded. We would leave at 8p.m.

By 8p.m. the baggage of all the other passengers had been loaded. But the driver discovered that the headlights of the lorry were not working correctly. *Pazienza!* We would leave at 6a.m. the following day.

Arturo had already stripped bare the house.

"It doesn't matter," he told me. "We will have supper at Palmira's and doss down in her kitchen."

I liked Rina's fat, jovial sister who was one of those who believed that I came from the north. Since her husband had been captured on the Russian Front, she and her brood of children had shared a house with two old uncles, Zio Zompa and Zio Ettore.

"I shall ask the *PAI* officer and his sergeant to join us for supper," Arturo continued.

"*Madonna mia!* Is that really necessary?"

"*Stai tranquillo*, don't worry, Gianni. There is really no danger. I want to make quite sure that they take us with them in the morning. There are lots of others who want a lift in their lorry, you know."

I could see that a little of Palmira's food and wine would help to ingratiate us with them, but I did not relish the prospect of our supper party. The officer was an educated man who must notice that my accent was odd. I decided that I would try and keep silent and, if necessary, again play the part of the village idiot.

Fortunately, there were at least ten of us assembled in Palmira's kitchen when the two men of the *PAI* joined us. I sat in the semi-darkness at the far end of the table, beside Palmira's young son and old Zio Zompa, who found the presence of policemen at his table as distasteful as did I. I was thankful to find that the policemen showed no interest in my presence; they chatted together, making jokes about the primitiveness of our table manners, and for all the attention they paid us, we might have been animals. Their own manners disgusted me. They consumed Palmira's food and wine without a word of thanks. They smoked their own cigarettes and never thought to offer one to us, who had not had a proper smoke since the rations lorry had been bombed. Their air of smug superiority made me long to reveal my identity.

At last they left us. There was a bed upstairs for Rina and Marilanda, but Arturo and I had to make do with the kitchen furniture. I made a pillow with a rug and stretched myself out on the long wooden table at which we had eaten.

I had hoped that the quantity of wine which I had drunk would compensate for the hardness of my bed and that I would fall easily into sleep. But I was far too excited. My thoughts jerked backwards and forwards in time like the dials of a fruit machine, unable to credit the fact that I was really going to Rome. A thick mist obscured my future; my past, previous to my arrival in

Nespolo, seemed infinitely remote. Only the intervening days had any reality. I counted them up and found that they totalled forty-six. I tried to remember myself as I had been when I had arrived in the village under the shelter of Ida's blue umbrella. What had I expected to find? Certainly not the kindness and courage of the Platano family. For a few minutes I let my memory bask in the warmth of their friendship towards me and dwell on the sunny days which we had spent together gathering chestnuts; and on the evenings, rich with laughter, when we had sat round the fire roasting the shiny nuts and quaffing the rough red wine.

I shuddered at the memory of the other side of the picture: of the agony of my long walk under arrest back through the woods, when I had been tortured by indecision and appalled by the proximity of death; and of the fear which had pervaded the village during the days when the Germans had threatened its destruction.

Had the experience of these forty-six days in Nespolo left their mark on me? At the moment I could not tell. Any more than I could tell if there were other escaped PoWs in the surrounding mountainside who were experiencing adventures similar to my own. What had happened to the train after I had jumped from it? Had others followed me through the ventilator high on the side of the cattle truck?

One day, perhaps, I would know the answer to these and other questions.

★　★　★

We got up at 5a.m. In readiness for our arrival in Rome, we shaved our stubbly chins and washed as best we were able.

It was still dark as we walked through the rain to the lorry parked at the lower end of the village. Arturo carried a suitcase, Rina carried Marilanda and I a basket containing our two hens. By the time dawn had broken, a dozen others had assembled round the lorry. We were already wet and cold when the *PAI* officer, with his sergeant and driver, joined us shortly after six. The sourness of the officer's temper suggested that he had slept as fitfully as I had done.

There was a space in the lorry of perhaps four feet between the level of the top of the load and the roof. The officer lined us up in order of priority, for there were more people hoping for a lift than could possibly be squeezed inside. A ladder was positioned against the baggage at the open back of the lorry. The first to go up was a nun. Our party followed. We had to crawl right down the length of the constricted space between sacks and roof, a claustrophobic experience for me if for no one else.

Others joined us until we were packed head to feet down the length of the lorry. In addition to the nun, the passengers included the village lawyer, one of the tarts who had been staying with *la spia*, three children and several peasants reeking of pig manure. The back door was swung up and bolted, the lorry lurched over the bridge and down the rough road into the valley. Discomfort is a great leveller and soon we were as merry as a band of Canterbury pilgrims. Cramped but

129

happy, I bumped about on top of the sacks in the semi-darkness. At my head was the basket of hens and at my feet little Marilanda, squealing with rage and pissing on the sacks of flour.

The lorry's pace quickened as we joined the main road at Carsoli. At Tivoli and again at the gates of Rome, it was stopped by German military police. To my relief, for I was dubious as to the adequacy of my document, the *PAI* officer's testimony for our credentials was accepted at both halts.

We had been driving for more than five hours when we halted for the last time. The back door of the lorry was swung open and, as the passengers climbed down one by one, we crawled slowly back towards the open door. When it came to my turn to jump down, I found that I was so stiff that I stumbled on landing. I picked myself up and saw in front of me the plinths and arches of the Roman Forum.

My recollections of my first few hours in Rome consist not of a logical sequence of events, but rather of a series of visual impressions engraved with the vivid, yet distorted, characteristics of a dream, and separated from each other by blank patches in my memory. There comes to my mind a picture of myself, Arturo and Rina, the latter with Marilanda in her arms, standing among a multitude of sacks on a broad pavement alongside the Colosseum. Pedestrians stream past us, trams rattle along broad avenues towards the huge monument to Vittorio Emanuele II, confusing me with their unfamiliar noise.

In the next tableau I see myself strap-hanging beside Arturo in a crowded tram as it crosses the Tiber and runs south alongside the Janiculum gardens. I catch a glimpse of the Castel Sant'Angelo and the great dome of St Peter's. Other landmarks, familiar only in my imagination, cross my field of vision. I am bewildered by so vast and wonderful a scene. Two years have passed since I have seen a shop, a café or a well-dressed woman; and my astonishment is that of a peasant faced for the first time with the wonders of civilization.

Between these two scenes, we must have made some practical arrangements. How, for example, did we dispose of our seven sacks? I have a vague memory that Arturo spent some time in a telephone box and that a cousin of Rina's, a butcher by trade, came to our assistance.

In the final tableau, I am sitting in the living-room of Arturo's little ground-floor flat. The fields run up to within sight of the window, because the modern block in which he lives lies on the extreme south-western outskirts of the city. The front door opens and Lucia walks in. She has come to fetch me and take me to La Nonna's flat. She is small, dark-haired and vivacious, and as pretty as the image of her which I have fashioned from Arturo's descriptions. Her urbanity makes me feel shy and boorish, but she soon puts me at my ease by laughing at my tattered trousers and long, unkempt hair.

"Never mind, Gianni," she says, "I'll have you looking like a Roman in a day or two. Meanwhile

131

Arturo must lend you an overcoat. I won't be seen on the tram with you looking like this."

The thread of my memory, from the moment of my meeting with Lucia, is continuous. I borrowed from Arturo a coat which, though far too small for me, covered up most of my shabbiness, and with Lucia I set off on the long tramride to the family flat. We changed trams at Piazza del Risorgimento and alighted about half a mile north of the Vatican. A short walk brought us into Via Famagosta, a small street lying between, and parallel to, two large boulevards, the Via Giulio Cesare and the Viale delle Milizie.

We stopped outside the archway to No 8. In order to avoid being noticed by the porter who lived in the lodge beneath the archway, Lucia had timed our arrival to fall within the one hour of darkness which preceded the 7p.m. curfew. After she had checked that he was not standing beneath the arch, we passed through it into a dark courtyard and from there turned right into a second, smaller yard. I followed Lucia to Staircase G.

"*Coraggio*, Gianni," she said, "there are a hundred and forty steps."

The stairs were uncarpeted and our steps on the cold stone rang out and echoed up the long shaft where there should have been a lift. There were two flats on each landing, one on either side of the central shaft. We climbed to the top floor.

"*Eccoci, finalmente arrivati!*" said Lucia, pressing the bell of the door on our right with three short, staccato bursts.

The door opened. La Nonna was on the threshold, dressed as always in black with a shawl draped round her shoulders. She threw her arms around me.

"*Bravo*, Gianni, I told you that you'd get here safely, didn't I? You see how *il Papa* has guided you to our home."

"*Il Papa*? Don't talk nonsense. What on earth has the Pope got to do with it? It's you and Arturo who have arranged it all!"

"*Disgraziato!*" she admonished me. "I can see that you have not changed at all."

PART THREE

Rome

CHAPTER
ONE

Throughout the summer and early autumn of 1943, the men who shaped Italy's political pattern had been scattered and reassembled in the manner of the glass pieces of a kaleidoscope. With each twist the centre pieces, round which the pattern took form and colour, had been dislodged from their positions of power and banished to the peripheries, their places being appropriated by others of a different shape and hue. With the King's dismissal of Mussolini on 25th July, the true-blue Marshal Badoglio had been thrust into the centre of the circle. Around him had gathered, in the places previously occupied by the Fascist hierarchy, a group of dedicated monarchists and senior officers of the armed forces. At a further distance from the centre, but prominent enough to give a pink tinge to the new political kaleidoscope, were a number of distinguished anti-Fascists who had returned after the change of government from prisons on the Lipari Islands where they had been confined by Mussolini, or from enforced exile in Switzerland.

The kaleidoscope had again oscillated violently as the Germans fought out the battle for Rome during the days which followed the declaration of the armistice on

137

8th September. Mussolini was rescued from the ski-hut in which he had been imprisoned on the top of the Gran Sasso mountain. The Italian Royal Family, together with Marshal Badoglio, fled south to join the Allies, and within a week all opposition within Italy to the Germans and Mussolini had been driven underground, except, naturally, in the southern extremity of the peninsula which was occupied by the Allies. Prominent Fascists, who had been arrested or had gone into hiding on 25th July, were reinstated in positions of authority, while those leading anti-Fascists who managed to avoid arrest were forced back into the shadows from which they had so recently emerged. The pieces of the Italian kaleidoscope had re-formed in a pattern similar to that which had been shattered by the overthrow of Mussolini in July, with this difference: that the central position was occupied now, not by Mussolini, but by the Commander of German troops in Italy, Field Marshal Kesselring. Kesselring's first act had been to place Rome under martial law and appoint General Maelzer as its military commander, in place of General Calvi di Bergolo, who was locked up in Rome's ancient prison, the Regina Coeli.

The city which I reached on 15th November was therefore ruled, in name as well as practice, by Germans rather than Fascist Italians. There had been few changes since Arturo's flight to the country seven weeks previously. Anti-German feeling had hardened and a fillip had been given to the underground resistance movement by Marshal Badoglio's declaration of war against Germany on 17th October. Kesselring's headquarters remained at Frascati, ten miles away in the Alban hills; General Maelzer continued to rule the city with an iron hand. He was a rubicund, wine-swilling bully who lived in the Hotel Excelsior where, according to popular gossip, he spent his nights in feasting with his cronies and mistresses, as though bent on driving from his mind the odium in which he was held by the million and a half citizens of whom he was absolute master.

The most dreaded gaol in Rome, in which Mussolini's most dangerous enemies were incarcerated, was the Regina Coeli prison on the west bank of the Tiber. The *Gestapo* torture chamber operated from a house in the Via Tasso which had previously been the seat of the German Institute of Culture; the Fascist equivalent was established in a house in the Via Romagna.

The Italian Ministries, dependent officially on Mussolini's newly-constituted Republican-Fascist Government, based near Verona, were in practice the tools of General Maelzer. Those departmental heads appointed during Badoglio's tenure had been replaced by dyed-in-the-wool Fascists who had spent the months of the late summer in prison.

The turn of the kaleidoscope in September had also tumbled from their chairs the editors of the Roman Press and raised in their places a sycophantic group of newspaper men, who were prepared to publish in the pages of their dailies — the *Popolo di Roma*, the *Messaggero* and the *Giornale d'Italia* — a version of the news twisted to please their German masters. The

139

Carabinieri, a police force which took its oath to the King, had been disbanded, most of its members having deserted. An Italian secret police force, modelled on the German *Gestapo*, had been formed from a few genuine supporters of Mussolini and a rabble of juvenile and other delinquents released from the city's prisons.

A curfew operated from 7 P.M., after which hour anyone out in the streets was a legitimate target for the rifles of the police; trams and buses ceased to run half an hour earlier. It was forbidden to pass the night in the houses of others, to cross certain streets in the neighbourhood of the German-infested Via Veneto, to enter or leave the city without a permit, or to telephone outside Rome. The use of bicycles was also forbidden, because of the partisans' practice of tossing hand-grenades from them as they pedalled past groups of German soldiers. It was a crime to listen to radio broadcasts from London and also from Bari or Palermo, both of which were in Allied hands, and a capital offence to conceal a political refugee, a deserter from the armed forces, or an escaped prisoner of war. It was even dangerous to look like a Jew, to be shabbily dressed, or to carry a parcel which looked as though it might contain a hand-grenade.

Fortunately it was impossible for the authorities to enforce all these laws. The majority of dwellings housed a refugee of one sort or another, a deserter, a civil servant evading the new Fascist republic, a Jew or a north Italian who had come south in September in the hope of crossing the Front Line. Some of these "wanted" men so feared arrest that they never left their dwellings for weeks on end; a few even walled themselves up in concealed rooms. But the curfew was stringently enforced and each evening the streets would resound with the sound of shots aimed at stragglers. It was at least expedient to shut the windows before listening to an Allied broadcast.

The economic situation was equally grim. For geographical reasons it would be difficult to imagine a less suitable location for the siting of a capital city. Rome stands in the centre of a barren and thinly populated plain, on the banks of a river liable to flood but incapable of being navigated. It is only twelve miles from the coast, yet enjoys none of the advantages of a maritime port. It is cut off by surrounding mountains from easy communication with the rest of the peninsula. In the days of which I write it enjoyed the support of neither agriculture, industry nor commerce.

These geographical disadvantages, comparatively unimportant in peacetime, were exacerbated by the war, which also reversed the benefits derived in peacetime from the ancient adage that all roads lead to Rome. For now the city became a bottleneck through which all German lines of communication with the Front on the west side of the Apennines had to pass. It was inevitable that the Allies should bomb and strafe the many roads which radiated from the heart of the city. In consequence, supplies of gas, water and electricity were in constant jeopardy and the Romans were virtually isolated from the countryside which, in normal times, provided the bulk of their food. A black market thrived, but its prices were too high for the pockets of the man of modest means. Its presence provided another source of intrigue for a people who were contemptuous of all authority save, possibly, that of the Pope.

This picture of the Roman situation began to take shape in my mind during the course of the long conversation which I had with Lucia on my first evening at Via Famagosta. It was a pleasure to talk with someone both so intelligent and well-informed; and her wit made me realize that at Nespolo I had fallen into the habit of thinking, as well as dressing and acting, like a peasant. It was now up to Lucia to give me the new identity which would transform me into an inconspicuous inhabitant of Rome.

No. 8 Via Famagosta, where the Platanos lived, was a group of about one hundred and fifty flats built at the beginning of the century on what had then been the extreme north-western outskirts of Rome. The blocks of flats which made up the group were built around two intercommunicating courtyards, in the first of which a sick palm tree, planted in the centre of the irregular yard, added to the general air of neglect and decrepitude which radiated from the peeling stucco of the walls and the flaking paint of the window shutters. The tenants of the flats were for the most part *piccoli borghesi*, white-collar workers, tram conductors, shop assistants and suchlike.

The Platanos' flat was in the second courtyard, on the top floor of Staircase G. It consisted of four rooms, a kitchen and a lavatory. The front door led into a passage, on the left of which three rooms looked south on to the courtyard; the first was occupied by La Nonna's husband; the second, the brightest room in the flat due to the size of the window, was Lucia's. The third room contained two beds, usually slept in by Ida and Maria. But since Maria had not come to Rome with us, La Nonna was able to move into her bed to allow me the use of her own usual bedroom which was on the other side of the passage next to the kitchen and lavatory. The tall, shuttered windows of this room looked north on to the Viale delle Milizie, a wide boulevard flanked with pollarded plane trees. It was furnished with an old-fashioned sideboard topped by a mirror, an oak wardrobe and a divan bed.

All the floors of the flat were made of a cheap version of terrazzo and were uncarpeted. The solid furniture made no concessions to beauty or comfort. No dash of colour relieved the sombre tones of the curtains and walls, and there was neither sofa nor armchair to invite one to relax. Yet to me, accustomed to the rigours of Chieti and Nespolo, the flat seemed the acme of urban comfort.

I slept late on my first morning at Via Famagosta and, when I had dressed and made my way to the kitchen, I found that La Nonna, Ida and Lucia had already breakfasted. The old lady heated me up a cup of barley coffee and gave me a slice of bread.

"Do you see what a nice kitchen I have here?" she said to me. "I have gas and water, not like at Nespolo."

I looked around me. Along one side were ranged the gas cooker and the table at which, except on special occasions, we were to have all our meals. On the other side were a sink and a row of shelves and cupboards. My eye came to rest on a big aluminium tub beneath the sink.

"It's to take the bath," said La Nonna. "We have no bathroom and no hot water. But I can always heat some up for you when you want to wash or shave."

After I had breakfasted, Lucia took me up to the roof terrace, which was the common property of the tenants of our staircase. From this vantage point she was able to point out to me the famous landmarks of the city. Beneath us to the north the Via Trionfale pierced its way through modern shops and flats to the foot of Monte Mario, a bare cone-shaped hill crowned by an observatory. From a short distance to the south of us, the eastern wall of the Vatican ran down to Bernini's great colonnade. Beyond the Vatican City, which was dominated by the dome of St Peter's, the green gardens of the Janiculum glowed in the November sunshine. To the south-east, across the twisting Tiber, lay the heart of Rome, studded with monuments long familiar to me from photographs: the Spanish Steps, the Pantheon, the Capitol Hill, the huge, hideous monument to Victor Emmanuel II, the Colosseum and the Forum. Beyond the city curled the arid plain of the Roman Campagna, backed in the north-east by a gallery of snow-capped mountains and, in the south-east, by the spires and domes of the little towns which clustered on the Alban hills.

As there was no communal living-room in the flat, Lucia suggested that I should have the use of her room in the daytime. There were many disadvantages to my own bedroom. It never got the sunshine, it had no table and it housed the telephone, which was used frequently by one or other of the eleven Neapolitan refugees who lived in the four-roomed flat across the staircase from us. Lucia's room was quite the nicest in the flat, facing as it did south on to the courtyard and having in its centre a large oak table ideal for writing. In it was the family wireless set, kept in this room because none of the walls adjoined neighbouring flats, which prevented our neighbours from knowing that we listened to Radio London. I knew that I could be happy in this room, and spent the rest of the morning there, sorting out the scraps of diary which I had scribbled at Nespolo, listening to the radio and generally taking stock of my surroundings.

Something of the personality of Lucia was reflected in the atmosphere of her room, which was furnished with more taste than the rest of the flat. My evening's talk with her had made me realize that she had educated herself to a level far beyond that of her brother and sisters and had raised herself several notches on the social scale. Evidence of how Lucia's mode of life differed from, for example, Rina's was indicated by the presence in her room of books and a typewriter, and by the content of many snapshots of Lucia with her friends, picnicking on the beach at Ostia or dancing in the garden of a Roman *trattoria*. In spite of her obvious ambitions, she was both feminine and amusing.

The walls were hung with studio photographs of the whole family, including one of her father dressed in his Sunday best. He was known in the family as Babbino; we had decided that he should not be told that I had come to stay and that, in order to spare him the worry, my identity should be concealed from him. It would be easy, so I was told, to fulfil this apparently tall order because it might be several weeks before I came face to face with him, as he played no part whatsoever in the day-to-day life of the family.

Babbino had retired five years earlier from his work on the railways. Although he was seventy years old, he was still remarkably active. Each morning he would leave the flat at seven, wearing a collarless shirt beneath his hairy suit and a dirty old brown hat on the back of his head. After a long constitutional walk, he would join his cronies in a local wine-shop, where he would pass the day smoking his pipe and playing cards. He would return home in the late afternoon, have something to eat in his bedroom and go straight to sleep.

I studied his photograph with interest and saw a tall upright man with fair hair (his eyes, I was told, were blue) and a rather gruff expression. He looked anything but the southern Italian he was; his stature, colouring and heavy cast of features made a startling contrast to La Nonna's fine-boned darkness. I could now understand why their four daughters, whose portraits were aligned before me, were so different in appearance and, as I was already beginning to guess, in character. While Maria and Iolanda had both inherited their father's stature, Maria's features were finely modelled,

146

her hair black as pitch. Only the tall, auburn-haired, handsome Iolanda, whom I was yet to meet, resembled her father physically in every respect. In her own way, Iolanda was as successful as Lucia, her services as a qualified midwife being much in demand among the rich Roman families. She was working now as a child's nurse, having broken her usual custom and stayed on with a family after her successful delivery of the baby.

The photograph of Ida showed that she had inherited her father's fair colouring, but she had none of his stature and presence. Lastly I examined the photograph of Lucia whose bright, dark eyes sparkled at me with the intelligence of an attractive monkey.

Although we still clung to the idea that the Allies would be in Rome by Christmas, we were all agreed that I must have a measure of fresh air and exercise, unlike many young men who, in their determination to avoid the manhunt at all costs, remained permanently indoors. So that I should not attract attention in the streets, it was necessary to alter my rustic appearance. With this in mind, Arturo had borrowed a suit from a friend who was about my height and brought it round to Via Famagosta, where I tried it on. We decided that, like the overcoat which Arturo had lent me, it could be altered to fit me reasonably well.

Our first expedition was therefore to a tailor. Lucia went ahead of us through the courtyard to make sure that the porter was not hanging round the door of his lodge. I followed with Arturo at a discreet distance. I felt very much the country bumpkin as I dodged through the traffic in the Via Giulio Cesare to the tailor's shop in a neighbouring side street.

I let Arturo explain what was needed and stood in silence while the tailor took my measurements. Despite my greater height, Arturo's overcoat needed only minor alterations, having been cut in the Roman fashion of the time to hang nearly to his ankles. The suit, a grey worsted, presented more of a problem. But by dint of turning down the cuffs of the trousers and lengthening the sleeves, a passable fit was attained. Lucia insisted on buying for me a pair of socks and a white shirt.

Our next visit was to Arturo's barber, where my hair was trimmed behind but left long at the side, smothered with oil and brushed back over my ears in the fashion favoured by Roman *giovanotti*. Finally we went to a photographer, who took photos of me of a size suitable for transference to Antonio Maggi's identity and ration cards. Throughout the expedition I was given confidence by the knowledge that many Romans were at this time trying to change their appearance, and that no tailor, barber or photographer was therefore likely to ask embarrassing questions.

When the alterations to my wardrobe had been completed and my army footwear replaced by a borrowed pair of black, ultra-pointed shoes, we were satisfied that, with my dark hair and straight nose, I looked not out of place in the streets of Rome. Lucia criticized only my walk and I tried to adopt a more Roman ambulation whereby the right shoulder tends to swing forward with the right leg instead of with the left.

I soon evolved a simple routine to ease the monotony of my days. I would get up late, usually at ten o'clock when a siren sounded to announce the morning break at a nearby factory. La Nonna would be in the kitchen to give me breakfast: a cup of black *ersatz* coffee and a nibble of bread, should I have succeeded in preserving any of my ration from the previous day. This consisted of a roll, about the size of my fist, and until such time as Antonio Maggi had drawn his ration card bearing my photograph, I had to depend for this, as for all my rations, on the charity of Iolanda who, being fed by her employers, gave me hers.

After breakfast I would shave and dress with considerable ceremony and do a few gentle exercises. This would take me to eleven o'clock when I would shut the windows in Lucia's room and tune in to the morning news from Radio London. If Lucia was at home, she would then give me an Italian lesson, otherwise I would study or read one of her few Italian novels till it was time for lunch. Meanwhile La Nonna would dust the furniture and sweep the floors. She kept the flat spotlessly clean and, by so doing, confounded my English prejudice that the Italians were dirty. Only Babbino's room, crowded with trunks and boxes, escaped her dusters and brooms, for the old man liked to live higgledy-piggledy among his possessions.

Sometimes I would help La Nonna in the kitchen, learning to roast and grind ears of barley into *ersatz* coffee, to make sauce for the *pasta* from the meagre materials at our disposal and to first boil and then fry with a sliver of garlic the greens which we had bought in the market. At this time we had just enough to eat, thanks to the potatoes, flour and chestnuts which we had brought with us from Nespolo. The rations to which our cards entitled us were completely inadequate. Apart from the 150-gram roll of bread issued daily, they consisted of a small quantity of macaroni, spaghetti or rice issued (in theory) once a week, two ounces of meat and one egg issued once a month, and a small quantity of sugar which never lasted us for more than a few days. All kinds of food were available on the black market, but at prices well beyond our pockets. All that we could afford to buy were vegetables: dried beans and peas, cabbage, beetroot and turnip tops, chicory and fennel.

In the afternoon Arturo would usually pay us a visit. More often than not, he and I would go out together for a walk, and at least once a week we would go, with Lucia, to the local cinema. I enjoyed these expeditions not only for the films, which were usually Italian or German, occasionally French and, once, Hungarian, but also for the feeling of wellbeing and security which I got from relaxing in the dark in a comfortable seat. The only moments of danger came as we left the cinema. It was a favourite trick of the labour-hungry Germans and Fascists to cordon off cinema exits and we were always on guard against being caught in that kind of *rastrellamento*.

I made a point of returning to Via Famagosta during the short period of darkness immediately preceding the curfew in the hope of escaping the eye of the porter. In accordance with Roman custom, he was an official of the State and, as such, expected to spy on his tenants. From time to time, German or Fascist police would visit him to check on any new lodgers.

After I had got my Roman ration card in the name of Antonio Maggi, I was able to obtain another document, one which allowed me to buy forty cigarettes each week at the controlled price. This was a privilege extended to men only, as Mussolini did not approve of women smoking. I tried to limit my consumption to six a day, but before the end of the week I was always reduced to smoking the butts of my cigarettes, which I would store in a tin during the day and re-roll each evening.

I would have supper with La Nonna, Ida and Lucia each evening at about 8 o'clock A normal meal would consist of *pasta* or potatoes or dried beans, with some green vegetable and what remained of the bread ration. During my first month there was wine and chestnuts brought from Nespolo. After supper we would sit in the kitchen and talk. I might tell them about life in England, of which they knew next to nothing, far less than of America to which so many peasants had emigrated; La Nonna might recount stories of miracles which she had witnessed during her childhood in Apulia; Lucia would relate the gossip of the day. Often we would play at cards, either *scopa* ("broom") or *briscola* ("trump"), two excellent games requiring both card sense and that tactical slyness — *furberia* — at which the Italians excel.

Both games were played with the Neapolitan pack of cards which was the oldest in Europe, originating as it did in the fourteenth century and deriving from the

151

emblematic *tarot* picture cards. The pack had ten cards in each of the four suits: numbers one to seven and three picture cards — king, chevalier and valet. The suits were *spade* (swords), *coppe* (cups), *denari* (money), and *bastoni* (clubs).

I was greatly intrigued by the Neapolitan pack and spent pleasant hours speculating how the symbols and names of its suits had developed into the modern packs of England, Italy and France. After the war I checked my deductions in *Chamber's Encyclopaedia* and was interested to find that certain anomalies defy explanation. It seems that the origins of the symbols of the Neapolitan pack are emblematic, that swords stood for justice, cups for faith, money for charity and clubs for fortitude. But odd things happened in the transmission of these symbols to the modern pack. In England, for example, we use the word "clubs" (a direct translation of the Italian word *bastoni*) to describe the suit which the Neapolitans marked with a caveman's weapon but which has evolved in the modern pack into a suit represented by a trefoil and called *trèfles* in France and *fiori* (flowers) in Italy. And we call the suit, now marked by a wild plum and known in France as *piques* and in Italy as *picche*, by the name of "spades", which is a transliteration of the Italian word and Neapolitan suit "swords".

The derivation of our red suits is less obscure. The Neapolitan cups have become "hearts", both in symbol and name, in all three countries, and money has become "diamonds" in England, *quadri*, or "squares" in Italy and *carreaux*, or "small squares", in France.

★ ★ ★

My daily routine was broken every Sunday when, together with at least one of his sisters, I would visit Arturo. First we would go to Mass at our local church, then take two trams to the south-western outskirts of the city where Arturo lived. After the order of Via Famagosta, I found the anarchic confusion which characterized Arturo's married life stimulating. Rina would lie on the sofa bawling at her husband and trying to flirt with me, while the little girls screamed incessantly.

This was the best meal of the week for all of us. Usually there was something other than *pasta* or potatoes. Once we had tripe. On another Sunday we ate one of the hens which we had brought from Nespolo. But despite the food and the stimulation I was often glad when the time came to leave, so strident was the atmosphere which Rina created, so wearisome to me the pretence with her that I was other than English.

After lunch we would, if the weather was fine, take the little girls on an expedition, usually to the Janiculum gardens but once by tram across the Tiber to the gardens of the Pincio where we watched the Romans boat on the lake and fly their elegant coloured kites in the high Italian sky.

After the dramas of Nespolo my first month in Rome was restful, if a little dull. For all I knew I was the only escaped prisoner of war in Rome. And if at times I queried my lack of enterprise in not pushing south towards the Front, I could still console myself with the spurious dream that the Allies would be in Rome by Christmas.

CHAPTER
TWO

"Not bad, Gianni," said Lucia. "But *balcone* is masculine, not feminine, and you think *to* not *of* someone."

She had been correcting my Italian composition and I had bet her a cigarette that there was no mistake.

"Rot the dogs!" I said, to show her that at least I had mastered some Italian slang, and tossed her a cigarette. "Just wait till I start giving you English lessons!"

"You can start next week, but not on Monday. That's St Lucia's Day — the 13th of December — on which I was born, and I am giving a birthday party. About fifteen people, all good friends of mine, are coming and I don't see why you shouldn't appear."

"*Vengo con piacere.*"

"I will tell them that you are a friend of mine from Sicily. Nobody will notice your accent with the gramophone playing. I have a girl friend for you to dance with, and I want you to meet Enrico."

Enrico was an army lieutenant who had gone into hiding after the armistice. Lucia had already told him about me.

"Good, I want to meet him."

"He has promised to give me a bottle of *spumante*. And Iolanda is bringing wine and cakes."

The party was to be held in my bedroom, and we spent the Monday morning moving furniture around and wiring up the gramophone. La Nonna used the last of the flour which we had brought from Nespolo to make a *pizza*. She tried to hide her excitement with some characteristic digs at Lucia's friends.

"You'll see, Gianni, how grand they all are. *Tenente* this! *Maestro di Musica* that! What do they want with an old woman like me?"

"Never mind, I'll dance with you."

"*Cretino*! Do you think that I can dance the foxtrot?" She put her skinny arms above her head and spun into a pirouette. "This is what I call dancing."

I took great trouble with my appearance. It was evident to me that I was going to be produced as a boyfriend of Lucia's. It was therefore important to her that I should not *fare brutta figura*, and for the first and only time during my stay with the Platanos I felt class-conscious. I remembered the infinite gradations which in every industrialized society divide the middle class into strata. Lucia was anything but a snob, but she was conscious, in a way that the rest of her family were not, of the social gap which divided me from the peasants of Nespolo among whom I had been living. She did not realize that it was probably easier for me than for her to bridge this gap. I was a little afraid of meeting her friends and unsure of the social mannerisms which I should assume if I was to fit naturally into the background of her friends.

In fact, as soon as they started to arrive, I lost my misgivings, so pleasant and friendly were all Lucia's guests. Nevertheless it was a comfort to see La Nonna hovering in the background, ready at a moment's notice to rescue me from any conversational impasse which might arise. But it was easy to say *piacere* and shake hands with the people to whom I was introduced. The laughter and music were loud enough to drown my mumbled invitations to dance, my gestures alone proving sufficient to make clear my intention. And should I fail to understand my partner's remarks I could cover my confusion by clasping her tighter to my chest.

I danced with Lucia's blonde girl friend who had worked with her in the Ministry of Culture. This girl was half Austrian, so that it was hardly surprising that she was now working with the Germans. I also exchanged a few words with Iolanda, whom I was meeting for the first time. She had heard so much about me, and me of her, that it was like meeting an old friend.

After a dance or two I was glad to take a glass of *spumante* and withdraw to Lucia's room with Enrico. I took an instant liking to him. He was small and dapper, with curly brown hair, and a sad mouth. As we did not wish to draw attention to ourselves by a prolonged absence from the party, our conversation was unnaturally hurried. But in the course of it I was able to discover that, like me, he was a gunner, and that his regiment had spent the siege of Tobruk sitting outside the perimeter of that desert fortress and lobbing shells

156

at me and the twenty-five thousand others who were besieged therein. We arranged that he should visit me later in the week, when we could have a leisurely talk.

I went back into the other room and stood beside La Nonna, watching the couples dance. But now I was far away, back in those stirring days of 1942, wandering in rocky caves and sand-swept dug-outs. I could taste again the brackish water, feel the blistering heat of the sun, hear the thud of bursting bombs and shells.

Ever since the failure of the attack which the Fifth Army had launched against the Gustav Line in early December, I had guessed that Rome would not be liberated by Christmas. The Rome Press carried graphic descriptions of this defensive line, which straddled the peninsula eighty miles south of Rome and pivoted on Monte Cassino. I had read in the *Messaggero* a scathing editorial which stressed that the *anglo-americani* had underestimated both the tenacity of the Germans and the strategic possibilities of the Italian terrain.

A visit with Lucia to our local cinema, which was showing a German documentary film, *The Heroes of Smolensk*, was enough to shatter any doubts which I might have entertained concerning German tenacity. And when Enrico came to see me a few days after Lucia's party, the first thing which he told me was that, for the past seventy years, Cassino had been quoted in Italian military manuals as an ideal winter defensive position.

Enrico's anti-tank regiment had been stationed near the mouth of the Tiber on the day of the armistice. He told me that it was one of the many units taken by surprise at the announcement. Instead of withdrawing to the north, as Enrico's colonel had expected, the nearby German HQ had threatened to attack his regiment unless it surrendered. In the face of a lack of clear orders, Enrico's troop had blown up their guns and dispersed into the countryside.

Enrico had discarded his uniform and gone into hiding in Rome, so that in the eyes of the Fascists and Germans he was a deserter. His own home and family being in Naples, on the other side of the line, he had been forced to ask friends to give him shelter. He was living from hand to mouth and, to add to his troubles, was suffering from ulcers.

Over a cup of mint tea which Lucia had made for us, he told me that he had recently joined an underground organization known as the *Centro Militare*, which had been built up by Colonel Montezemolo, a brilliant and courageous staff officer who had been Calvi di Bergolo's Chief of Civil Affairs during the latter's short-lived command of the Open City in September. When the Germans had occupied Rome, Calvi had been arrested, but Montezemolo had escaped and formed the nucleus of his organization from other officers, such as Enrico, who had gone into hiding.

The *Centro Militare* coordinated the sabotage operations of invisible bands of *militari*, ex-Army men operating against the Germans and Fascists in Lazio and Umbria, and collected intelligence which it transmitted by clandestine radio to the Allied Command. It also collaborated with Rome's other resistance organization, the military committee of the *Comitato di Liberazione Nazionale*. The *CLN* was later to coordinate all the partisans of Italy. Inspired by the five anti-Fascist political parties (from left to right the Communists, the Socialists, the Action Party, the Christian Democrats and the Liberals), the *CLN* controlled several groups of saboteurs within the city. Unlike the *Centro Militare*, which called itself apolitical (a term which, as is often the case, implied a right-wing bias), the *CLN* aimed not only to defeat the Germans but to provide the nucleus of a democratic government ready to rule the country after the end of the war. There was some rivalry between the two organizations.

All this was of great interest to me, for I was, at this time, totally ignorant of the Italian Resistance Movement. My newly acquired knowledge compensated for the depressing nature of the rest of Enrico's news. He confirmed that the Germans had just issued another manifesto ordering all able-bodied men to report for conscription in labour gangs. The manifesto went on to state that all deserters from the Armed Forces who failed to give themselves up by the end of December would be shot "whenever possible in their own homes". The Jews, too, were now being persecuted. Enrico believed that we were in for another wave of *rastrellamenti*, of which we had been comparatively free since my arrival in Rome. The Germans had announced that they would take a census in Rome on 30th December; for the first time I realized

159

the full extent of the Roman conspiracy and that I was one of many thousands who were leading clandestine lives. The predicament of some of them was worse than mine as their names were on a list of "wanted" men. Many made a practice of changing their addresses frequently to prevent the enemy from catching up with their movements.

I asked Enrico what he did for money. He told me that he had been able to borrow just enough from friends to buy his food on the black market. Naturally he was unable to use his ration card as he had been posted as a deserter.

"I gather that the price of food is soaring," I said.

"Inevitably. For one thing Rome is swollen with refugees from the north. Thousands came south in September hoping to cross the line."

"Are they still coming?"

"Only in driblets. The Germans and the republican Fascists, the *Repubblichini* as we call them, are making it as difficult as they can."

"Is food coming in from the countryside?"

"Not much. That's the real trouble. As the Germans don't want more people in Rome, they are levying a tax on it at the city gates. And, of course, your bombing raids on the roads leading to Rome help to isolate the city."

"Don't the Allies recognize Rome as an open city?"

"As I see it, you are prepared to do so as long as the Germans stick to their side of the bargain. But you and I both know that a lot of Germans are living in the city and that the marshalling yards are full of war material on its way to the Front. Still, it's a long time since you bombed the centre."

We changed the subject to a less depressing topic and reminisced about Tobruk. For eight months we had faced each other across a stretch of sand, two men behind guns, enemies cloaked in anonymity. But we had shared the same privations and experienced, too, the same beauty which night brings to the desert. In those days both of us had been sustained by the strength which comes from being one of a group. We had been relieved of the necessity to make decisions, whereas now we were two lone individuals, each responsible for his own fate. I drew comfort from the bond created between us by the similarity of both our past and present predicaments.

As Christmas approached we began to worry about how we were going to feed ourselves in the New Year. During the past month we had had just enough food to keep us healthy. But now the flour and chestnuts which we had brought with us from Nespolo were finished and we could see the bottom of our sack of potatoes. In future we would have to rely on windfalls to supplement the totally inadequate rations to which our cards entitled us. The family had spent nearly all their savings and the cost of food on the black market was beyond their modest means. The price of cooking oil, for instance, had increased forty-fold since the 8th of September. On the open market there was little to buy except vegetables in various stages of decay.

Undoubtedly we would have to tighten our belts. We needed money urgently.

"I'm starting to work in the New Year," announced Arturo one day. "The bank have agreed to take me back."

To excuse his sudden disappearance on the 1st October he had stuck to his story that he had been picked up in a *rastrellamento* and conscripted into a labour gang at Frosinone, from which he had only recently escaped. How much of this his bank manager believed, I could not tell. I myself could never quite believe Arturo's stories.

"I, too, must start work again," said Lucia. "The trouble is that the only jobs I can find are with the Germans."

"Don't worry, we'll manage somehow," said La Nonna. "*Dio provede*, you'll see."

God, in the shape of Iolanda, certainly provided us with a Christmas feast. She brought us a baby lamb, a present for us from the family for whom she worked, and with it some eggs, cakes, oranges and wine which she had bought on the black market. Arturo produced the last of his flour from Nespolo.

I spent the morning of the 23rd December in helping La Nonna to make enough *fettucine all'uova* for ten people. Together we kneaded the eggs and flour into a dough which we rolled out on the kitchen table and sliced into long, thin ribbons of golden paste. These we spread on a newspaper on the floor of my room. All night I had to struggle against the temptation to eat the twisting ribbons, which were setting into a perfect consistency for consumption on the following day.

On Christmas Eve I lunched at Arturo's and travelled back in the late afternoon with him, Rina and their little girls. They were all dining and spending the night with us, though where they would be sleeping I could not imagine. The start of curfew had been put back till 9 P.M. for the Christmas holiday, but we grumbled all the same that we would not be able to attend Midnight Mass at St Peter's, in normal years the highlight of the Platanos' Christmas.

We had decided to have our big meal on Christmas Eve and that night ten of us sat down for dinner in Lucia's room. Iolanda was staying with us and Babbino had been persuaded to postpone his usual bedtime. Apart from two brief confrontations in the passage, it was the first time I had met him. He had put on a tie in honour of the imminent arrival of the infant Jesus.

The menu remains printed in my memory, for it marked the last time for several months that my stomach was to be comfortably distended. All of us were ravenously hungry. We disposed quickly of the mountain of *fettucine* and attacked the baby lamb like a pack of wolves. Only when we had sucked the bones dry and moved on to the cake and oranges did we find time to talk. The wine had loosened La Nonna's tongue and mellowed Babbino's gruff manners.

"And when do you think the English will arrive?" she asked her husband.

"They come slowly, the rascals."

"And if I were to tell you that one of them was in Rome already?"

"What do you mean, woman?" Babbino scoffed. "They are all stuck in the snow at Cassino."

"Not all of them."

Rina looked as mystified as Babbino. The others were laughing at their confusion. There was no stopping La Nonna now.

"There's been an Englishman in your home for six weeks!" she shouted, waving her hand at me.

I turned my head towards Babbino.

"It's true," I said.

The old man got unsteadily to his feet.

"*Porca miseria!*" He looked me up and down. "*Inglese, tu?*"

"Yes, I'm English."

He thrust his horny hand across the table.

"*Bravo!*" he said. "*Bravo!*"

Rina was flabbergasted.

"*Madonna mia!* And to think that I never guessed!" she exclaimed. I could tell that she was thinking of Nespolo. "No wonder Arturo and Maria were so frightened when Gianni was arrested. And my cousin the *podestà*! What would he have felt had he but known!"

La Nonna explained to Babbino how I had pretended to be the village idiot. To illustrate her story, she pranced round the room, twisting her old body into monstrous shapes and grimacing horribly.

I am glad that cat is out of the bag, I thought. Perhaps now I will get on better with Rina.

After dinner, some of us played *scopa*. I could recognize in Babbino's play the hand of the expert and realized that it was not for nothing that he spent so many hours in the *osteria*. The key card in *scopa* is the seven of "money", *il sette bello*, and when Babbino held it he would rise to his feet and slap it on the table with a force calculated to scare his opponents into submission. It was a technique which I was later to employ in my games with La Nonna.

Just before midnight our laughter subsided as La Nonna brought out the infant Jesus from the box in her room where He spent most of the year. She had already assembled her *presepio* in Lucia's room and placed in position the Madonna, Saint Joseph, the three wise men and many wooden animals. When the bells of St Peter's chimed the hour of midnight, she placed the infant Jesus in His crib.

All over Rome the church bells were ringing as we opened the bottle of *spumante* which Iolanda had given us. We drank first to the *bambino Gesù* and to his mother, the Madonna. Then to the Pope, to the *inglesi*, the *americani*, the *italiani*. We drank to each other, to my family in England, to Maria at Colle Giove, to the people of Nespolo. We drank to peace and goodwill on earth.

165

CHAPTER
THREE

In the Viale delle Milizie beneath my bedroom window, a group of German revellers shot in the New Year with a midnight hail of bullets. I peeped down at them through a crack in the shutters, half expecting to see a corpse sprawled on the pavement. But no, for once the Germans were firing at the open sky.

Events in the past week had borne out Enrico's forebodings of trouble ahead. Once again the manhunt was in full swing. On Christmas morning the SS had cordoned off the Piazza Barberini and caught a large number of men within their net. On Boxing Day hand-grenades had been thrown in the course of a scuffle outside our local cinema. On the 29th the Allies had bombed the outskirts of Rome, their first raid since my arrival in November, and according to the *Popolo di Roma*, killed fifty civilians.

January 1st, 1944, dawned crisp and sunny. Sitting at the table in Lucia's room I reviewed the slowness of the Allied advance since my escape and registered some New Year resolutions. Heavy snowfalls along the length of the Gustav Line had increased the difficulties of crossing that formidable barrier which lay between me and liberty. I must sit tight in Rome, I decided, avoid capture, keep alive. There was really no alternative. I resolved to go out less and not run unnecessary risks.

Three months had passed since I had jumped over the hedge which had bounded my previous existence. To mark their completion I wrote in English a summary of the diary which I had started to keep in Nespolo and which I had written in a form of abbreviated Italian devised to safeguard its secrets. So unversed in the use of my native language had I become that I never noticed the Italianized spellings which I was frequently using: for instance, I was writing giornalist instead of journalist. Ninety-three days had passed since I had read, spoken or, except on the radio, heard a single word of English. I was thinking in Italian. And so absorbed had I become in the role assigned to me by necessity that I had half come to believe that I was indeed the adopted son of a peasant from Apulia and the brother of a Roman bank clerk. My performance had become the reality; my past and my questionable future had assumed the phantom quality of a dream.

I realized, dimly, that I was a very different person from the officer whose uniform I had buried at dawn on that hilltop above Carsoli. Only at night, stretched in a bed, the comfort of which contrasted so strikingly with the austerity of the upright chairs on which I passed my days, did I recapture something of my "real" personality and slip behind the cover of that protective skin which I had grown during my thirty years of life as an Englishman.

I would lie in bed, my body relaxed and warm, my mind at rest in the knowledge that I had survived another day. I developed a trick of projecting myself into a more comfortable future from which I could look back at the present through that haze of glamour with which we like to contemplate the past. Seen from a point in the future, my present was exciting, even exhilarating, its very discomfort and monotony endowing it with an interest such as grips one when watching a gloomy play by Strindberg, if only because one is curious to know the end of the story.

Never in my life have I slept more soundly, dreamt more pleasantly. As I drifted into sleep I would, in my imagination, hover over the dark, deserted streets of Rome and follow my thoughts south to the hills above Cassino or north to the prison-camp in Germany where I imagined so many of my friends from Chieti must be. Often in my dreams I would visit this imagined camp and recount my adventures to my friends, conscious always that I could float back into my strange existence at Via Famagosta at will.

I would wake with the hooting of the 10 o'clock siren, rise from my bed and assume again the clothes, speech and habits of a Roman refugee. The actuality of the present would blow away the air of romance in which I had wrapped it in my dreams, and I would ask myself for the hundredth time whether it was prudence or cowardice which stopped me from trying to reach the Front. Then I would recall my mental torment when I had expected that the Platanos would be shot on my account at Nespolo and wonder whether I had the moral right to involve other Italians in my adventure, as I inevitably would should I decide to leave Rome. The Platanos were already involved with me. They wished me to stay with them and, indeed, took umbrage whenever I suggested that I should leave them and make my way south. Provided I acted with prudence, the risks which they were running on my behalf were not now great.

In the New Year the newspapers devoted much space to the census which had been taken on 30th December. La Nonna and Lucia were both alarmed by the persistent rumours that German and Fascist police in civilian clothes were making a house-to-house search in order to check the figures. Their fears were intensified when one day the Germans entered the flat below us and arrested a young man who was staying there. I tried to convince them that, in this case, the Germans had acted on information previously received. Experience on racecourses before the war had taught me something of the mathematics of chance and it seemed to me that the odds against our, or any other, flat being entered in the course of a routine check were astronomical. So that it was principally in order to set the minds of the others at rest that I agreed to make a hiding-place to guard against such a contingency.

We spied out the roof and failed to find a suitable place of concealment or a line of escape to a neighbouring flat. The thought of walking along the ledge beneath our windows filled me with vertiginous horror. Eventually we hit on the idea of hacking a hole, similar in shape and size to that of my standing body, out of the wall behind the wardrobe in La Nonna's room.

This wall was an outside one and backed on to the courtyard; it was made of stone and was two feet thick. I moved forward the wardrobe and sketched out a silhouette of my figure with my feet six inches above the level of the floor. Then I set to work with a hammer and chisel.

It was slow work because I had to make as little noise as possible for fear of rousing the suspicions of the tenants of the next-door flat. To lessen the noise I padded the handle end of my chisel. Much of the stone and rubble broke away easily beneath the blade, but here and there I came up against a large stone or brick which I had to hew round and extract in one piece. As the outline of the recess assumed the silhouette of a figure, I tasted a little of the sculptor's joy. Should the hole be of no practical value, I thought, at least its construction is occupational therapy.

Arturo was now back at work in his bank and Lucia had taken an inferior job with the *anagrafe* — the register of births, deaths and marriages. Consequently I was alone in the flat with La Nonna for much of the day. She acted as my builder's mate, sweeping up the rubble into sacks and, occasionally, taking a turn with hammer and chisel. Each evening, as soon as it was dark, we would carry the sacks down to the Viale delle Milizie and dispose of their contents beneath one of the plane trees.

It took us five days to excavate a space sufficient to admit the depth of my body. When I stepped up into the coffin-shaped recess, I found that my torso was so wasted that my nose and toes projected beyond my chest. We staged a dress rehearsal for Arturo who was visiting us on his way home from work. When he rang the bell (the family always gave it three staccato pushes), I climbed into the hole. La Nonna and Lucia pushed back the heavy wardrobe close against the wall and, in doing so, closed the lid of my upright coffin. I was assailed by an irrational fear that the wall behind me would crumble and allow my body to catapult backwards into the courtyard beneath me.

Arturo peered down the crack between wall and wardrobe, then got on his hands and knees and looked underneath it. No one could guess, he declared, that a man was concealed behind it.

It was a brilliant January morning. I sat at the table in Lucia's room and spread before me on its solid oak surface an English-Italian dictionary, the exercise book in which I listed Italian words and wrote out the dictations which Lucia gave me, and my morning ration of two cigarettes. This room had become for me a kind of sanctuary, not unlike a monk's cell, behind the doors of which I practised my morning routine. I never visited my own dark bedroom during the day. In it there was nowhere to sit, and I knew that if I once allowed myself to take an afternoon siesta, it would become a habit which would prevent me from sleeping at night.

Because the day was a saint's day and a national holiday, Lucia was at home. Before she had taken the job with the *anagrafe*, she had been in the habit of giving me a daily lesson in Italian. She was an excellent teacher and had rubbed off many of the rough edges from the mixture of dialect and Italian which I had learnt at Nespolo. Today she suggested that we should read Dante together. It would not be for the first time and I was beginning to appreciate the swinging metre of his three-lined verses. But this morning I could not concentrate, perhaps because I was distracted by the shafts of sunlight which were flickering across the table at which we were seated. My thoughts kept straying back to Lucia and to the question of why she had never married.

There had been a time, soon after my arrival in Rome, when I had wondered whether I was falling in love with Lucia. I had felt a current of understanding between us from the moment of our meeting, a knowledge that we shared at least some of the same dreams. Perhaps I had been a little in love with the idea of her before we even met. It was a classic romantic situation. The English soldier on the run meets the pretty daughter of the peasant who has befriended him, a girl whose intelligence and ambitions are far above the circumstances to which she has been born.

There is usually a moment of truth before the start of an affair of the heart. In our case, the moment came and passed without anything happening. Perhaps I was held back by the knowledge that with Lucia it would be all or nothing and that our backgrounds were too dissimilar for a deep relationship. I realized, too, that, even had she so wished it, a love affair between us would have been difficult to pursue in the constricted family life in which we were forced, by circumstances beyond our control, to spend our days.

Lucia was thirty-one, a year older than me, and yet there had apparently been no great love in her life. She must have had many chances to marry, I decided. Her sparkle and vitality were enough to banish any man's depression. Perhaps, I thought, her gifts were too exuberant for the taste of the average Italian man, who likes to dominate his marriage. Certainly Lucia would require as a husband a man of strong character, ideally a man dedicated to his profession, such as a doctor or an artist. Behind her gay façade lay a deep need for self-expression, evidenced by the passion with which she wrote fiction. It often happened that, a few minutes after she had returned from her office, hungry and tired after her day's work, she would confide in me that she had an exciting idea for a short story. Then she would get out pen, ink and paper and seat herself down at the table. For half an hour the ink would flow smoothly and swiftly. It was almost as though the pen was writing the story and not Lucia at all. Indeed, she confessed to me that this was what did seem to happen — a phenomenon which appears less improbable in the light of the knowledge which I later possessed that she had psychic gifts.

My musings were interrupted by their subject.

"What is the matter, Gianni? Your Italian is hopeless today. You're not concentrating at all."

"I know, I'm sorry. It's the fine weather, I expect."

"*Si. Certo è una bella giornata.*"

I shut up Dante with a bang.

"Let's go for a walk," I said, "a long walk. I want to see more of the centre of the city. Let's pretend we are a couple of tourists."

During the past week, I had been so busy making the hole in the wall that I had scarcely been out.

"*Va bene*," Lucia agreed. "We'll do exactly that."

Up to now my expeditions had been limited in scope. I knew well the district inside the triangle formed by St Peter's, the Castel Sant'Angelo and Via Famagosta. I was familiar with the Janiculum gardens, where I had admired Tasso's oak tree and Garibaldi's statue. On one occasion I had entered St Peter's, which was closed to the general public. In order to convince the Swiss guards that we had legitimate business inside, Arturo had had to give them a letter addressed to a priest who lived in the Vatican. This priest, whom Arturo had known well during the time when he had been an acolyte in St Peter's, had sent back a message that we should be admitted. Once inside, Arturo had shown me the door which led from a corner of the great nave into the Vatican City. I had been tempted to pass through. But having little idea what would happen to me should I declare my presence in neutral territory, and not wishing to be interned for the rest of the war, I had contented myself with storing away the knowledge of this door for use in an emergency.

Until this morning, I had seen little of the centre of Rome, and had certainly never set out with the undisguised object of sightseeing. So it was with a sense of excitement that I followed Lucia past the porter's lodge. We took a tram to Piazza Cavour. Owing to the petrol shortage, there were no taxis and very few private cars on the streets; there were a few horse-drawn *carrozze*, but the main means of transport were the buses and trams, which were always incredibly crowded. I had by this time mastered the technique of travelling on them. One boarded them at the rear, bought a ticket at the barrier and shoved one's way forward, muttering "*permesso*" until one reached the exit platform at the front.

From Piazza Cavour, we skirted the Castel Sant'Angelo, built by the Emperor Hadrian as a burial place for the Imperial family and later converted into a fortress. We crossed the Ponte Umberto, pausing in the centre to watch a group of urchins playing at the edge of the muddy water of the Tiber. From there we walked through narrow streets to the Renaissance Piazza Navona which, despite its air of faded splendour, was inhabited by poor people.

"That's where we used to live," said Lucia, pointing to the top floor of a crumbling palace on the east side of the lovely oblong *piazza*. "It was cramped and dirty and I hated it." For Lucia romance lay in the future, not in the past.

We passed Bernini's Fountain of the Rivers and the Pantheon, and came to the Piazza Venezia, dominated by the huge, garish monument to Victor Emmanuel II, the building which was later to be so aptly nicknamed The Wedding Cake by British troops. Lucia pointed to one of the balconies of the adjacent Palazzo Venezia.

"That's where *Il Duce* used to make his famous speeches. What a disaster he was, the great big

175

buffone!" Did I detect a shadow of nostalgia behind her mockery? Unlike the rest of her family, Lucia had once believed in Mussolini. There was nothing surprising in this. She belonged to the class to which Fascism had most to offer. Her nature, at once practical and idealistic, required some goal on which she could set her sights. She wanted heaven on earth, not in the afterlife as did her mother.

Two German officers passed us. It was here, in the centre of the city, that their presence was most in evidence. We followed them down the Corso Umberto and turned right towards the Fontana di Trevi. Like a good tourist I threw a coin into the water and made my wish — that I would see it again in more normal circumstances. We made a detour to see the Royal Palace and walked round the courtyard of the Palazzo Barberini. We drank an *espresso* in a café in the Via Veneto and watched two girls flirt with a party of Germans. We went inside the Capuchin Church and inspected the vaults, which are decorated with the skulls and bones of 4,000 Capuchin monks.

While we were standing in a queue waiting for a bus to take us back across the Tiber, a woman standing in front of us turned round and stretched out her hand.

"*Ciao, Lucia!*"

"*Ciao!*"

"*Come vai?*"

"*Non c'è male, e tu?*"

"*Si va avanti.*"

While they were talking, I had turned away from them in the hope that Lucia's friend would not have noticed that I was with Lucia. I decided that I would take the tram, which drew up at this moment, and rejoin Lucia at the end of our journey. Only as I walked in after them did I realize that I had thrown my last coin into the Fontana di Trevi. Fortunately, Lucia spotted my predicament and was able to slip some *lire* into my hand, unnoticed by her friend.

We got off near St Peter's and were joking about the incident as we walked between the colonnade and the Vatican wall. Suddenly Lucia nudged my arm.

"Do you see, Gianni!" she said with excitement, pointing to the words on a door. "Post Office of the Secretary of State of the Vatican! And it's not even inside the walls. Come on, let's go in."

I followed her inside the building. It looked like any other post office. The same thought was in both our minds.

"Do you think there is any chance that we can send a cable to my mother?" I asked her.

"At least we can try."

She turned to the man behind the counter.

"Is it possible to send a message to my aunt in England? *Poveretta*, she is married to an Englishman. We have had no news from her since the war began."

"Certainly it is possible. You can send her a telegram. I don't know how long it will take to reach her, but it will arrive one day."

He handed Lucia a form, which she put in her handbag. "*Molto bene*. I'll come back with it tomorrow."

Even as I walked back to Via Famagosta I was composing the telegram. Later in the evening Lucia wrote on the form: "To Mrs Miller, Banchory, Scotland", and continued in Italian: "Giovanni is with us and is well. How are you, Rosalinda and Emilia? Love from your niece, Lucia Santini."

We mentioned the Italianized names of my sisters to make it quite clear to my mother that the telegram was from someone well-acquainted with me. Lucia signed it with a false name and address to avoid the embarrassment which might result from a reply. Next day she went back to the Vatican Post Office and handed in the telegram.

Later, out of curiosity, I looked up "Miller" in the Rome telephone directory. I found that it contained four Millers and only three Santinis.

It seemed (and still seems) incredible to me that there should have been a post office in Rome, outside the Vatican, from which it was possible to communicate with an enemy country. Presumably the message was transmitted through Switzerland, or possibly Cairo. Whatever the method, it did eventually reach my mother — more than three months later.

The day after our successful despatch of the telegram, Allied planes launched another attack on Rome. It was rumoured that there was a munitions train in a siding. I stood on the roof with La Nonna and watched an air battle high in the sky above Monte Mario. She had refused to go down to the air-raid shelter in the courtyard, preferring to wave at the Liberators and shake her fist at the attacking

Messerschmitts. We could see the silver gleam of sunlight reflected on the clustered bombs as they dropped around the marshalling yards in the north of the city. With their explosion La Nonna's excitement changed to dismay.

"The planes looked so beautiful, Gianni. Why must they drop bombs?"

As I was wondering how to answer so imponderable a question, we noticed that one of the Liberators had been hit. Two of the crew managed to bale out before the plane crashed in flames, and we watched their parachutes open and swing gracefully down to the green slopes of Monte Mario.

Next day the newspapers made much propaganda out of this raid. "Terroristic aerial attacks on Rome by the *anglo-americani*," the headlines screamed. "More than a hundred civilians killed."

But the propaganda fell largely on deaf ears. "This is an open city," the Romans maintained. "You Germans have no right to be here. Get out and the raids will stop."

Yet I could not help appreciating the Fascist jibe concerning the name which the Americans had given to their largest bomber. "Liberators they may be," wrote the leader-writer in the *Messaggero*, "for they certainly liberate the soul from the body!"

The raid had cut off our supplies of water and gas. For the next week we had to fetch our water from a pump in the street and carry it up six floors, and cook our meals on an open wood fire on the landing outside our flat.

CHAPTER
FOUR

"During the night Allied troops made a landing on the west coast of Italy SOME DISTANCE behind the Front."

I silently cursed Radio London for not being more precise and seized my map of southern Italy. Just how far was "some distance"? Rome was eighty miles behind the Front. Had we landed to the south or north? Or at the mouth of the Tiber?

The day was 22nd January 1944, the time midday. I was alone in the flat with La Nonna. I rushed into the kitchen where she was stewing chicory for our lunch and told her the news. Would she telephone Arturo immediately, I asked her, and get him to come round as soon as possible? I was in a dither of excitement and half in mind to go out into the streets and walk blindly to the coast.

Arturo arrived at half-past two. The city was seething with rumours, the most prevalent being that the Allies had landed at Anzio, thirty-five miles south-west of Rome. Some people swore that British armoured cars had been sighted on the southern outskirts of the city, others that the Germans were already withdrawing. I could only hope that these rumours were true, in which case Rome should be liberated in the course of the next few days, unless our landing force was driven back into the sea. There seemed little case for attempting to walk to the coast at this late hour. It would have been a different matter had I heard of the landing at dawn.

Wrongly, as it transpired, I decided to play safe and sit tight. During the afternoon Radio Rome confirmed that a landing had taken place between Anzio and the mouth of the Tiber and that it was "being contained". In the evening Radio London announced that the beach-head had been consolidated and that the Fifth Army had launched a full-scale attack on the Cassino front.

Hubris overwhelmed me for the next two days as I crouched over the wireless set, inhaling hope over the ether from Radio London. German counter-attacks on the beach-head had been repulsed and our troops had pushed inland for several miles. Already their guns were in range of the Via Appia, one of the two main roads linking Rome with the front at Cassino; in the quiet of the night I could hear the boom of their fire. If they could cut this road, the battle was surely won.

The reactions of the Germans in Rome confirmed my optimism. The curfew was put forward to 5 P.M., the Tiber bridges were being mined, and Staff Officers were openly admitting to their Roman friends their belief that their days in Rome were numbered. All the signs indicated that the Germans were preparing to concede victory and abandon the capital.

Yet with the passing of each successive day my optimism dwindled, until one morning about a week after the landing, I woke in an agony of doubt. During the night the streets had resounded with the rumble of German transport travelling south. It was evident that Kesselring was rushing up all his available forces and that the battle for Rome was far from won. The morning news from Radio London confirmed that our troops had again failed to break through the Gustav Line at Cassino. I telephoned Enrico and together we went to the Piazza del Popolo, which was always a good place from which to gauge German military activity. Sure enough, an armoured column was wending its way south through the "open city". The crews looked fit and jubilant. Their confident bearing was in sharp contrast to the dejection which I had noticed, on the day after the Anzio landing, in the bearing of the Germans stationed in the city.

Enrico and I agreed that the Allies' plans had miscarried. What exactly had gone wrong?

Military historians have been attempting to answer the question ever since. Enrico and I could only presume that the overall plan demanded that the Fifth Army crack open the Gustav Line at Cassino before it was safe to unleash the beach-head troops against the Appian Way. To us, in Rome, it seemed that over-caution had allowed a great prize to slip through our fingers.

We had sound reasons for our belief. We knew that the landing had achieved complete surprise. There had been no opposition and nothing to prevent a scout car from driving up to the gates of Rome on that first morning, as the Romans believed had happened. We felt reasonably sure that German troops garrisoned in Rome had anticipated a withdrawal to the north and that Kesselring's original intention had been to abandon the capital. The Field Marshal could hardly believe his luck when the beach-head troops failed to exploit their advantage by advancing and cutting the Appian Way. Only then did he bring up all his reserves and throw them, with a gambler's desperation, into the defence of Rome.

Our opinion that the beach-head troops could have cut and held the Appian Way before the Germans had time to rally their reserves was reinforced by the knowledge, acquired by Enrico from the *Centro Militare*, that on the morning of the landing a partisan band of ex-*Carabinieri* had descended from the Lepini hills and occupied Velletri, a small town less than twenty miles inland from Anzio. They had held it for two days before being overcome by a superior force of Germans.

Once it had become clear beyond all measure of doubt that the beach-head had been contained, I was seized by a depression which was aggravated by a gnawing regret that I had not tried to reach Anzio on the day of the landing. The Germans now launched a counter-attack on the beach-head and, for two terrible days, I was almost convinced by the jubilant tone of the Roman Press that they would drive our troops into the sea. To add to my misery, I was both cold and hungry; as a sad little entry in my diary for 8th February reads: "Wind and sleet continue. The flat is so cold that I now wear my overcoat throughout the day. The consumption of gas has been rationed to two hours a day — not that we have anything much to cook. Our lunch consisted of turnip-tops but for supper we gave ourselves a treat and opened a tin of sardines."

Each day the newspapers recounted further acts of violence. On the 8th, the Germans entered the extra-territorial Basilica of St Paul Without the Walls — the first time that they had violated Vatican territory — and arrested a number of refugees living in its sanctuary. On the 11th, Mussolini shot the eighteen rebels of the Fascist Grand Council, including Ciano and De Bono. On the 13th, American planes bombed the Monastery of Cassino, reducing it to a pile of rubble. The next day, Radio London announced that the Germans had just arrested and shot five escaped PoWs in Italy.

I retired to bed with a sore throat and violent neuralgia. My morale had reached its lowest ebb.

Re-reading my diary, I can detect the first signs of returning interest in life in my entry of 22nd February: "Weather fine. Radio London says beach-head secure. Ida buys flour on the black market. Continue to study Renaissance art. Go for long walks alone."

The last two items were not unconnected, for the book which I was reading provided the inspiration for the long, solitary walks which were to be the central motif in my life for the next few weeks.

Many months previously, somebody had lent Lucia the art book which had so captivated my imagination.

La Storia Generale dell'Arte was, if I remember rightly, the work of three men and covered the history of the visual arts in Europe, Asia and Africa. The section on Europe was written by a Hungarian, Ladislao Eber, and I immersed myself in his account of the Italian Renaissance as though my sanity depended on its successful comprehension, which it may indeed have done. Despite my fondness for painting, I had never studied either the history or the theory of art. My ignorance made me fertile ground for Eber's theories.

I felt an immediate sympathy with Eber's predilection for the aesthetic vision of Michelangelo and the new spirit of unrest which the latter seemed to represent. The violence and misery of the Roman winter had attuned me to the turbulence inherent in Michelangelo's art. I was seething with introspective doubts. My scale of values had been turned upside down by the experiences into which I had been catapulted. If art was to have any meaning for me, it must dig beneath the surface of reality.

The realization that so much of Michelangelo's best work was on my doorstep filled me with excitement. I persuaded Lucia to borrow a guidebook to Rome and, from it, made a list of the buildings which he had designed and of the churches which housed his most famous works. I continued my researches with a study of Bernini. According to Eber, the master of Roman Baroque was a direct descendant of Michelangelo's revolutionary genius. With the works of these two artists as my principal objectives I embarked on a series of long, solitary walks.

The fine March weather was unusually cold, but I was well protected by Arturo's grey overcoat. I grew a short imperial beard, persuading myself that it made me look more Italian. (Actually it merely drew unwelcome attention to me, and a psychiatrist might diagnose that I was subconsciously pretending to be an art student.) Each day I set out immediately after lunch, took a tram to Piazza Cavour, crossed the Tiber on foot and made my way into the centre of the city. Most of the buildings which I wanted to view were either in the fashionable Ludovisi quarter or in the neighbourhood of the Palatine and Capitol hills.

I remember the joy of discovering the broad and gentle stairway leading up to the Campidoglio, and how I was admiring the equestrian statue which stands in the centre of Michelangelo's beautiful square when two culture-conscious soldiers of the *Wehrmacht* came and sat beside me on the balustrade. I would have liked to talk to them and disclose my nationality, for it seemed absurd to me that the universality of Michelangelo's genius should not override national enmity. But good sense prevailed and made me retreat into the sanctuary of Santa Maria in Aracoeli.

On another day I had lost my way in the maze of narrow streets between the Pantheon and the left bank of the Tiber when chance led me into a *piazza* dominated by a massive, golden-brown palace, topped by an enormous cornice. From photographs in Lucia's guidebook, I was able to identify it as the Palazzo Farnese, one of Michelangelo's supreme works. I knew that it was now the French Embassy and wondered what sort of reception I would get should I declare myself to the Vichy Government's representative.

Why, during those weeks in Rome, did sightseeing stir me in so unaccustomed a manner? Was it all due to the unique beauty and history of Rome? Or to the fact that my senses, starved by four years of war, now seized hungrily on the only stimulant available? I think that a third factor contributed to my excitement: that my senses were given an extra exhilaration such as that said to be experienced by shoplifters, by the element of risk involved in securing my prizes. Certainly I enjoyed the exercise of plotting the safest routes to the objects of my pilgrimages. As far as was possible, I steered clear of places which, perhaps quite illogically, I associated with danger. For instance, I distrusted the Piazza Barberini because it was there that a friend of Arturo's had been picked up in a *rastrellamento*; the Piazza del Popolo reminded me of an occasion when a tram conductor had queried my ticket; while in the Corso Umberto it seemed that strangers always picked on me to ask the way.

On all my excursions I had to keep an eye on the hour, because the trams stopped running half an hour before the start of the curfew. I had no watch, so I had to depend on street clocks.

By the middle of March I had, in tourist phraseology, "done" most of Bernini and Michelangelo. I had left till the last, because it was situated in a locality both distant and dangerous to reach, the church of San Pietro in Vincoli, which houses Michelangelo's Moses, one of the most famous of all his statues. I approached

187

it from the Colosseum, successfully skirting a column of German transport; their presence made the sanctuary of the church doubly welcome. But on this occasion my pilgrimage was frustrated because I found that the massive marble effigy was concealed behind a scaffolding erected as protection against bombs.

My sightseeing was not confined to Renaissance and Baroque Rome. I spent other afternoons exploring the Forum and the Colosseum. I walked down the Via del Impero, built by Mussolini across the open space which he had cleared to reveal more fully the grandeur of ancient Rome, and inspected the triumphal monument erected by him to mark the foundation of his short-lived Ethiopian Empire. I climbed the Spanish Steps and wandered in the Pincio gardens. I made a complete circuit of the walls which guard the Vatican, making a mental note of a point which I could scale should the necessity arise.

At some stage in my afternoon excursions I would rest for ten minutes or so in one of the city's innumerable churches, partly to enjoy their architecture, but principally in order to relax. I welcomed the feeling of security which came from my belief that no one could arrest me when inside their sanctuary. I was intensely moved by the naturalness with which the people of Rome used their churches, and by the way in which they slipped into them at all times of the day. Inside their churches, they did not assume a special mode of conduct, as Protestants are apt to do in theirs. I am not a Roman Catholic, but I was greatly impressed by both the ritual and the simplicity in Rome's churches; I often watched and listened to Mass.

Returning home, exhausted physically and mentally from my expeditions, I would slump into a chair in the kitchen and recount to La Nonna, Ida and Lucia where I had been and what I had seen. Lucia would tell us some of the jokes which were circulating in Rome, not all of them complimentary to the Allies. I remember laughing over a song about the Crown Prince Umberto, who had lost much sympathy on account of his hasty flight, along with his father, to the safety of the Allied-occupied south immediately after the armistice. Most Romans thought that he should have stayed in Rome to face the music. The song was sung to the tune of "Who's afraid of the big bad, wolf?" and started

"E Umberto, bel Apollo,
se n'è andato con padre al collo."
("And Umberto, that handsome Apollo,
Has skipped off, with his father round his neck.")

La Nonna would show me what she had bought for our supper, as likely as not the green tops of turnips which normally one would expect to feed to animals. We would clean them with care, boil them and fry them with garlic in a drop of oil. Or perhaps we would have dried beans, when it would be my task to pick out the grit and the desiccated insects with which they were mixed.

Immediately after supper I would smoke the last of my daily ration of cigarettes and by so doing signal to my stomach that it had had its food for the day. I found that my perpetual state of hunger increased my craving for tobacco in any form. In this Lucia sympathized with me, for she also liked to smoke. She bought cigarette papers and we both became expert at rolling the tobacco which we had saved from the butts of our cigarettes.

Ida did not smoke. She had no vices and few interests. Though she lacked Maria's passion and Lucia's dynamism, hers was in no way a negative personality. She talked little but her company always gave me a comfortable feeling that conversation was unnecessary, presumably because she radiated some of her own happy, easygoing nature. Although never apparently exerting herself, Ida got things done with a minimum of fuss. There were times when her passivity proved irritating to both Lucia and La Nonna. Rather than lose her temper should other members of the family try and impose on her, as they sometimes did, she would shrug her shoulders, smile and walk out of the house.

Our thin diet was having a beneficial effect on Ida's squat figure; her face had lost much of its roundness, and one day, when she had taken the trouble to make herself up, I realized how pretty she could have looked if she had so cared.

CHAPTER
FIVE

One day in the middle of March an old friend of La Nonna's came to see us. She was so thin that she reminded me of the starving camel which I had once seen in the Libyan desert. She had the same scraggy neck and angular, projecting bones. Despite her physical appearance, her voice positively chirped as she told us how she had been living with other refugees in the Benedictine monastery of Monte Cassino when Allied bombers had razed it to the ground.

The great monastery, which was founded by St Benedict in 529, had dominated the German defence system at Cassino. After the air bombardment, the Allied Command defended its action on the grounds that the Germans had been using the monastery's abbey as an observation post for their artillery. The Axis Press had made much propaganda out of what they described as the "dastardly action of the self-styled liberators," asserting that no German had ever set foot in the monastery. The Vatican newspaper, *L'Osservatore Romano*, which could be depended on to report news accurately and without bias, had said much the same thing. I believed that for once the German propaganda was correct and that Allied Intelligence had been guilty of a tragic error.

La Nonna's friend confirmed my fears. She assured us that the only inhabitants of the monastery had been the monks and a number of refugees like herself who had sought and found sanctuary there from the war-devastated area of the Front Line. During her several weeks in the monastery, she had never seen a German inside the precincts. In the course of the raid, the cell in which she had been sheltering had collapsed on top of her. When, a few hours later, she had been dug from the rubble, she had been surprised to find that she was suffering from nothing more severe than shock, a truly miraculous escape. But what struck me as even stranger was that she could now be so deathly thin and yet, apparently, healthy. For three weeks after the raid, so she assured us, she had eaten nothing but grass. We drew comfort from this proof of the body's strength.

A day or two after my meeting with this scarecrow of a woman, the Fifth Army attacked Cassino yet again, and it became obvious that, whatever the rights and wrongs of the decision to bomb the monastery, it had gained us nothing from the military point of view. The huge pile of rubble, which crowned the mountain where the monastery had once stood sentinel, gave excellent cover to the German troops, who once again defended the position with suicidal courage.

The measure of the German victory was soon made clear to me. On the next Sunday I lunched as usual at Arturo's, eating the blind hen which we had brought with us from Nespolo. (The toughness of this scraggy veteran increased our pleasure by prolonging the period of mastication.) After lunch, as we walked to the Janiculum gardens, we came across eight German armoured cars parked beneath the trees at the side of a square. Arturo engaged one of the crew in conversation. At the mention of Cassino his comrades crowded round him, jubilant as strutting cocks. "*Cassino immer Deutsch!*" they crowed. "*Americani, inglesi, alles kaput!*" Even Arturo, who had lost his fear of the Germans ever since he discovered the efficacy of the faked document which exempted him from conscription in a labour gang, was too daunted by their confidence to continue the conversation.

On the next day Vesuvius erupted with a violence unknown in the century, and threw up a cloud of cinders which formed a dark, threatening umbrella high above the volcano. I read in the newspapers how this cloud had drifted in the wind across the peninsula to Bari on the Adriatic coast. Here it had halted and hung stationary above the city, creating an effect of darkness at noon.

The ancients would have divined that the gods were angry and would not have been surprised when, next morning, Allied planes bombed Rome's railyards and once again damaged the city's water and gas supplies. On the same day there was a commotion outside the barracks close to Via Famagosta when a crowd, consisting mostly of women, protested against the incarceration therein of their sons and lovers, who had been caught in a recent manhunt. In the ensuing scuffle, hand-bombs were tossed into the barracks while Fascist guards opened fire on the crowd. Two Fascists and three women, one of whom was pregnant, were killed and many others were wounded.

This affair was said to be the reason why the Germans cut down the plane trees beneath our window in the Viale delle Milizie. This vandalism upset La Nonna out of all proportion, perhaps because she bore the name *Platano*, which means plane tree. She worked off her indignation by pinching some of the branches for firewood.

Altogether it was a week of ill omen, and, had I been superstitious, I would have waited for a favourable astrological portent before challenging fate with another of my long walks.

Instead, the late hours of the March afternoon found me leaning over a parapet of the Lungotevere and staring across the shallow, sluggish water of the Tiber at the island of Tiberina.

This island made me think of the Ile de la Cité, and I began to make a comparison in my mind between the beauties of the Seine and the Tiber. There seemed little doubt but that, as regards both its colour and the speed with which it flowed, the Seine at Paris was more attractive than its Roman counterpart.

Leaning on the parapet, recalling happy memories of Paris, I failed to realize that two young men, wearing long overcoats and with hats pulled down over their eyes in the manner of American gangsters, were asking me a question. What time was it, please?

I was accustomed to being addressed by casual strangers. Usually I answered as briefly as possible. On this occasion, perhaps because my thoughts were far away, perhaps because I sensed something furtive in the bearing of the two youths, I merely shrugged my shoulders and pulled up my sleeve to show that I was not wearing a watch. They moved back a few paces and started to whisper together in a manner which I did not like at all. I walked the few steps which separated me from a newspaper kiosk and studied the headlines with as much deliberation as I could muster. Then I started to stroll away.

As I did so, the men blocked my path.

"*Documenti, per favore.*"

At least they have said "please", I thought, remembering the bark with which the Feldwebel had demanded my papers at Nespolo. And at least they were not pointing a machine-gun at me.

I handed them the Fascist Youth card which Lucia had forged for me.

One of the youths scrutinized it carefully.

"But this is not good enough. Have you no other identity card?"

I shook my head and drew my wallet from my pocket. From it I extracted a piece of paper inscribed "*sono muto*", a doctor's certificate which confirmed that I was dumb, and a long letter addressed to Signore Maggi at a fictitious address.

This letter, which began "*Carissimo* Antonio", was a masterpiece of Lucia's, a triumph of feminine sympathy for the disaster which had befallen Maggi. Inspired by

195

my Nespolo adventure, it referred to the destruction of all Maggi's possessions in an air-raid and gave encouraging news about a doctor who had a new method of curing "tracheismo tonico", the disease with which Maggi had been afflicted as a result of a beam falling on the back of his head. Lucia and I had laughed a lot during the composition of this letter and I doubt if either of us had seriously considered that I might one day make use of it. Now, in the Roman twilight, the story appeared ludicrous. But at least, while the letter was being read, I was gaining time to think.

Both the youths were small and, apparently, unarmed. I was familiar with the nearby church and knew that it had an exit at the back. Should they order me to go with them, I decided that I would punch a right and left into their faces and dive across the street into the church. A typical Roman crowd, composed of hollow-faced men and a few housewives whose loosely hanging clothes indicated that they had once been fat, had gathered round us. I felt that I could depend on them to obstruct my pursuers.

As the youths read Lucia's letter and whispered together, I stared straight into the eyes of the more formidable-looking of the two. Perhaps he gleaned what was passing in my mind, for he handed back my papers and muttered that I was free to go. I slipped into the church, offered a silent prayer as I walked down the nave, and went out at the back door. I took a circuitous route to Trastevere and found that I had missed the last tram. I hurried back to Via Famagosta on foot. I reached the flat with one minute to spare before the curfew and found La Nonna waiting for me anxiously in the doorway. One look at my white face told her at least half the story.

We agreed that only the inexperience of those teenaged youths had saved me from arrest. Probably they were two of the many young criminals whom the *Repubblichini* had recently released from gaol on condition that they worked for the secret police.

After supper I shaved off my beard.

The next day was 23rd March, a memorable date in the calendar of the Italian Resistance Movement. That afternoon two men disguised as roadsweepers parked a cart in the Via Rasella, a small street near the Royal Palace. They had previously placed forty pounds of explosive, wired to a one-minute fuse, beneath the rubbish with which the cart was laden. One of the roadsweepers stood beside the cart, the other took up his position at the end of the street. He stood there waiting for the arrival of a German police platoon which he knew was coming that way at a certain hour. As the platoon came towards him, he judged the moment when they were within a minute's march of the rubbish cart, then raised his hat as a signal to his accomplice to light the fuse.

The explosion killed many of the platoon. Others were hit by hand-grenades thrown from the window of a nearby house. In all, thirty-two Germans met their death.

In a matter of minutes German and Fascist police swarmed into the Via Rasella and rounded up passers-by and occupants of the adjacent houses. They shot a few on the spot and removed the others to prison. Field Marshal Kesselring immediately ordered that 320 Italians must die, in conformance with his rule of ten reprisals for every German killed. About seventy people had been arrested near the scene of the attack. The balance was to be made up from inmates of the notorious Regina Coeli gaol.

In fact, an extra fifteen were taken the next day from the Regina Coeli, making a total of 335 men, including the hostages arrested on the spot. They varied in age from boys in their teens to the very old. Most of them were political prisoners or men arrested during the past few months for anti-Axis activity. They were chained together, hurled into lorries and driven south to some caves near Ardea. There, with their hands bound, they were made to kneel in rows one behind the other and shot in the back of the neck by the Gestapo. Many of them were not killed instantly and only died — of suffocation — when the entrance to the caves (later known as the Ardeantine Caves) was dynamited.

The Via Rasella action had been planned by the Roman Committee of National Liberation and executed by one of their killer squads, known as a *Gruppo Azione Patriotica*. I learnt these details two days later from Enrico, whom Lucia had brought to drink a cup of mint tea. He was by no means convinced that the action was justified, an opinion which I understood to be prevalent throughout the *Centro Militare*.

"The trouble with this kind of action," Enrico said, "is that retribution falls on the heads of innocent people and not on those of the men who have perpetrated it. I am all for killing thirty-two Germans. But in this case 335 men, people of outstanding merit, paid for the deed with their lives. Those who planned the action, and the ones who lit the fuse or threw the hand-grenades, were well-placed to make their escapes."

Viewed in this light, the incident left a nasty taste in the mouth. But I sensed a flaw in the line of argument which, surely, told only part of the story.

"But you can't condemn an action on the grounds that its execution requires no physical courage. The concept of chivalry is a luxury which we can't afford in this war," I said.

"I suppose that is what I regret."

"Of course one regrets it, just as one regrets that a bomb dropped on a city kills women and children. There is no place for sentiment in total war, particularly in the only kind of war which the Resistance can fight. If you decide to resist, you must be prepared to use every low trick you can think of."

"I get your point," said Enrico.

"You know, I came up against this dilemma at Nespolo. I have often wondered whether Paolo and Riccardo were right to kill those two Germans. They got clean away, but I still wonder what has happened to the twenty hostages. But just think. If every peasant in every Italian village had acted like those two Nespolini

199

did at the time of the armistice, the Germans would have been driven out of Italy long ago."

"*Gia*. That's true," said Lucia, "I hadn't thought of it like that."

"I'm still unconvinced," said Enrico. "Has any individual the moral right to set in motion a chain of events such as that which ended in the Ardeantine Caves?"

"That's another question," I said. "A pacifist would answer 'no', and his conclusion is perfectly tenable. But surely, once the decision to fight a war has been taken, there can be no half measures, neither on moral nor on practical grounds. It was the Germans and not the partisans who made the rule that ten civilians must die for every German soldier killed. Whenever it is possible, the partisans try to ensure that no innocent people suffer for their acts."

"With that I agree."

"I don't see how you can draw up a balance sheet for each individual action of the Resistance," I went on. "You must judge each action in the context of the whole. I agree that the Via Rasella affair had disastrous repercussions. But in the final resort, the justification for the Resistance throughout Europe will be gauged only by the number of days by which its existence has shortened the war and the number of lives consequently saved."

"I expect you're right. To come back to the Via Rasella, did you know that Colonel Montezemolo, who started up our *Centro Militare*, was one of those massacred in the Ardeantine Caves?" said Enrico.

"Lucia told me. What happened?"

"He was arrested at the end of January and taken to Via Tasso. The Gestapo tortured him day after day but he revealed nothing. Then they moved him to the Regina Coeli. Of course they had to pick him for the Ardeantine Caves massacre."

Kesselring imposed another and less drastic punishment on the Romans for the Via Rasella incident. He decreased our daily bread ration by a third.

In one respect the Ardeantine Caves massacre backfired on the Germans, for it turned many Romans, who had previously disliked but tolerated them, into active enemies. During the last week of March, the papers were full of stories of the arrest of partisans, deserters and escaped PoWs; tales of torture and shootings abounded. It was said that 2000 SS and security men had been brought into Rome after the Via Rasella incident, and partly on this account, but also because I had been shaken by my narrow escape from arrest on the banks of the Tiber, I decided that I must forego my daily walks and confine my expeditions to Sunday jaunts to Arturo's flat and an occasional sortie with a member of the family.

Another deterrent to my expeditions was the presence, throughout most of the day, of the porter in his lodge at the entrance to our block of flats. Until now, I had been able to depend on his absence during the many hours of the day which he had spent drinking in the wine-shop at the end of the street. But now the wine had run out and, like Cerberus at the gates of

Hell, he was constantly hanging round the archway in search of a victim on whom he could vent his spleen. Nor was it any longer possible for me to come home under cover of darkness, because it was still daylight at the hour when the curfew began.

The coming of spring mitigated against my expeditions in other ways. I could no longer wear Arturo's old overcoat, which had disguised the poor fit of my grey suit, itself conspicuously thick for the warmer weather, and my furtive passage through our courtyard was jeopardized by the presence there of many women and children who had been attracted out of their flats by the sunshine.

During the past month my life had revolved round my walks, and without their stimulus I grew bored. I had read all of Lucia's books. I was tired of studying Italian, of listening to the radio and of playing the few gramophone records which the family possessed. There was nothing for me to cook and no jobs about the flat for me to do; it was not safe, even, for me to fetch water from the pump in the courtyard.

I was also lonely. La Nonna spent most mornings standing in food queues, and in the afternoons she either went to St Peter's or took a nap. Babbino, too, was either out of the flat or in bed. Lucia and Ida were at work all day and, apart from Sundays, I rarely saw Arturo. Forced back on my inner resources, I started to write down all the poetry that I could remember.

CHAPTER
SIX

"April is the cruellest month, breeding
Lilacs out of the dead land, mixing
Memory and desire, stirring
Dull roots with spring rain."

I looked down on the courtyard, the opening lines of
T.S. Eliot's "The Waste Land" surfacing from my
subconscious. Spring rain was indeed falling — it
always did in Holy Week, according to La Nonna, who
had just made the traditional pilgrimage on her knees
up the steps of the *Scala Santa*. I wondered how the
"dull roots" would compare with the withered
vegetables which made up most of our diet. At this
time, food was scarcer than ever; even the scrawny stray
cats had vanished, presumably into cooking pots, and
we were only saved from starvation by the soup
kitchens just set up by the Pope. From one of these La
Nonna could, on most mornings, collect a tureen of
stewed vegetables; she and I always found it a
considerable strain to put half of this aside for Ida and
Lucia to eat on their return from work.

The fact that this food came to us through the good
offices of the Pope made it doubly nourishing in La
Nonna's eyes. I was beginning to share her admiration
of Pius XII who, in my opinion, behaved throughout

the German occupation with dignity and courage. The help which he gave to anti-Fascists and Jews was never fully appreciated in England, where many people believed that his sympathies lay with the Axis.

Domani (tomorrow), always a well-used word in Italy, was now constantly on our lips. Tomorrow the water supply might return, or a new attack might breach the Gustav Line . . . tomorrow Iolanda might bring us some food. Instead of *domani*, La Nonna often used the Apulian word *crai*, a derivative of the Latin *cras*. For *dopo-* or *pos-domani* she would say *puscrai*. So far, there was nothing very strange about this; it was her use of the continuation of the sequence (non-existent in modern Italian), which could be guaranteed to bring forth peals of laughter from the rest of us. For such was the richness of the Apulian dialect that La Nonna also had a word — *puscridri* — for the day after *puscrai*, and another word — *puscrodri* — for the day after that; and, as a final fence in this verbal steeplechase, a word which, by La Nonna's own admission, was too exotic for everyday use, namely *puscrudri*, which in English can only be translated as the day-after-the-day-after-the-day-after-the-day-after-tomorrow.

I was reminded of La Nonna's splendid sequence when I wrote down, as one of my morning exercises, the opening lines of Macbeth's famous speech:

Tomorrow and tomorrow and tomorrow
Creeps in this petty pace from day to day . . .

The lines of the complete speech had, I believed, inspired the titles of more books than any other in the English language. Now I was struck, also, by the aptness with which they caught the atmosphere of this Roman April. I had never read the speech in Italian, and decided to attempt a translation. But I stopped after the first line. *"Domani e domani e domani"* sounded both pedestrian and unharmonious. How much more elegant — and pleasing to the ear — the line would sound in La Nonna's Apulian: *"Puscridri e puscrodri e puscrudri"*!

In between eating the Pope's soup and writing down poetry I toyed with two schemes for leaving Rome. The first was built on a suggestion of Enrico's that he might be able to arrange for me to join a partisan band operating in the mountains near Spoleto. But I could not bear the thought of going fifty miles north when at night I could hear the sound of Allied gunfire only sixteen miles to the south. The second scheme had a certain mad appeal. A friend of Lucia's, who made maps for the authorities but also worked secretly for the partisans, suggested that he might, on one of his official trips, be able to give me a lift in his car as far as the French frontier, from where I might be able to find my way to Spain. But again it seemed crazy to embark on a long and hazardous journey just at the moment when deliverance seemed to be on my doorstep.

Both these possible courses of action were, however, really nothing more than mental exercises, for I knew quite well that I had already decided to wait in Rome and hope for early liberation. Surely the Allies would soon — perhaps in the moonless final week of April — open another attack on Cassino?

My problem, then, was to remain at large and passably fit for another month. To replace my daily walk, I forced myself to do exercises, but soon found that I was too weak for such unaccustomed exertion. I spent one whole weekend trying to fit a totally unfunctional third wheel on to Lucia's bicycle, to convert it — because of the German ban on the use of bicycles — into a tricycle. Being hopeless when it came to mechanical tasks, I had to call in Arturo to help me.

By the middle of April I had written down all of the scraps of poetry which I could remember and was searching for another pastime. The inspiration for this came in the course of a largely sleepless night, when my restless thoughts were interrupted by a faint noise. It sounded like the baa-ing of a flock of sheep, and swelled to a crescendo directly below my bedroom window. For several minutes I lay in the darkness, thinking of Don Quixote and of how he had mistaken a flock of sheep for "a prodigious army of divers and innumerable nations", but, unable to think of any logical reason why a flock of sheep should be walking through the centre of Rome at such an improbable hour, I wondered if I was making an analogous error.

I got up, padded to the window, and cautiously opened the shutters. Beneath me I could see, in the thin moonlight, an apparently endless procession of shaggy rumps, white woolly backs and horned heads surging along the broad avenue. They were going in the direction in which I liked to see Germans go — from south to north.

I went back to bed, baffled by what I had seen. I felt sure that the half-crazy Don would have conceived a fantastical explanation for this strange manifestation. Were the sheep, perhaps, partisans in disguise, or German deserters from the front at Anzio? Had not Ulysses and his men escaped from the giant, Cyclops, covered in the fleeces of slaughtered sheep? Stimulated by such Quixotic speculations, I spent most of the remainder of the night awake, my body pleasantly relaxed and my brain functioning with such an unnatural clarity that I later wondered if I had been in a state of hallucination. Abstract political and philosophical arguments rose one by one to the surface of my mind, the syllogisms resolving themselves with such dialectic clarity: thesis, antithesis, synthesis. Several hours later, deluding myself that I had solved every problem, I fell into a deep sleep.

Next morning I wrote down the skeletons of these hypothetical theories which had come to me as if by magic during the night, and later expanded them into essays. Rereading these essays some years later, I found it impossible to recognize the man who wrote most of them as my normal, extrovert self; I could only assume that the inactive and lonely life which I endured in April 1944 had temporarily disturbed the balance of my mind. However, some were fairly logical, particularly those concerned with the broader issues of the war, or rather of the two wars, for it seemed to me that as well as the nationalistic war between the Allied and the Axis powers, a civil war was being fought throughout German-occupied Europe; the dilemma of whether to support one's country or one's beliefs was inextricably woven into the lives of millions of people of occupied Europe. I also criticized the concept of representing the political spectrum in the form of a straight line; my own visual picture was that of a spiral, in which Communism and Fascism lay at the extremes of the spiral but at the same clock hours.

The occupation of writing these essays was therapeutic, and left me with some understanding of the connection between meditation and fasting — though in my case the fasting, unlike that of hermits, was anything but voluntary.

For a few weeks the abstract world of my imagination was more real to me than were the actualities of my life. It became a retreat which alone saved me from collapse. Even so, I grew morose and testy; any interruption to my daily routine angered rather than diverted me. I even resented our Easter celebrations, fearing that they would upset both my mental equilibrium and my digestive system. I was content in my self-ordained monasticism, indifferent to hunger and discomfort. It was as though I had put aside my desire to return to the world.

Even with Lucia, to whom I was devoted, I now found conversation tedious, being unable to share with her the theories which so absorbed me. Only with La Nonna could I happily converse. With her I had built another world of fantasy based on make-believe and surrealist jokes. We played cards together with the light-hearted intensity of children.

My secret thoughts found no place in my diary and I had little else to record in the month of April. On the 8th Lucia brought an English-speaking friend to see me; I was shattered to find how haltingly I spoke my native tongue. On the 10th we received a meat ration, the first for three months, and consumed it in one meal; counterbalancing this pleasure, the weekly cigarette ration failed to materialize. On the 21st a group of Roman housewives stormed a bakery and made off with a large quantity of bread. Laughing over the report of this event in the *Popolo di Roma*, I recalled a similar incident in Manzoni's *I Promessi Sposi* which I had recently been reading. It struck me how closely Rome resembled the Milan of 1630 described in the novel. Both cities were under the yoke of a detested foreign domination, both were suffering from near-famine. Now the bread riots, a feature of Manzoni's Milan, confirmed the similarity. I hoped that we would be spared the climax of Milan's miseries, which had been an outbreak of the plague.

On the 24th the factory workers of Rome went on strike for an hour in memory of the 335 people shot a month previously in the Ardeantine Caves. On the 26th, my birthday, La Nonna cooked a *pizza* for me and brought a flask of wine. She hid them under my bed, so that the family would not know of this extravagance. Enrico brought me a summer suit which he had borrowed from a friend whose waistline was evidently twice the circumference of mine. I celebrated May Day with a sunbathe on the roof.

During April the Allies had bombed only the perimeter of the city, but I knew from a macabre incident that these raids were exacting their toll of lives. One Sunday Ida went to lunch with a girl friend in her flat. On her return she made our mouths water with her account of the meat she had eaten.

"*MEAT!*" exclaimed La Nonna. "How could your friend afford *meat?*"

"It was very cheap," said Ida, stating the price.

"But that's not possible."

"I don't understand either. Anyway, I have the address of the butcher. Here it is." She handed us a scrap of paper.

"And was it good?" we asked.

"*Si, si, molto buona. Deliziosa!*"

"Describe it," said La Nonna.

"Lean, quite tender, very light in colour." We listened voraciously to the succulent adjectives.

"Rabbit, perhaps?"

"No, it wasn't rabbit. More like veal."

"But the price! It couldn't have been veal!"

"Cat?" I suggested, remembering how the cats had vanished from our courtyard.

"Much too good. And too white. Not that I have ever eaten cat!"

The problem seemed insoluble. No matter. La Nonna would go to the butcher on the morrow.

But she never did. Next morning the headlines screamed at us from the *Popolo di Roma:*

"TRASTEVERE BUTCHER ARRESTED FOR SELLING HUMAN FLESH. VICTIMS BELIEVED CASUALTIES OF AIR-RAIDS BY ANGLO-SAXON CRIMINALS!"

Feeling slightly sick, we checked the butcher's address with that on Ida's scrap of paper. It tallied.

One afternoon La Nonna burst into my room.

"I've just come from St Peter's . . ."

"Yes?"

"I've made a confession . . . to a Polish priest."

"Polish?"

"*Si, un Polacco*. He's a good man, Gianni."

"I'm sure he is. But what did you confess to him?"

"I told him about you, that you were living with us."

"*Bravissimo!* What did he say?"

"He congratulated me. He told me to come back tomorrow."

"And?"

"I am to bring him a letter from you, to give to the British Minister in the Vatican. Oh, Gianni, I hope I've done right?"

"Done right! You are the only one of us with any brains."

I danced her round the room. Why, in the course of nearly six months, had I never thought of this simple manoeuvre?

With the hesitancy which comes from lack of practice, I composed a formal letter to HM Minister to the Holy See, giving the bare facts of my escape. Dear God, I had forgotten my Army Number!

CHAPTER
SEVEN

"Gianni! Gianni! Get up, you lazy son of a pig!"

I pulled the blankets over my head and muttered a curse. I knew that it was long before ten o'clock, my usual hour of rising.

The intruder threw open the tall louvred shutters and walked back to my bedside, where she stood above me, glowing like a visitor from another planet. I rubbed the sleep from my eyes and saw that it was Maria.

I crawled out of my bed, embraced her and followed her into the kitchen where I found La Nonna, Babbino, Ida and Lucia weeping tears of joy over a huge pile of bread, potatoes and flour. Beside the sunburnt Maria, they looked like shadows.

"Eat, Gianni, eat," Maria commanded, thrusting a hunk of golden bread into my hand and breaking an egg into my barley coffee.

She had travelled up from Colle Giove overnight in a lorry which had been machine-gunned on the outskirts of Tivoli. Later she had managed to get through the control post at the gates of Rome without paying duty on the food which she had brought for us. Her elation at seeing us was slightly dampened by her obvious dismay at our appearance.

212

I had forgotten how La Nonna had looked when I first met her. I had not realized how little flesh covered the bones of her body because of the many black jerseys she wore over her serge dress. But her face, framed as usual in the black scarf, told the story of the recent hungry months. Her chiselled features were drawn and yellow-ivory in colour, reminding me of a painting by Goya of the horrors of war. As for Lucia, without her make-up she looked tired and sallow, while Ida's once buoyant breasts sagged like pillows that had lost their stuffing. Babbino, too, had thinned appreciably since Christmas.

After Ida and Lucia had set off to their offices, La Nonna and I continued to gorge ourselves with bread and butter while we listened to Maria's news of Colle Giove and Nespolo. The two "murderers" had never been caught and it was believed that they had succeeded in crossing the Front Line. The twenty hostages had been removed to a concentration camp in Germany. Sometime in January three escaped PoWs had been picked up in Nespolo and, because of this, Rina's cousin the *podestà*, the man who had saved me by swearing that I was Arturo's dumb brother, had been arrested and incarcerated in the Regina Coeli prison in Rome.

We had previously guessed, from an obscure reference to me in a letter from Maria, that there were some escaped PoWs living in or near Colle Giove. Now Maria told us the whole story. Recalling the state of her nerves when I had last seen her in mid-November, I marvelled at the resilience of the human spirit. Around

Christmas time, two young South Africans had reached Colle Giove, having walked many miles south down the Apennines. As they were both suffering from frostbite, Maria had taken them into her house and nursed them back to health until they were fit enough to join a group of other escaped PoWs who were living in caves and shepherds' huts above the village. Thereafter she had carried food up to them three times a week. Before a round-up, which had resulted in the capture of three of their number, the group had consisted of fifteen, each with his "godmother" in Colle Giove who supplied him with food. They comprised men of six nations and included an Indian, a Yugoslav and a German doctor who had deserted from the *Wehrmacht*.

It was primarily to obtain medicines for the South Africans that Maria had made the dangerous journey to Rome.

At midday La Nonna went to St Peter's to keep her appointment with the Polish priest and collect from him a reply to my letter to the British Minister. What would be in it, I wondered? Congratulations? A reprimand for not trying to cross the line? Financial aid? I realized with mixed feelings of pleasure and alarm that the letter which I was awaiting was the line which might fish me out of my watery limbo. My excitement was tempered by anxiety lest I should fail to adapt myself to the unaccustomed element of air.

While I waited impatiently for La Nonna's return, Maria kept me amused with stories about her South Africans Daniel and Eric, whom she planned to bring to Rome after the liberation. The prospect of meeting them disturbed me. I was still well entrenched in the world of ideas which I had created as a retreat from the despair of my physical reality. But the excitement, caused first by La Nonna's contact with the Vatican and now by Maria's arrival, had roused me from my lethargy and made me long to be drawn back into the normal world of people and events.

The surprise contained in the letter which La Nonna brought back to me from the Polish priest jerked me completely out of my private world. I opened the envelope, expecting to find a few formal lines from the British Minister to the Holy See. Instead I found a scribbled note starting "Dear John" and signed "Sam, same regiment as yourself, collector of the SBO's *vino*". An enigmatic footnote instructed me to "address answer to Toni". In between salutation and signature the writer presumed that I was "the same John Miller who had been Chieti Q Liaison Officer, high jumper, etc"; that, if so, several of my old friends were in the city "including the small, playwriting accountant and the young Scotsman". He told me to stay where I was at present and concluded "I am sending you 6,000 *lire*. Let me have a photograph and I will try and send you some documents."

So surprised was I by this unexpected communication that I had to read it through several times before it made any sense to my bemused brain. For a few moments I even wondered if it was really intended for me. But indeed I had once been a Cambridge "blue", though it now seemed improbable. For I saw myself as the adopted son of an Italian peasant, a thin, unathletic man, dressed in a grey suit several sizes too loose for him. As for Sam, who on earth was he? And why had he collected the *vino* for Chieti's Senior British Officer?

Bit by bit the identity and personality of Sam surfaced in my memory. He was Major Sam Derry, a gunner like myself, and he had played a leading part in the Chieti escape organization. In his letter he had told me that he had jumped from the same train as I had. Presumably he had got into the Vatican from where he was running some kind of organization to help escaped PoWs. I was trying to piece together the identities of the other two Chieti men who, according to Sam's letter, were now in Rome, when I realized that La Nonna and Maria were still leaning over my shoulder.

"Is it all right?" asked La Nonna anxiously.

I came back to the present with a jolt. The world of Sam and the SBO's *vino* might still be unreal to me, but the money enclosed in the letter was concrete enough — six crisp notes of one thousand *lire*, equivalent to about a month of Arturo's wages and, to us, untold wealth.

"It's wonderful," I said, handing one of the notes to Maria. "Go out immediately and buy us *meat* for dinner. Meat and lots of wine."

I handed the other five notes to La Nonna.

The afternoon passed in a flurry of preparation for the great dinner which we planned to eat in the evening. Yesterday we had been too poor to buy *pasta*. Now, thanks to Maria and Sam, we were rich twice over. Arturo and his family would dine and spend the night with us to celebrate Maria's visit and my sudden wealth.

By 10p.m. I was just sober enough to tune in to Radio London. The bulletin rounded off this day of unbelievable happiness. The Fifth Army had launched a massive attack on the Gustav Line. Units of the Eighth Army had been brought over from the Adriatic section of the Front to strengthen the attacking forces. This time it really looked as though the Allies meant business.

From now on we all had sufficient to eat, drink and smoke. For me it was wonderful to be able to give rather than receive. It did not take me many days to realize how little 6,000 *lire* was when it came to feeding ten mouths. No wonder that the Platano family had long since exhausted their savings.

I had spent every penny by the following Tuesday, when La Nonna had her third assignation with the Polish priest. She had previously taken to him a long letter which I had written to Sam Derry, explaining our numbers and our poverty, and enclosing a photograph for the identity card which he had promised to get for me. Now La Nonna came back from St Peter's with another package of notes, this time amounting to 8,000 *lire*, and another letter from Derry, suggesting that he should arrange a meeting for me with the "small, playwriting chartered accountant" to whom he had referred in his previous letter.

Since first hearing from Derry, I had thought much about the week which we had both spent at Sulmona

217

prior to the departure of the train to Germany. "Several of your old friends are in the city," he had written. I was surprised that I had never come face to face with any of them during the weeks when I had stalked the streets of Rome, and I was most curious to know who they might be.

I had already identified in my mind the two officers whom Derry had described. "The small, playwriting accountant" was undoubtedly John Furman and I looked forward to our proposed meeting. I had played bridge with him at Chieti a few times and, purely by chance, had witnessed his escape from Sulmona.

It had happened like this. I was sitting one afternoon on top of an old well close to the main gate of the camp, studying the routine of the sentries. I watched some German guards march a party of other-rank PoWs towards the exit. Though at the time I did not know it, they had just finished some particularly squalid fatigue and were being taken to wash themselves down in a cattle trough a few hundred yards outside the camp.

No sooner had the sentry opened the gate and waved the party through, than a figure dressed in a khaki shirt, shorts and a pair of gym shoes jumped down from the well where he had been sitting beside me. It was John Furman. Frantically waving a towel above his head and shouting "Hey there, wait for me!" he ran through the gate, slowing down only momentarily to explain to the sentry, in the excellent German which he spoke, that he was one of the washing party. Once through the gate he jogged along behind the others. This was the last I saw of him. Presumably he had taken care not to close the gap between him and the armed guards at the tail of the marching column and had dived into a ditch as soon as he was out of the sentry's view. In any case we never saw him again at Sulmona.

The whole astonishing act had been completed in a matter of moments, though, doubtless, hours of thought and observation lay behind it. Furman's hobby at Chieti had been writing plays and I suspected that the drama which I had witnessed had been carefully planned and rehearsed.

I was not quite certain if I had correctly identified the officer whom Derry had described in his letter as "the young Scotsman". But I was fairly certain that he was Bill Simpson, whom I remembered chiefly for the nonchalance with which he had plucked and slapped deep, fruity notes from a string bass in the Chieti dance band. I knew that he had escaped because his feat had been the talk of Sulmona. When the Germans had moved us there from Chieti, they had done so in open trucks each containing twenty PoWs and two armed guards. Escape had seemed impossible under these conditions and Simpson was the only one of the six hundred of us who had succeeded. He owed his success to sheer nerve combined with perfect timing, achieved, no doubt, as a result of many hours of application to his chosen instrument. As his truck, which was one of twenty in the convoy, had swung round a sharp corner close to the camp at Sulmona, he had leapt to freedom in one huge bound which took him over a hedge into the cover of a ditch.

219

Presuming that I had identified Furman and Simpson correctly, there remained the question of which of my other friends might be in Rome. One candidate was a close friend of mine at Chieti — Gilbert Smith, a lieutenant in the Royal Tank Corps. About a month before the armistice, Gilbert had been afflicted with a skin disease, the symptoms of which were of so disgusting a nature that the sight of him brought to mind a biblical scourge of boils and sores rather than a twentieth-century disease such as might be described in the clinically impassive pages of a medical journal. His whole face had swelled up to such an extent that it was almost impossible to discern on its convex surface of suppurating sores any resemblance to his own features, nor even the demarcation lines between any features at all. Admittedly, a slight protuberance indicated the spot where Gilbert's rather handsome nose had once served its purpose as an air imbiber. But his eyes had completely lost the function for which they had been designed and had been abstracted into two thin lines such as Picasso might have been pleased to draw. He had been removed to the civilian hospital at Chieti, much to the relief of myself and the rest of us who shared his room. He had returned to the camp shortly before our move to Sulmona, recognizable at least as a human being, though one would have guessed him to be a leper of considerable seniority. Fond as I was of Gilbert, it had therefore not been my happiest moment when I discovered that he had chosen to occupy the bed next to mine at Sulmona. The sight of him lying on his back picking at the yellow scabs which still disfigured his face was no help to my digestion.

"For Christ's sake, stop scratching!" I had shouted. "Anyone would think you wanted to sabotage yourself."

"But that's exactly what I'm trying to do."

"What do you mean?"

"If I pick off the scabs, I'll start oozing again. Then, with a bit of luck, the Germans will move me to the civilian hospital at Sulmona. And when you are all moved to Germany, I'll be left behind."

I had to congratulate him on his enterprise. It was a much braver plan than I could ever have contemplated. And it had worked. Two days later, Gilbert had been moved into the civilian hospital. That was the last news I had of him.

I mentioned to Arturo that there were evidently several of my friends somewhere in Rome. "It's a funny thing that I have never run into any of them," I said, in a tone of regret.

"It's just as well that you haven't," he retorted. "You know how it is, people talk and the next moment the Gestapo are on your tail. Don't you remember our motto, 'To trust is good, not to trust is better'?"

There was something to be said for this point of view. But even though I knew that the Platanos would not approve I was determined, if possible, to meet John Furman.

I now spent many hours crouched over the radio, always remembering to close the window of Lucia's room first. I marked the progress of the battle on a map. On the 18th May the Allies broke through the Gustav Line. Particulars of the units engaged in the battle brought home to me the international composition of the American-commanded Fifth Army. The Poles were now in Cassino. French Moroccan troops (the Goums) were also in the news. Italian civilians were terrified of these Goums, for rumour had it that their sexual manners were as forceful as their military prowess, tradition apparently permitting them young people of both sexes as legitimate booty. German propaganda had played up this unsavoury rumour by depicting on a huge poster captioned "*Il Liberatore*" a coloured soldier waving a machine-gun high above his head in his right hand while with his left arm he encircled the waist of a pretty girl.

The Germans fought for every inch of ground but, as the month of May progressed, one could tell from an understanding of the conventions of the Roman Press, that they had lost the battle. From "German Forces Resist All Enemy Attacks" the headlines changed to "The New German Alignment Halts The Enemy" to "German Resistance, Ever Determined, Favours The Manoeuvre For The Defence Of Rome". On 23rd May our troops at Anzio broke out from the beach-head. On the 25th American troops crossed the Pontine marshes and linked up with the Anzio forces. By the 1st June, British units had captured Frosinone and the Anzio garrison were attacking a German stronghold in the Alban hills, only twelve miles from the centre of the city. We could hear, distinctly, the rumble of battle. Two armies were fighting at the gates of Rome.

CHAPTER
EIGHT

I stood on the roof-top with La Nonna. Beneath us, bathed in the high sunlight of summer, the city nestled on its seven hills, its skin of red-brown roofs broken here and there by gleaming spires and golden domes. The streets and squares immediately below us were empty, making me suppose that others were, like us, staring at the distant horizon from balconies and from the windows of upper storeys.

The diameter of Rome alone stood between us and the fulfilment of our long dream; already Allied spearheads were approaching the south-eastern outskirts of the city. From our vantage point we watched the cloud of dust and smoke creep steadily towards us across the yellow plain which lay between Rome and the Alban hills. We could hear the dull crump of exploding mortar bombs interspersed with the rattle of machine-gun fire, and the drone of planes as they swooped and circled above the battle.

We were alone on the roof and could talk freely.

"Will they come today?" La Nonna asked me. It was the 4th June.

"Yes, today they will come."

"*Caspita!* It doesn't seem possible, Gianni. Perhaps tomorrow or the next day?"

"None of your *poscrai* or *poscrudri*," I teased. "They will come today."

And this time I felt sure. For much of the night I had lain awake and listened to the noise of gunfire and the rumble of German convoys as they withdrew through the city, heading north.

"I am afraid, Gianni. Will there be a battle in the streets? Why don't the *tedeschi* run away?"

"Some of them are running away," I said. "The others are only fighting in order to give their pals more time to escape. And, if the rumours are true, there will be no fighting in the streets and no demolitions. They say that the Pope has promised to do what he can for the German casualties, in return for Kesselring's assurance that he will spare the city."

"You see, Gianni. *Che bravo il Papa!*"

I was inclined to believe that the Pope had played a big part in persuading both the Allies and the Germans to treat Rome as an "open" city. During the past two days I had inspected two of the Tiber bridges and had seen no signs that they had been mined, as had happened at the time of the Anzio landing, though it was possible that mines had been laid and subsequently removed by partisans. These thoughts reminded me of Enrico. He had promised to let me know if I could be of any use to the *Centro Militare* in the event of the German garrison getting tough. Among other actions, his Command planned to guard the bridges, to save them from demolition.

"Let's go down to the flat," I said. "I want to telephone Enrico."

"Why?"

Too late I realized my mistake. I had not disclosed my plans to La Nonna, knowing that she would disapprove of them. She had nothing against Enrico, except that he was an officer, a *pezzo grosso* and therefore a source of possible trouble.

"He may have some news."

"But you have already told me that the Allies will arrive today!"

"He may think differently."

"*Mascalzone!* I believe you are hatching up some plot with him. Don't you dare to get killed on the last day!"

I was feeling anything but heroic and was relieved to hear from Enrico that my services were not at present needed. Nor did he think that they would be, as it seemed that the Germans had called off their demolition programme.

Later that morning La Nonna and I together cooked and ate our solitary lunch for what was to be the last time. I think that we both sensed that the next day would bring to an end the simple intimacy of our relationship by severing the umbilical knot of conspiracy which had bound us together for so many months.

"Will you go home when the Allies arrive?" she asked me.

"Yes, I will go home. But not, I hope, immediately."

"Why can't you stay here with us? Why become a soldier again?"

"I must go to my own family, my own country. *Ognuno a casa sua*, you once told me."

"*E già!* You must go to your mother, *poveretta*. Just think of her excitement."

Soon after we had lunched, Arturo, Lucia and Ida arrived at the flat. Everywhere offices were closing their doors, and shops putting up their shutters. It was said that, during the previous night, all the "*pezzi grossi*", both German and Fascist, had fled, taking with them the most important of their prisoners and a quantity of personal loot. Among them had been the commander of the open city, the pig-faced General Maelzer who, according to rumour, had been too drunk to step unaided into his car. The Germans were now fighting a rearguard action on the south-eastern outskirts where the Appian Way penetrated the city. But west of the Tiber, in our quarter of the city, all was quiet, and it seemed that the spearhead of the attack would miss us as it swept north after the retreating enemy.

I went down into the street with Arturo and Lucia and walked south towards the Vatican. There was little to excite us until we had reached the Via Ottaviano; there we saw a sight which brought home to us the extent of the German disaster. A long column of stragglers, scattered remnants of a crushed army, was moving north along the street. Some were travelling in cars or trucks; others on bicycles or on foot; some were towing guns, others pushing carts laden with kit and equipment. They had in common only their look of utter exhaustion. Their tunics were covered with dust, their eyes red-rimmed and heavy with fear. Every now and then one of them would look back over his shoulder, as though fearing pursuit.

Groups of Romans stood on the pavements and watched the retreating Germans as if unable to believe the evidence of their own eyes. Mingling with them, the three of us felt stunned; this moment, which sometimes we had secretly doubted we would ever see, had actually come.

A sudden burst of machine-gun fire snarled over our heads. Two British fighters were tailing a Messerschmitt. The roar of engines as they dived above us snapped the taut nerves of a group of battle-weary Germans who were dragging their kit along the street. They swept us up in their stampede and bore us with them into the shelter of a courtyard. We were enveloped by the smell of sweat and fear, caught at the throat by the panic of the herd. I put my arm round Lucia as a fair-haired private, with the eyes of a frightened schoolboy, pressed us hard up against the wall of the courtyard. I could feel the texture of his grey tunic with my nose.

As the roar of the engines receded, the panic left us, snapping the chain which had momentarily linked us to our enemy. In my mind the fair-haired private was no longer a frightened boy but once more the symbol of a hated régime.

We watched the men of the *Wehrmacht* pick up their kitbags and troop back into the street. They joined the

227

long column moving north. I turned to Arturo who was standing beside me, pale with excitement.

"Well, there goes the master race."

"*Puzzno*," he said, tapping the side of his nose with his forefinger. "They stink — like badgers."

There was no answer to this beyond agreement. I tried to curb the sudden rush of sympathy which I felt for these defeated men whose plight reminded me so vividly of my own circumstances when Tobruk had fallen.

We walked on down to the Tiber, along empty streets. At the Ponte Umberto we came across a group of Fascist police whose orders were evidently to prevent us from crossing the river. We retraced our steps to Via Famagosta.

We found La Nonna dancing with excitement. Iolanda had just telephoned from the other side of the Tiber to say that some American armoured cars had passed down the street in which she lived, pursuing Germans. An hour later we heard a roar of cheering in the Viale delle Milizie. It was past the hour of curfew. We crowded on to our balcony and craned our necks, the better to see down the long, dark street. As an armoured car drew towards us and passed beneath the window, the cheers subsided and turned to laughter; we could see clearly the swastika painted on its bonnet.

After supper, we sat on the roof for several hours and watched fires burning on the approaches to the city. Columns of smoke twisted upwards and drifted towards us across the roof-tops. From time to time we would hear the distant rumble of tanks and the throb of aeroplane engines. But in the streets beneath us, all was quiet. It seemed that we had been forgotten, abandoned in a military vacuum.

There was no alternative but to try and sleep. I lay fully clothed on my bed, too excited to lose consciousness. It was nearly five in the morning before I heard the noise for which my ears had been straining throughout the long night and, moving to the window, saw a single scout car drive along the Viale delle Milizie. I woke up Arturo and together we walked out to meet the dawn. At a corner in the Viale, parked beneath a plane tree, was a huge American tank, bigger than any I had ever seen. A steel-helmeted GI sat in the gun turret gazing steadfastly at the vista on which his gun was trained. A small crowd of admirers was examining the tank.

I shoved my way to the front and shouted up to the tank turret.

"Hullo there! I'm English."

My words, in the unaccustomed tongue, sounded immensely affected. The GI continued to chew his gum and keep his eyes fixed down the street.

"I guess everyone round here speaks English," he said.

"But I am English! I'm an escaped prisoner of war."

"Oh yeah!"

Covered with embarrassment I faded back into the crowd. Why should he believe me, I thought? He has a job to do, other things to think of. Too late did I realize what a *brutta figura* I was making in the eyes of Arturo.

"*Caspita*, Gianni!" he exclaimed. "Don't you know how to speak American?"

"Come on," I said. "We'll find some others."

And, indeed, in the Piazza del Risorgimento, we came across a group of armoured cars, their American crews standing beside their vehicles and conversing with a crowd of excited Romans. I chatted with several of them and outlined my story. They gave me cigarettes and gum. They gave everyone cigarettes and gum. A girl gave one of them an Italian flag which he planted on the top of his turret.

I had not slept at all during the night and my stomach was knotted with excitement and nervous tension. The strong American cigarette made me sick and dizzy. I went to sit on a bench at the foot of a plane tree with my head between my hands. This is the moment, I told myself, the moment on which your thoughts have been concentrated for eight months. Relax, rid yourself of this tension. Your troubles are over, you can do what you like now. Vomit if you want.

At this instant I felt the pressure of a hand on my shoulder. It belonged to Arturo.

"Bend over, *cretino*," he said.

And I did. Just in time.

PART FOUR

Liberation

CHAPTER ONE

Most escape stories end with the protagonist successfully crossing either into the lines of his own army or over the frontier of a neutral country. Then he is interrogated, congratulated, fed, washed and, finally, fed into an assembly line which will convey him as rapidly as possible to his own country and reunion with his family. The account of these happenings is essentially an epilogue to the period in his life which started with his escape and ended abruptly at the moment when he crossed the frontier to freedom.

There were many reasons why my adventure did not end when I was sick under the plane tree in the Piazza del Risorgimento. Principal among these were the facts that I had not actively crossed a front line (for the line had, so to speak, crossed me) and that I was but one of a large number of escaped PoWs of many nations who rejoined their armies in Rome. My position was not so very different from that of the millions of people who had lived unwillingly in German-occupied Europe and been liberated by the advancing Allied armies, a comparison made real by the fact that I had taken eight months to complete my escape, during which period I had lived with and identified myself with one family of Italians.

I neither wanted nor intended to leave Rome immediately after the liberation. For one thing, I wanted to make sure that the Platano family were suitably rewarded for the help which they had given me. I was also curious to see how occupation by the Allies would compare with that which I had experienced under the Germans, and whether or not the anti-Fascist Italians, whose hopes I had come to admire and even to share, would gain political power in the emergent Italy.

Nor had I any urgent personal reason to go home. My father was dead, and my mother, to whom I was devoted, had lost her memory to such an extent that I was afraid that she would not recognize me on my return. I had no wife or fiancée, and both my sisters were happily married and had their husbands with them.

As it turned out, there was never any question of my being whisked away from Rome immediately. Such were the numbers of escaped PoWs liberated by the Allied advance that the unit responsible for our repatriation was delighted to find someone like myself who was prepared to fend for himself until arrangements had been completed for his return to England. Consequently, I was able to stay on at Via Famagosta for a period to which my memory has given an importance out of all proportion to its two weeks' duration. In the course of it I lived vicariously the adventures of other escaped PoWs and experienced both the joys and torments of a return to a more normal existence.

I felt better after I had been sick under the plane tree. The sun crept up above the eastern rim of the city and warmed the *piazza* with the promise of another hot June day. As more and more people woke up, looked out of their windows and ran down into the streets to greet the liberating army, the crowd around me thickened. I became impatient with the role of spectator and begged a lift to the centre of the city from an American sergeant. I asked Arturo if he wanted to come with me, but he said no, he would go home to Rina. I felt that I had disappointed him in the hour of triumph; he would have liked to have been acclaimed as the man who had saved an Englishman, placed beside me on the top of a tank, and driven triumphantly through the streets. He may even have expected that this would happen.

The sergeant set me down outside one of the big hotels in the Via Veneto. I walked into the huge front hall, the floor of which was covered with sleeping soldiers. They lay where they had dropped in their tiredness. Their heads pillowed on haversacks, their arms encircling rifles and tin helmets, they slept like men who had reached the final stages of exhaustion. For the first time I pictured the battle through their eyes and not through those of the people of Rome.

I managed to find an American Intelligence Officer. A few minutes' talk with him confirmed my belief that I had no information of any immediate value to impart.

235

He suggested that I should return next day, by which time he might be able to tell me to whom I should report.

There seemed no point in hanging around the Via Veneto at this early hour, so I hitched a lift back across the Tiber and walked the remaining distance to Via Famagosta. La Nonna, Lucia and Ida had just woken up and I was able to surprise them by making for breakfast a cup of real coffee, a present from an American. Then I went to bed and slept till lunchtime.

While I slept, the city came to life. Like butterflies which had been confined for nine months in dreary chrysalids, the people of Rome shook off their skins, polished their wings and emerged into the streets to link hands with the troops of the liberating army. The spirit of *festa* had, for the moment, made them forget that these troops were conquerors as well as liberators.

We had heard that the Pope was to appear on the balcony of St Peter's to offer a prayer for the safe deliverance of the city and to bless the assembled crowd. After lunch we joined the crowd which was sweeping down the Via Ottaviano towards St Peter's. The traffic thickened at each intersection. Tanks, jeeps, horsedrawn carriages and bicycles weaved their way through the crowd. A light wind fluttered the flags of many nations which hung from balcony and window. Huge coloured streamers were draped high across the street and boldly proclaimed their messages of welcome in two languages — "*Vivano gli Alleati!*" and "Hurrah for our gallant liberators!" — against a background of bright blue sky. American soldiers sat smiling on the tops of their tanks and threw packets of cigarettes and chocolate to their admirers who, in return, showered them with kisses and pressed into their hands bunches of flowers and flasks of wine. Jeeps, piled with pretty girls in summer dresses, honked their way through a sea of people. A fat GI sat on the bonnet of his truck with a girl on either knee, and parried the good-natured chaffing of the crowd with wise-cracks and snatches of dialect acquired in the streets of Naples. A little boy climbed along the barrel of a heavy gun and triumphantly planted a bunch of roses in the muzzle.

In the Piazza del Risorgimento we were joined by a long column composed of representatives of the anti-Fascist political parties; they walked in formation and bore with pride the flags and banners of their parties. The hammers and sickles of the Communists and Socialists mingled with the crusaders' shields of the Christian Democrats. Like the rest of us, these men of the underground were on their way to pay homage to the Pope.

We reached St Peter's Square and joined the multitude thronging the foreground of the great church. The bells stopped ringing. A frail figure, dressed in white, stepped out on to the balcony high above the crowd.

A mighty storm of applause burst forth and echoed round the arches of Bernini's colonnade. It expressed the people's thanks for the safe deliverance of their city, and their tribute to the constancy, in a world of shifting values, of the Catholic faith. With a movement of his arm the Pope stilled the crowd and waved us down onto our knees. He thanked God for sparing the city from destruction. Then he blessed us.

I looked at Arturo beside me and tried to read his thoughts. Did he believe that he was listening to the words of Christ transmitted through the lips of His representative on earth? Or to the words of a good and brave man who was, nevertheless, just another able politician? I knew, of course, what La Nonna was thinking and envied her the certainty of her belief.

The *piazza* was so densely packed that we feared little Stellina would get crushed; La Nonna decided to take her back to Via Famagosta. The rest of us let ourselves be borne by the crowd across the Tiber towards the centre of the city. I felt like an actor in a crowd scene of a Cecil B. de Mille epic of ancient Rome, in which the parts of centurions, returning in triumph from some foreign war, were played by American soldiers. I was swallowed up in the carnival spirit. This Roman crowd was celebrating the end, not only of the German occupation, but of twenty-two years of Fascist dictatorship, during the last nine of which the country had been almost continuously at war.

As I walked towards the Piazza Venezia I marvelled at the presence of the happy throng where two days previously only a few gaunt men had stalked the broad avenues. I wondered from what retreats these joyous Romans, of seemingly healthy appearance, had emerged. I looked at Lucia walking by my side and, in her bearing, saw the answer to my question. She was wearing her one good dress, kept chic and fresh throughout the years, and walked as though she owned the world. Few could guess that, behind the make-up, was the girl, sallow of face and sick with tiredness, who had so recently wept over the basket of worm-eaten greens which were all that she had been able to buy for our supper.

When we arrived back at Via Famagosta, we found two GIs sitting with La Nonna in the kitchen, eating the *pizza* which she had cooked for our supper and drinking from the flask of wine which we had put aside for the liberation in the days before I had money. Like so many Roman housewives, La Nonna had been unable to resist the appeal of the young American fighting troops. She had found these two hanging round the door of our local wineshop, which was closed because it had run out of wine.

To their enquiry "Where wine?", she answered "Come! Come!" as she would still have done had we been too poor to buy another *fiasca* for ourselves. For she still honoured the peasant custom of hospitality to strangers.

They were two nice boys who hailed from Texas and had come to Rome by way of the Anzio beach-head. I was amazed by the ease with which they could communicate with La Nonna. Like so many Allied soldiers, they had learnt a few Italian words from the peasants as they fought their way up the peninsula — enough, when seasoned with the right gestures and intonations, to get their message across. They made us a present of candy and a carton of cigarettes.

In the evening we entertained the family of eleven Neapolitan refugees who lived in the flat across the landing and whose ages ranged from seven to seventy. I knew many of their voices well, for in the course of the past months most of them had used our telephone from time to time or entered our flat for one reason or another. I found it a curious experience to fit faces and names to the familiar voices. The memory of what we talked about has burnt to ashes in the glow of the great happiness which filled our hearts. I can remember only that the Neapolitans were piteously grateful for the food and wine which we were able to give them, and that some of us went wandering down the Viale delle Milizie, ill-lit because the Germans had blown up one of the dams on which the city depended for its electricity supply, in order that we might bring an element of reality to our newfound freedom.

Because of the curfew, I had never before seen Rome by night.

CHAPTER
TWO

Next morning came the news of Allied landings on the beaches of Normandy. I heard it from a British captain who was collecting information from escaped PoWs. I had tracked him down in the lounge of a luxurious Via Veneto hotel, which had just been requisitioned by the Americans.

The news, for which I had waited so impatiently for so many months, fell curiously flat on my ears. Such was my contentment that, for all I cared, our troops might have landed on the moon, a contingency which in those days appeared unlikely. I felt like a space traveller myself, as I surveyed the alien scene. The hall of the hotel was heaped with the paraphernalia of the US Army — packs and valises of strange design, crates of PX rations, steel helmets shaped like inverted chamber pots — all unfamiliar to me who had never seen an American soldier until the previous day. Two GIs, rifles slung on their shoulders, paced up and down the lush carpet between hall and lounge, where a number of Italians of both sexes sat drinking their morning coffee and gaping at the American officers.

The British captain confirmed that there were many other escaped PoWs in Rome and suggested that I should stay where I was until plans had been made for our repatriation. I agreed to write a report on the strength of pro-Allied sentiment in Italy, suggesting how we could use it for our better advantage. Then I made my escape down a passage in the direction of a neon sign bearing the words *Bar Americano*.

The small bar which I now entered was of a magnificence such as I would have been unable to conceive of two days previously, when my imagination could aspire no higher than to a dream pub dispensing unlimited quantities of beer. Standing before a regiment of gleaming bottles, lined up with military precision on shelves of glass, a barman in a white coat was pouring the contents of a silver cocktail shaker into the glasses aligned on the bar before him. Sitting with their backs to me on high stools were three immaculately dressed young men. Otherwise the bar was empty, for the hour was comparatively early for morning drinks.

The barman eyed me superciliously. Conscious of my frayed collar and crumpled suit, the trousers of which hung in loose folds over my skinny thighs, I was about to make a discreet withdrawal, when one of the young men turned his head in my direction.

"John, you old bugger! How nice to see you. Sam told me that you were somewhere around. Have a drink."

I stared at the gleaming figure in the brick-red suit and saw that it was my old friend, Gilbert Smith, now no longer blemished by the yellow scabs which had so nauseated me at Sulmona.

242

"Good God, Gilbert! When did you get here?"

"I've been tooling around for months." He waved his hand towards the two men sitting beside him at the bar. "You remember these Chieti types?"

I had no difficulty in recognizing Bill Simpson because Derry's letter had led me to believe that he was in Rome. I had a vague recollection of having met the third man, who was now handing me a cigarette from a silver case, in Chieti bridge tournaments.

"Yes, of course. How good to see you all."

They ordered me a gin sling and then started to bombard me with questions.

"When did you escape?"

"Where have you been hiding yourself all this time?"

"How long have you been in Rome?"

"Where did you get that appalling suit?"

Their exuberance embarrassed me, and I took a long swig at the drink which Gilbert had pressed into my hand before attempting to sketch the outline of my story. Told in a couple of sentences it sounded very dull.

"Funny we never met," said Bill. "We've all been here for months too. Did you never go out?"

"Oh yes, often."

"Never saw you at the Orso," said Gilbert.

"Or at the Opera."

"Or at Millie's."

"Shut up, you clowns," said Bill. "Give the man a chance."

I had a thousand questions to ask. But I wished first to get the feel of their talk, which was so different to anything to which I was then accustomed.

I was confused not so much by the strangeness of speaking in English as by the speed and sureness of their repartee. I had forgotten that conversation was a matter of thrust and return, of intercept and volley, and when I attempted to play the game, my words fell like drop shots on the verbal tennis court. And so I chose to sit on the sidelines and pick up clues as I listened to their stories. Bit by bit I began to put together the jigsaw puzzle which had intrigued me ever since a piece of it, in the form of 6,000 *lire*, had come into my hands by way of the Polish priest in the Vatican.

I learnt that they had been in touch with Sam Derry in the Vatican ever since their arrival in Rome in December, and that they had all stayed in many Italian households, sometimes together, more often on their own. In particular, Bill Simpson had frequently changed his address and, at one period, had rarely slept for two consecutive nights under the same roof. He and John Furman had been the chief links between Sam Derry, who lived inside the Vatican, and the many escaped PoWs who were hiding in the city. Bill had found them billets with Italian families and had taken them food, clothes and money. The Gestapo had caught up with him in April and imprisoned him in the Regina Coeli. But the documents which he carried had been impeccably forged: they showed him to be an Irishman who had lived in Rome for many years, and the Gestapo had failed to break down his alibi. Unlike

244

some of his fellow prisoners, who had been shot, he had been mysteriously released from prison on the day before the liberation. Gilbert had had his adventures too, and shared with Bill a host of Italian friends.

By the end of my second drink I was beginning to relax and to form a picture of the danger, excitement and high living which had made up the pattern of my friends' lives. I knew now that they had all been able to cash cheques with rich friends; that the Orso was a black market restaurant at which they had often lunched; that they had been a few times to the Opera; and that their suits had been made for them at the establishment of a naval commander, named Ciro, who before the war had made suits for the then Prince of Wales. It seemed impossible that their gaudy lives should have been lived at such a short distance from Via Famagosta where I, at the same time, had been living on bean soup. It would be futile, I decided, to attempt to interest them in the unique personality of La Nonna or the flights of imagination to which hunger and despondency had driven me.

Nevertheless, the impact of each gin sling on a head deprived of spirits for two years soon loosened my tongue. A glimpse in the mirror behind the bar of my thin figure in a crumpled suit no longer humiliated me, and when Bill suggested that we should move on to the Grand Hotel to meet some of the Italians about whose exploits I had been hearing, I had identified myself with my friends to such an extent that his suggestion seemed to be the most natural in the world.

I followed them out into the street, outwardly composed but inwardly marvelling at the sudden transformation of my circumstances. I had arrived at the Hotel Flora lonely and on foot. I left it cock-a-hoop, in a white Lancia.

As we drove down the Via Veneto, I questioned Gilbert about the people whom he expected to find having drinks at the Grand. He told me that several Italians who had played a part in Derry's organization were likely to be there, together with the escapers whom they had helped, and that his particular date was with Renzo and Adrienne Lucidi. Adrienne was French by birth. She and her husband had both played a big part in the Roman underground movement and Derry had used their flat as a kind of transit camp for escaped PoWs on their arrival in Rome.

"You'll love Adrienne," said Gilbert. "She's brave as a lion and mad as a hatter. But it's utter hell walking down a street with her — she's always shouting *salles Boches* at Germans."

We found the Lucidis among a large party of men and women who were sipping dry martinis in a corner of the baroque foyer of the Grand Hotel. There were at least three escaped PoWs among them, one of whom I recognized as an American pilot who had been at Chieti. When I had been introduced all round, and given a dry martini, I sat down between Adrienne and a tough-looking little man whose shabby suit looked as out of place as mine did in the sumptuous setting. At the other tables a few Allied officers, mostly American, mingled with a gathering of sleek, elegant Romans. The thought crossed my mind that most of the latter had probably been drinking here with their German protectors only a few days before.

The conversation ricocheted round our group of tables in three languages. Everyone seemed to be unnaturally handsome and witty. Adrienne, with true Gallic intuition, sensed my diffidence and quickly put me at my ease. She spoke good English with an attractive French accent.

"Which is your husband?" I asked her, for I had missed his name in the round of introductions.

She pointed across the table to a man of about forty who had the look of someone who both worked and played hard.

"That's him over there, talking to the prettiest girl as usual. He's a film director, though nobody has made any films during this last year."

She went on round the table, giving me short, incisive portraits of everyone, explaining that the thin, elderly count had an Irish mother; that the faded beauty with blonde hair and high cheekbones was an Austrian Jewess, a refugee from Vienna, and that the Englishman on her right, another acquaintance from Chieti, was her present boyfriend.

"Who's the lovely redhead?" I asked.

"She's a *marchesa* from Piedmont, I think. *Elle est très belle, n'est-ce pas?*"

"She certainly is. Tell me about the little man on my left."

"The partisans call him Mario. He was exiled by Mussolini and fought in Spain with the International

Brigade. He is very shy — you'll have to get my husband to tell you his story."

The gin had by now conquered my inhibitions.

"They certainly seem a mixed bag."

"You're quite right. A year ago you would never have found all of us together. That is one good thing that the German occupation has brought about."

"You mean you've been drawn together by your hatred of Mussolini and the Germans?"

"*C'est ça*. We have all been fighting them in one way or another. And most of us have been hiding people like you, sent to us by the Vatican organization. I hear that you have been living alone all the time with one family."

"Yes. I only got in touch with Derry a few weeks ago. I had no idea there were so many escaped PoWs around. How many are there in Rome?"

"At least a hundred, I should guess."

"Good God! As many as that? And I flattered myself that I was a kind of freak!"

"You are," she laughed. "Derry thought he knew the names of all the escapers in Rome until he got your letter."

Later, a number of us, including Bill Simpson and the Lucidis, moved on to the Orso where Adrienne introduced me to Felix the barman. It was through her friendship with him that a small group of British officers had first come to lunch in this black-market restaurant. Felix had made a habit of giving them a table which was discreetly screened from the other customers, most of whom, because of the Orso's expensive menu, were German officers.

248

Over a meal of a kind which I had forgotten existed I got Bill to explain the background of the organization which Sam Derry had controlled from inside the Vatican, and to tell me about the Irish priest, Monsignore Hugh O'Flaherty, who had been the inspiration behind it.

He started by telling me how he and my other friends had come to be in Rome. After he had jumped from the German truck just before the convoy from Chieti had reached Sulmona, Bill had been hidden by friendly Italians, and a few days later had run across John Furman, whose escape from Sulmona I had myself watched; the two of them took on the job of finding safe houses for the many other escaped PoWs who were hiding in the hills around Sulmona. They also contacted Gilbert Smith, whose plan of sabotaging the sores on his face (so as to be moved into the German hospital at Sulmona) had worked; using knotted sheets as a rope, he had escaped through a hospital window with several other patients, some of whom were seriously ill.

By the middle of November — at about the time when I was moving from Nespolo to Rome — the pressure of the Germans' hunt for escaped PoWs increased. It culminated in a day of terrible *rastrellamenti*, during which many escapers were recaptured; whole families of Italians were also arrested, and in some cases executed. Gilbert, Bill and John decided that they must leave the district.

Shortly before this Gilbert, badly in need of money to buy medicines for the sick escapers, had persuaded an attractive girl — who said she was a singer on Radio Roma but whom he suspected of following a far older profession — to take with her, on her next trip to Rome, a letter addressed to Sir D'Arcy Osborne, the British Minister to the Holy See. She was to give the letter to an Irish priest in St Peter's, in the hope that it would be passed on to Sir D' Arcy inside the Vatican.

When she returned from her next trip to Rome, the girl brought with her an envelope stuffed with bank notes. Uncertain exactly who in the Vatican had provided this money, but keen to follow up the lead, the three friends decided to try to get to Rome. The girl singer helped them make the train journey, and showed them exactly where they could find the helpful Irish priest; within days, John Furman was smuggled into the Vatican, and found himself face-to-face with an old friend from Chieti — Sam Derry. The meeting took place in the Vatican office of Monsignore O'Flaherty.

"Haven't I seen this Monsignore somewhere?" I interrupted.

"You might have — when he visited Chieti with the Papal Nuncio. He's an official of the Holy See — he's been there about twenty years. They were making a tour of prison camps."

"That's right — I remember winning the camp raffle, for a set of Vatican stamps that the Nuncio gave us. I had to leave them behind when I jumped off the train. I wonder who's got them now. But go on — tell me about the Monsignore."

"He's a tremendous fellow. He wasn't particularly anti-Fascist before the war, but when Mussolini joined

250

forces with Hitler and started rounding up the Jews, he got really mad. Since then he's been a kind of Scarlet Pimpernel."

I realized that the Monsignore was the key to many things that had been puzzling me ever since La Nonna had been given the 6,000 *lire* by her Polish priest, but by the time Bill had got to this part of the story my head was swimming, for I had drunk a great deal of alcohol to which I was totally unaccustomed. Later I learnt that Sam (who had escaped by jumping from the same train as me) had himself been smuggled into the Vatican to see the Monsignore, whose organization — already extremely busy with its work of helping anti-Fascists, Jews, and other persecuted people — badly needed to recruit someone who would be able to work full-time on the task of getting aid to escaped PoWs. The two men had taken an immediate liking to each other, and it had been agreed that Sam should move permanently into the Vatican, and build on the solid foundation of aid already laid down by the Monsignore; in this he was greatly helped by a colourful character of great ingenuity, called John May. May was Sir D'Arcy Osborne's butler, and was responsible for much of the financial side of the organization, the full story of which is told in Sam's own book (*The Rome Escape Line*, by Sam Derry, Harrap, 1960).

Bill turned the conversation to less serious subjects, and described to me how, one day in the Orso, he had become involved with a party of German officers which included the champion boxer, Max Schmelling. He had resolved what could have been a dangerous situation in a characteristic way — by standing the Germans a round of drinks. On another occasion, he told me Gilbert had been ticked off by a Hauptman for ordering a drink in English at the Excelsior bar. Such wild behaviour was not as mad as it would appear and could, indeed, be said to have provided a measure of security, for no German would ever imagine that an escaped PoW could be crazy enough to seat himself on a bar stool beside his enemy, let alone ask the barman for a dry martini in English, a tease which Gilbert had copied from some of the Roman aristocracy. The big bluff always worked. And though a number of Bill's friends had been arrested at one time or another, a disaster had never befallen them in any of the elegant bars or restaurants which they had frequented.

It must have been after four o'clock when we rose from the table at the Orso. Someone, I forget who, drove me back to Via Famagosta. As I crossed the familiar courtyard, passing serenely but unsteadily between the usual bands of urchins, and climbed the steep steps — so hard and cold compared with the plushly carpeted stairs of the Grand Hotel — I realized that I was exceedingly drunk. This did nothing to assuage the feeling of guilt consequent upon my reawakened knowledge of how the rich lived, a feeling which mounted with each step and multiplied tenfold when I met La Nonna on the landing. She was carrying an empty bucket in either hand.

"*Ben tornato*, Gianni," she said. "I'm just going down to the pump to fetch some water."

The supply to our flat was still cut off. I gave La Nonna a big hug.

"Give me the buckets," I said. "I'm coming with you. I'm drunk, but not too drunk to fetch water. Where's Lucia? Where's everyone? I've had a wonderful day."

"It's good to see you so happy. Lucia has gone to see a girlfriend. But she'll be back for supper. Arturo is coming too."

"I feel as though I could never eat again. I've had the most enormous lunch, at a restaurant. How about that!"

"*Beh*! What would I know of restaurants!"

"Then have you ever heard of an Irish priest called O'Flaherty?"

"*Irlandese*? The Polish priest at St Peter's, the one who has been so good to us, talked of an *irlandese*."

"That will be him. I'll tell you all about him when we have fetched the water."

But by the time I had been down to the courtyard and up again, my head was spinning. I was afraid I was going to be sick.

"Better sleep it off, Gianni," said La Nonna. "I'll wake you up when it's time for supper."

"*Hai ragione*. I'll do just that."

I tumbled on to my bed. La Nonna, the Polish priest, Monsignore O'Flaherty, Bill Simpson, Adrienne Lucidi, Felix the barman. Their faces, real or imagined, spun before me like multi-coloured tops before I drifted into a dreamless sleep.

★　★　★

I felt ghastly when La Nonna woke me two hours later to tell me that Arturo had arrived and that we were going to have supper, not in the kitchen, but at the big table in Lucia's room. My head was still muzzy, which may have accounted for my failure to entertain the family with some of the stories which had so diverted me, but I told Arturo how three of my English friends had obtained General Maelzer's autograph on their single opera programme. On the night in question they had been taken to the opera by Adrienne Lucidi, who was a great lover of music, and found to their amusement that the German commander of Rome was occupying the adjoining box. The Frenchwoman was looking her most glamorous and had caught the eye of one of the General's ADCs. During the interval he had found an excuse to talk to her. And before the end of the performance she had been persuaded by her companions to get the General to sign their programme.

This story had delighted me when I had heard it at lunch. But in the re-telling of it, I amused only Lucia. Such high jinks were so far removed from the experience of Ida, Arturo and La Nonna that the frivolity and daring, which gave point to the episode, made little impact.

We ate for supper some of the tinned meat and vegetables which the two GIs had given us on the previous day. My shrunken stomach had been quite unable to cope with the huge quantities of food and drink to which it had already been subjected in the

254

course of the day; I had no appetite and had to force the meal down my throat in order not to offend Ida, who had taken great trouble in its preparation. The wine, which only yesterday had tasted like nectar, was rough and sour to my palate. I was appalled that a few hours of rich living could so speedily erase the standards which had been mine for many months. The Platanos' flat, I realized, was no longer the centre of my world.

CHAPTER
THREE

Next morning I stayed in bed late. I had spent a restless night and was suffering from an appalling hangover. For a long time I lay in a semi-comatose condition, turning over in my mind the extraordinary stories which I had heard on the previous day. Had I really seen that opera programme autographed by General Maelzer? And the photograph of Gilbert having tea with a German officer on a balcony overlooking the Piazza di Spagna?

I wished that I was lying in a bedroom in the Grand Hotel and could ring the bell and ask the maid to bring me a cup of strong coffee and turn on my bath. It was more than two years since I had had a hot bath, and yet this was the first time that my body had really screamed out for one.

I got gently out of bed and walked through to the kitchen to get my usual basin of heated-up water. I felt better when I had shaved and drunk a cup of coffee. La Nonna suggested that we should go together to St Peter's to see the Polish priest. She was looking forward to introducing us and I to meeting him. Before setting out, I reminded her that I would be out for lunch, as I had arranged to take Lucia for drinks at the Grand

Hotel. I hoped that by introducing her to some of my friends I might bridge the gap between my life with the Platanos and the new, exciting world which I had entered on the previous day.

I was determined not to jeopardize my friendship with the Platanos. Yet I was clamouring for the companionship of my English friends and for the society of some of the Italians, so fascinating to me, whom I had met at the Grand and the Orso. I also wished to know more of the wider background of the German occupation and to meet the personalities, such as Monsignore O'Flaherty and John May, the British Minister's butler, whose exploits, as recounted by Bill, had so amused me.

I imagined that Lucia would get a kick, as I had done, from the atmosphere of daring and elegance which, so it seemed to my starved senses, hung round the group of people in whose company I had spent most of the previous day, and that she would get the vicarious pleasure, similar to my own, from living their adventures at second hand. I had forgotten that, unlike Lucia, I had once been familiar with their way of living and that the Englishmen in their seemingly magic circle were old friends of mine. Nor did I realize at the time that the Italians among them, despite the diversity of their social origins, were bound together by the experience which they had shared during the recent past. Unlike them Lucia and her family had helped me because I was a human being in trouble and not on account of their patriotic or idealistic beliefs.

My idea that I could use Lucia as a bridge between Via Famagosta and Via Veneto was quickly shown to be an illusion. From the moment of our arrival in the Grand Hotel, everything went wrong. Neither Bill nor Gilbert was present. Nor was Adrienne Lucidi, who would have made the perfect catalyst. We joined a party of two other escaped PoWs and their charming but sophisticated hosts. The conversation was almost entirely in English, a language of which Lucia could not understand one word. The drinks were too bitter for her palate, the humour too cynical. For my part I lacked the self-assurance necessary to break down the embarrassment which she was obviously feeling in so unfamiliar an *ambiente*. There was no doubt that for her, and therefore for me, the party was a flop.

When we left the Grand it was after 2 o'clock, nearly time for Arturo's bank to close. I telephoned him and arranged for him to join us for lunch, choosing a blackmarket restaurant near the Pantheon which, so I had been told, was second only to the Orso. But our lunch, too, was a sad affair. The ornate food and the formality with which it was served chastened Arturo's usual volubility. I had to hide the bill from him, for it seemed so extravagant.

Transport was still a terrible problem. On the evening after my failure to bring together my two worlds, I set out from Via Famagosta on foot, heading for the Excelsior Hotel, where I had arranged to dine with Sam and John. Somewhere near the Piazza del Popolo I was lucky enough to grab a horse-drawn cab. As I was

258

driven in state up the Corso Umberto, two GIs hailed my driver. I told him to stop and asked the GIs to get in. Where did they want to go? To the Via Veneto? Fine, I was going that way myself. In they jumped and off we went. I told them who I was and explained how I had been hiding in Rome for many months. I thought we were getting on well together, and was surprised when they ordered the cab driver to stop in the Piazza Barbarini, beside an American Military Policeman.

"This guy says he's English," one of them told him. "It sounds like a phoney story to me."

"English, are you?" said the MP. "Then why are you wearing those clothes?"

"I am an escaped British officer, as I told these two soldiers."

"Escaped? And an officer!" There was no mistaking the ugly tone of his voice. "Where did you escape from?"

"A camp called Chieti."

"And you're British?"

"That's what I said."

"Show me your documents," he snapped.

"Now look here," I said, as politely as I was able. "How can I possibly have the right documents?" I resisted the temptation to show him my forged identity card. "I have, of course, reported to the British Army. But no one has got round to giving me any papers yet."

"You can't fool me with that cockeyed story."

"If you don't believe me, hop inside. I have a date at the Excelsior, just round the corner, with a British major. He knows all about me."

"Me come with you! You are coming with me, and right now."

Up to this point I had been sitting in my cab with as much dignity as I could muster. But as he spoke his last sentence, the MP seized me by the collar of my jacket, pulled me out and marched me across the *piazza* to the steps of a large building guarded by two American MPs.

I was spluttering with rage, not at the GIs for handing me over, not even at the MP for questioning me and taking me to his headquarters for a check-up but at his rudeness and the way in which he was treating me as guilty before he had any proof. If this is American justice, I thought, God help the Italians.

But now my luck turned. I saw, walking away from me along the street, an officer wearing the beret of the British Tank Corps. There were few British officers in Rome. To see one now was a chance in a hundred. I gave him a shout.

"Officer, you there!"

He went on walking away.

"ENGLISHMAN!"

I yelled the word at the top of my voice and for a moment I thought the MP was going to club me.

It was an unusual exclamation and the man stopped in his tracks and turned round. I waved him towards me. As he approached I saw with delight that he was a major and wore the ribbon of the Africa Star. I told him who I was and explained my predicament. After questioning me about the desert campaign, the major was able to vouch that I was the genuine article. The

MP retired in disorder. I asked my saviour to join me in a drink at the Excelsior but he had another engagement. I have often wondered who he was.

I pushed my way through the crowd of curious spectators who had gathered on the pavement. My cab and driver had vanished, so I walked up round the wide sweep of the Via Veneto to the Excelsior Hotel. As I did so, I tried to quell my anger and see my skirmish in its proper light, as a misunderstanding which would both divert my hosts and explain my lateness. But I knew that the incident would leave its mark. And I must confess that for some years even a photograph of an American Military Policeman was enough to make my hackles rise.

I found Sam and John waiting patiently for me in the bar of the Excelsior Hotel, and told them — rather breathlessly — of the reason for my lateness. They told me not to worry, as Monsignore O'Flaherty, who was to join us for dinner, had not yet arrived. I was delighted at the prospect of meeting the Irish priest about whom I had heard so much.

While we waited for the Monsignore, we reminisced about our escapes — for Sam and I had both jumped, at different moments, from the same train — and Sam went on to tell me that, while he was in the Vatican, he had listed the names of several thousand other Allied escaped prisoners who had, at one time or another, been at large in Italy; Michael Ardizzone's name had been on the list, but he had been recaptured and sent to a camp in Germany. Sam also told me that General

261

Alexander had asked him to form a unit — based on his existing Vatican organization — which would gather the information that the British Government would need in order to recompense Italians who had helped escaped PoWs. John Furman and Bill Simpson had agreed to join this unit, which was to be called the Allied Screening Commission.

Finally, Sam told me more stories about the Monsignore and his gallant band of priests, who had done so much — irrespective of nationality or political allegiance — for persecuted, sick or suffering people. One of these stories concerned an Allied soldier, though it would have made little difference to the Monsignore had the person in need been a Greek refugee, an Italian monarchist, or an Austrian deserter.

This soldier was a Cameron Highlander, one of a group of escaped PoWs living in caves near Subiaco, about thirty miles east of Rome. News reached Sam that the Scotsman was suffering from acute appendicitis and would certainly die unless he was operated on immediately. Sam put the problem to the Monsignore, who persuaded an old friend of his, a surgeon at a hospital to which the Germans were sending many of their wounded, to operate without telling the authorities who the patient was. To get the man from Subiaco to the Roman hospital took considerable ingenuity. The best way seemed to be to borrow a car protected by Corps Diplomatique plates; the Monsignore could hardly ask the neutral Irish Ambassador to lend him an official car, but he had nothing to lose by making a confidential appeal to the Ambassador's wife, and that evening an Irish car, carrying CD plates, drove from Rome to Subiaco. Sitting beside the driver was one of the Monsignore's priestly helpers, selected because his strong physique fitted him admirably for the role of stretcher-bearer. Lifting the sick soldier into the back of the car, the priest went with him to the Roman hospital, where the surgeon — who had already that night operated on four Germans — removed the inflamed appendix. Then the Scotsman, still unconscious, was whisked away to a safe house, where he made a complete recovery. The whole affair was handled with the Monsignore's typical daring and ingenuity, and I was still listening with admiration to the end of the story when the Monsignore himself hurried in, and apologized with a total lack of self-importance.

Although I had glimpsed him during his visit to Chieti, it was the first time I had actually met him. He was tall and blue-eyed, and made an impressive figure in his long black robes; I immediately fell a victim to his robust and beguiling charm. He had a tremendous sense of humour, allied to a rare sensibility and an almost Italian curiosity about human nature. At the end of the evening, happening to hear that I was living near the Vatican, he offered to drive me home, and on the way to Via Famagosta I explained to him how it was through La Nonna's confession to the Polish priest that I had got in touch with Sam.

"He's a great man, that Pole," said the Monsignore, in his rich Irish brogue. "But what a pity, my boy, that you didn't get in touch with him sooner. Imagine! There you were and there we were next door — it's no distance, ye know. And that old lady of yours — I'd like to meet her one day. She sounds a fine person."

It would have given me a great deal of pleasure to have introduced La Nonna to the Monsignore, for my instinct told me that they would have delighted in each other's company, but made wary by my disastrous attempt to unite Lucia with my English friends, and knowing how extremely busy the Monsignore was, I made no further attempts to intermix my two worlds.

CHAPTER
FOUR

A Repatriation Unit had arrived in Rome. It would issue me with an identity card (which I hoped would prevent further skirmishes with policemen) and arrange for me to go to a transit camp in Naples and then by ship to England. While waiting for this to happen, I divided my time between the simple family life of Via Famagosta and an uninhibited search for pleasure in the company of my Chieti friends and the Italians who had been involved in their adventures. I believed that only in the company of this group of people, who shared some part both of my background and of my recent experiences, could I piece together the chips of my splintered personality. They alone provided a line between my past and my present, and I craved their company with the single-mindedness of a dope addict.

Much of my time was wasted in rushing from one end of Rome to another, though "rushing" is hardly the word to describe the tortuous and frustrating movements of the public transport. Although I was sometimes able to hitch a lift, either in army transport or in the cars of my high-living friends, I covered many miles on foot. I got pains in my legs and blisters on my feet. These minor irritations increased my general indisposition which was caused by eating and drinking far more than my body was able to digest. I became moody and quick to take offence. And when I recall my only extant memories of the chaotic week in which I tried to reconcile my conflicting loyalties, I am struck by the ease with which little grievances could plunge me from gaiety to dejection.

One fine morning I was sitting in the bar of the Excelsior Hotel. Among the company was Monsignore O'Flaherty, for the priest, though a teetotaller himself, was tolerant of the bad habits of others. He had been telling us how it was the plight of the Jews which had first impelled him to declare his private war against the Axis and describing how the Principessa Pallavicini had helped him to forge identity cards for many hundreds of them. I asked him to tell me more about the Princess.

"I'll do better than that, me boy," he said. "I'll take you to tea with her this afternoon. Ye can't leave Rome without meeting that great lady. Many's the time I've had to hide her in the Collegio Teutonicum when the Fascists were hunting her."

Since the liberation, the Princess had moved back into her own home, from a rear window of which she had made her escape when the Fascists had raided it the previous winter. At her tea party were, among others, one of the leaders of the Greek underground movement, called "Liberty or Death", which had carried out some of the most daring actions against the Germans in Italy, and a Secretary from the Vichy

Embassy in Rome, a loyal Frenchman who had conspired against the German Allies of the Vichy government. We had thin buttered bread and cakes and china tea; and as we left her party, the Princess's footman put before us a silver bowl of hot water in which to wash our sticky hands.

I decided to walk back to Via Famagosta. It was a gorgeous evening. As I crossed the Tiber, I stopped in the centre of the Sant'Angelo bridge and let some of my happiness float down the river towards the sea and the future. It was nice, I thought, to meet a princess who was as brave and good as La Nonna. I wondered if there was any common ground on which they could meet and decided that Monsignore O'Flaherty alone could provide it. Or perhaps they could play *scopa* together? For I believed that they shared a love of cards.

I decided to tell La Nonna about the Princess at supper. But I found the old lady in the courtyard filling two pails with water and as I carried them up the stone stairs to the flat, I could not but remember the Princess's footman and the silver bowl in which I had dipped my sticky fingers. And the happiness drained out of me.

About this time, Maria arrived in Rome. She had driven up from Colle Giove in an American truck with her two South African boys. They had gone to the barracks which the Allied Repatriation had just requisitioned but they had promised to come to dinner with us at the flat.

267

When they arrived, they turned out to be tall, fair-haired, good-looking boys, both in their early twenties. One was a corporal, the other a private. They were sunburnt and looked fit. But their eyes showed traces of hardship endured and I guessed that they were well under their normal weights.

We felt self-conscious in each other's presence, as often happens when people who have heard a lot about each other finally meet. They told me how, after the armistice, the Italian guards at their camp near Bologna had deserted, leaving the prisoners free to disperse into the countryside. Many of them had been rounded up and sent to Germany, but the tough and lucky ones had moved slowly south through the mountains, living off the land or staying with friendly peasants. A few had joined partisan bands.

All had gone well with them until the snows came in December. When they reached Colle Giove they both had frostbite and only Maria's devoted care had nursed them back to health. They called her their *madrina*, their god-mother, and I could see that they were very fond of her. But, though they could speak some Italian, they made little attempt in the course of the evening to talk to La Nonna and Lucia, obviously preferring to talk and joke between themselves. I got the impression that they did not really like Italians. Because they had always been together, they had not felt the need, as I had done, to understand the Italians' habits and manners. They made it clear that their thoughts were already back in South Africa and that their adventure had become a bad dream which they wanted to forget.

There was nothing surprising about this. But I thought that they might have made it less obvious to Maria. I remembered the terror of her night drive to Rome through an air-raid, an expedition undertaken so that she could buy medicines for them, and I knew that, in Maria's mind, their friendship could not be summarily dismissed as just an adventure.

On Sunday I lunched, as usual, at Arturo's. It was the first time he had seen me wearing the uniform which I had just scrounged from a friend at Area Command. Khaki slacks and tunic, Sam Browne and gunner's cap.

"How different you look, Gianni," said Rina.

"Better or worse?"

"Better, *più uomo*."

I asked her what we were having for lunch.

"Spum."

"What's Spum?" I asked.

"It's your stuff — a present from your friends."

Spam had not been invented when I was taken prisoner. She showed me the tin and I recognized it as being the meat roll which we had sometimes got in our Canadian Red Cross parcels at Chieti. Young Pina started to fry it in oil and garlic.

Pina had become quite a competent cook. Although only just twelve, Rina had taught her to use lipstick. I could not imagine her back among the peasants at Nespolo and wondered what would become of her. We believed that her mother, one of the hostages, was in a concentration camp in Germany.

269

While Pina cooked, we drank a glass of sticky vermouth.

"How will you travel back to England?" Rina asked me.

"In a ship from Naples."

"Is it a long way? Farther than Brazil where my cousin is?"

"*Ignorante!*" said Arturo. "It's not very far. But Gianni has to go by boat because of the English Channel."

After we had lunched, Arturo took me to see a plot of ground, near his flat, where he wanted to build a coffee bar. There was nothing of the sort here, on the extreme outskirts of the city, and the project had much to recommend it. Arturo's idea was that I should put up part of the capital and that Ida and Maria, both excellent cooks, should run it. First he would have to get licences, both to build and to open a bar; this might require some judicious greasing of palms.

I told him that he could count on me for some money, and that he should go ahead with his plans.

I was determined that, before I left Rome, I would find Lucia the good job with the Allies which I knew she deserved. I took a lot of trouble to get what I thought was the right introduction, and went with her to the Allied Military Government HQ. We were shown into the room of the Personnel Officer, to whom, unfortunately, I took an instantaneous dislike.

Trying my best to curb my feelings, I introduced Lucia and explained how much I owed to her.

"Does she speak English?" he asked.

"No, I'm afraid not. But she is a first-class secretary. She worked for six years with the Italian Ministry of Culture."

"Why did she leave?"

You silly clot, I said to myself, has nobody told you that there is a civil war going on in Italy? And aloud, "Because she is on our side. If she had stayed with the Ministry after the armistice, she would have had to swear an oath of allegiance to Mussolini and the Germans. Instead, she threw up her job and looked after me."

"Yes, I see."

Did he? I watched his eyes run over her figure. He could see that all right.

He asked her a few questions in bad Italian.

"I can, of course, vouch for her loyalty," I went on. "And I know she's damned efficient."

"Well, I'll see what I can do. But I doubt if we can use her. Pity she doesn't speak English."

And a pity she won't go to bed with you either, I thought.

Lucia looked downcast as we left the office. She knew that her half-Austrian friend, who had been working for the Germans right up to the end, had already fixed herself up with an AMG job.

"*Corraggio*," I said. "I'll try somewhere else." We started the long walk back to Via Famagosta.

★ ★ ★

I was having a late drink one evening somewhere in the Via Veneto and wondering how on earth I was going to get back across the Tiber, when I walked down the bar into view of a tall, fair RAF officer, whose breast was covered with decorations.

"Good God!" he exclaimed. "You're John Miller, aren't you? What the hell are you doing in those clothes?" I was wearing my old civilian suit.

I focused my eyes on him, and recognized a friend I had not seen for several years.

"It's me all right. Have a drink, you old bastard."

While the barman filled up our glasses, I started to count the rings on his sleeve. There were an awful lot of them.

"Christ," I said. "You certainly are a *pezzo grosso!*"

"What on earth is a *pezzo grosso?*"

"You're a bloody Group Captain!"

"That's right." He looked me up and down, noted the unsteadiness of my legs and my rumpled, ill-fitting suit, then turned, smiling, to the RAF officer beside him.

"Do you two know each other?"

I shook the second man by the hand and began to count the rings, or rather the ring, on his sleeve. For there was only one and it escaped my notice that it was broad and edged with silver.

"*Buona sera,*" I managed to say. "Good evening, Flying Officer."

"Good evening to you," said the Air Vice Marshal with a grin.

★　★　★

272

"What about the hole in the wall?" I asked Lucia.

"Let it stay," cut in La Nonna. "*E un bel ricordo di Gianni*. We made it together, he and I. If the landlord notices it, shrug your shoulders, say nothing."

"She's right," said Lucia. "If necessary, Arturo can paper it over sometime."

"Very well," I said. "But remember to let me know if there is trouble."

"Have a drink, Captain," said the US lieutenant. "I sure go for this town. Been here long?"

"Two days," I lied. I was tired of telling my story.

"This place has got everything. And to think they told us the Romans were starving! My buddy and I have just had the best meal since we left home."

"Where?"

"Right here in the Grand. Try this Bourbon. It's the real stuff."

"Not many Italians can afford to eat in the Grand, you know. It's not exactly cheap."

"But lunch wasn't all that expensive. The chit for both of us was less than twenty dollars."

"That's about six thousand *lire*."

"I guess you're right."

"I have a friend here who's a bank clerk. Like to make a guess at his pay-packet?"

"I wouldn't know."

"I'll tell you. Exactly six thousand *lire*, the cost of your two lunches."

"Six thousand a week? Is that all he gets?"

"Not a week. A month."

"You're kidding, Captain."

★　★　★

"I've won!" said La Nonna, slapping down the *sette bello*.

"Yes, you've won again. It's not my night tonight."

"You're tired, Gianni. You've been drinking too much with all your smart friends."

"Yes, I've been drinking too much."

"Are you really leaving soon?"

"*Si. Devo andare a casa mia.*"

"*Già!* I will miss you, Gianni."

"And I will be sad to leave. But I bet you'll soon be hiding an escaped German!"

"*Mascalzone!* Now you are teasing me again."

CHAPTER
FIVE

One night I was unable to go to sleep. My legs ached and my liver grumbled like an overloaded camel. My bed, which for six long months had been a haven from the hazards of daytime, had lost its protective magic. In it I could no longer drift at will into a deep sleep, contented in the knowledge that I had achieved my immediate objective and survived at liberty for another day.

My mind was unable to grasp the happiness which I knew lay somewhere inside me. I was obsessed by the failure of communications, on both sides, between the Allied occupation troops and the people of Rome. I felt torn by conflicting loyalties, both of class and nationality, and riled by the dissensions which had replaced the conviviality of the first few days of the liberation.

I decided that, as well as Fascists and Germans, I now hated Military Policemen, AMG officers and drunk GIs. I resented the word "wop" as much as I did the inevitable requisitioning of an army which was still at war. And I loathed my own liver, for I knew that it was largely responsible for my irascibility. The night brought to the surface of my mind the knowledge, which I had previously refused to face, that I was not enjoying the process of being liberated as much as I had anticipated. It had made me conscious that I was suffering from the feelings of anti-climax which are apt to follow the fulfilment of a dream, in my case the arrival of the Allies.

I decided that it was time I left Rome.

Often since 1944 I have tried to place in perspective those features of the occupation of Rome by Allied troops — most of whom happened to be American — which at the time so disconcerted me. I have tried to make allowances for the fact that my judgement was blurred by poor health. Yet even now, when time has washed away the bitterness, I can still feel the impact of the anti-American bias which the occupation of Rome bequeathed to me. For all I know, occupation by the English might have produced a similar disillusionment, but I could not at this time make the imaginative effort necessary to visualize the ecstasy of a leave in Rome through the battle-weary eyes of an American soldier who might have spent the winter in the snows above Cassino. I came to share the dismay of the Romans, themselves not heavy drinkers, at the sight of scores of GIs lying blissfully drunk beside Roman fountains or under the shade of the plane trees which flanked the grand avenues of the city. If, as I suspected, many Romans were in some ways disappointed with the new chapter of their lives which had begun with the liberation, it was a small price to pay in return for the removal of the Germans.

No one in Rome seriously complained of the unavoidable shortage of food, though our radio propaganda had made quite unnecessary promises about the stocks which would be rushed into the hungry city in the wake of our troops. Few people at first objected to the requisitioning of hotels and offices (in what was called an "open city") on a scale which the Germans had never even contemplated. What did infuriate me and my friends was the total unawareness on the part of many senior Allied officers and members of the staff of the Allied Military Government of the psychological needs of the Italian people. They were apparently ignorant that anti-Fascism was a reality and that, for nearly a year, a state of civil war had existed in German-occupied Italy. To most of them, the Italians were a nation who had changed sides at the moment in the war when they realized that they were losing. Even if one admitted a measure of truth in this gross simplification, it was incontrovertible that, since the signing of the armistice, the large majority of Italians had either actively or passively assisted the Allied cause and only a small minority had collaborated with the Germans and the Republican Fascists. To anyone who had lived in Italy under the German occupation, the dividing line was definite and manifest.

Unfortunately, in Rome it was specifically the very rich, the collaborators and the black-marketeers who sought the company of unaware Allied officers and filled them, not only with food and drink, but with stories which gave a completely false picture of the Roman scene.

277

So it happened that partisans were sometimes arrested on the grounds of denouncement by a collaborator. Well-known Fascists obtained profitable business contracts from Allied Control Commissions. Girl secretaries were valued in terms of their prowess in bed. Linguists, aided by their knowledge of administrative liaison acquired under the Germans, had little difficulty in transferring their services to the unclued Allied Commands.

This was a double tragedy because there was a wealth of loyal talent available to work on our behalf. In our propaganda we had throughout underestimated the strength of pro-Allied feeling and held out nebulous inducements to convert those who were already our friends. Now we often failed to make use of their services and, instead, employed people who had recently worked for our enemies.

A further distortion was given to the Roman scene by the operations of the black-marketeers, who flooded the smart shops and bars of the centre of the city with luxuries and bottles of spirits which had been hidden away during the German occupation for this very purpose. The average GI came to Rome for a few days' leave, expecting to find a city on the verge of starvation. Instead he was confronted by an array of consumer goods such as he had not seen for months. To him, with his high rate of pay converted into AMG *lire* at an immensely favourable exchange rate, the prices were reasonable. He did not understand that to all but a few Romans they were prohibitive, and that it was for this reason alone that meat, wine and silk stockings were now available to him.

Another symptom of my malaise, which I think was fairly general among people in any way connected with the European Resistance, was the feeling of not belonging anywhere. I had supposed that, with the liberation, I would once more assume the outlook of an English captain. Now I realized the naïvety of this supposition. With the passing of each day since the capture of Rome, I had become progressively more conscious of a psychological barrier between liberators and liberated. I found that I identified myself first with other escaped PoWs, secondly with the people of Rome, in particular with those who had played an active part in the underground, and only thirdly with the liberating troops. In retrospect it is easy to understand why this should have been so. I had inevitably assumed many of the idiosyncrasies of the Italian whose role I had been playing for eight months. It was therefore to be expected that I should experience both the joys and griefs consequent on liberation from the same viewpoint as all the other Europeans who had lived in Hitler's Third Reich.

Lucia had admitted to me her surprise that my efforts to get her a job had availed nothing. This failure on my part had annoyed me more than anything else during the past week. Arturo was less surprised, because that was *la vita* — the way things worked out. Nor did he mind so much, for he was full of hope that his plans for opening a coffee bar would make all our fortunes. Up until now I had not broached the subject of life under the *anglo-americani* with La Nonna. But when she returned bearing a loaf of white bread but little else, I asked her to tell me the gossip of the markets.

She thrust the loaf under my nose.

"*Hai visto? Che bianco il pane!*"

I agreed that the bread was whiter than any I had ever seen. How it would taste to the Italian palate, I could not tell. But if La Nonna was typical, its colour alone would make it a focal point for the joys of liberation. I asked whether she had been able to buy anything else with our ration cards. She had to admit that so far little had been distributed and that the price of vegetables had risen again. I told her that I was feeling depressed and made a silly attempt to explain why the Allies had not brought in the millennium, talking as though it was my duty to apologize on their behalf. La Nonna lashed out at my absurdity.

"Don't be so impatient, Gianni. You're like all the young. *Pian' piano,* things will get better. Anyway, it's nothing to do with you what food the *americani* give us."

"*Già!* But I want to know that you are all right before I leave."

"Of course we are all right. The *tedeschi* have gone, haven't they? And with them the fear. Soon the war will finish, *non è vero?* Then the *anglo-americani,* too, will go back to their homes. *Ognuno a casa sua.*"

"Everyone to his own home," I repeated.

She clicked her tongue and handed me a potato to peel. It seemed infinitely long ago since we had lunched alone together.

"This is like the old days," I said.

"Yes. It's good to be quiet. You've been rushing round too much."

"I know. I've been a bit mad."

"E *naturale*. That you should want to be with your own people."

"What do you think of all the drunks lying round in the streets? Have you seen them?"

"No, I haven't been across the Tiber. But Lucia has told me about them. *Poveretti*, they are soldiers. They drink because they are far from their *mammas*, and because they are afraid."

She was much more indignant about the trucks and jeeps which were disfiguring St Peter's Square.

"*Sai*, Gianni, *la piazza è roba del Papa*. They have no right to be there."

She was right, of course, and a few days later the Pope asked the Americans to remove them.

I was much cheered by this conversation, by the wide humanity of her philosophy and her anarchic disparagement of every authority except the Pope. Since the liberation I had become conscious once more of my nationality, and had forgotten that to La Nonna I was a person and not an Englishman.

"Tell me," I said, "and I'm not joking this time, like I was before. If a *tedesco* came to you tomorrow and

281

asked you to hide him, you would, wouldn't you? Provided of course that you liked his face and that he was really in trouble?"

"*Scherzi!*"

"No, I'm serious this time."

"If he was good, well yes, I would hide him. Though I don't expect Arturo and Lucia would like it."

"I'm glad you would," I said. "But I would like to know why."

"Because, like you, a *tedesco* is *figlio di mamma*."

The next day was Saturday, which meant that Arturo, Lucia and Ida would all be at home. Maria, too, was still in Rome. I had arranged to go to Naples on the Monday but the whole weekend was before us. I had purposely already said goodbye to my other friends, though I expected to meet up with some of the English ones at the transit camp in Naples; Gilbert had borrowed a car in which to take to Naples his new suitcase packed with his Roman wardrobe. Bill Simpson and John Furman were already hard at work with the Allied Screening Commission.

I spent Saturday morning with Arturo, buying presents for everyone and visiting the barber who had twice before cut my hair.

At lunchtime Maria mentioned that she must find some way of getting back to Colle Giove on Monday.

I put down my knife and fork with a clatter. Why hadn't I thought of it before? If Gilbert could borrow a car, so could I.

"We'll go to Nespolo tomorrow," I said. "You, me, Maria and Rina, if she wants. I'll get hold of a car somehow."

"*Bravo*, Gianni. Imagine the surprise of the Nespolini!"

"We will see Palmira."

"And Berendina."

"And her sheep," said La Nonna.

"We can buy flour and potatoes," I suggested.

"That won't be so easy," said Maria. "There's not much to eat in Nespolo now."

"We'll find a way."

Everyone was excited at my suggestion. Now it was up to me to find some transport.

I telephoned the Allied Screening Commission which had set up office in the block of flats where the Lucidis lived. Bill and John were both lunching with them, I was told. I got hold of Adrienne, then Bill.

"You've got to help me," I said. "As far as I know, twenty Nespolini are still in a concentration camp in Germany. And I want to make sure that the *podestà* is all right. You remember my story of how he saved me? He must have been in the Regina Coeli when you were there."

"I'll see what I can do," said Bill. "But it won't be easy. Very short notice. Why not later in the week?"

"I'm going to Naples on Monday. Look, if you can't let me have an official car, could you borrow a private one? I don't mind paying for some black-market petrol."

"Don't worry, I'll manage something. How long will it take to get there?"

"God knows. It took me five hours coming the other way in a lorry. About three hours I should think, unless the road has been bombed to hell. It's near Carsoli."

"All right. I'll have something round at Via Famagosta about 9 a.m. I would come myself if I wasn't tied up. I'll probably send a driver with you. He could find some job to do in Carsoli."

"Bless you, Bill. See you next time I'm in Rome."

"*Ciao* for now."

"*Ciao.*"

CHAPTER
SIX

The car was a captured German Opel with plenty of room for the four of us: Maria, Arturo, Rina and myself. I sat in comfort beside the Italian driver and thought of the reverse journey which I had made seven months before — a journey which had required weeks of planning to arrange instead of five minutes on the telephone. I remembered how I had lain stretched on the sacks of flour in the darkness with little Marilanda squealing and pissing at my feet. I remembered the claustrophobia, the cramp in my legs and the overpowering smell of pig manure. Yet my physical discomfort had been swamped by the exciting knowledge that I was advancing rapidly in the direction of my single goal.

Now I was excited for other reasons. I knew that I was searching for something — tranquillity of mind, perhaps — which might recompense me for the loss of the singleness of purpose which had so simplified my behaviour both in Nespolo and Rome. I had a feeling that my return to Nespolo would help me find it.

I felt like a shipwrecked sailor who has sighted land, but who cannot yet decide on which side of a bay to ground his lifeboat. Nor was it clear how I could bring ashore with me those of my marine experiences — and in the months of March and April I had dived deep in the seas of introspection — which I wished to incorporate into my life on dry land. I wanted to take with me some of that instinctive wisdom and humility in the face of trouble which I had learnt from the Italian peasants, in particular from La Nonna. And I wished to preserve the ability which I had developed during my periods of enforced solitude to live my life without feeling the need for continuous distractions.

There must be many others, I mused, who had lost their identity in the war. People like myself whom chance had catapulted over the conventional hedges which had circumscribed their previous lives. In a way this had happened to everyone involved in the war, but not, so I believed in my egoism, to anything like the same extent. All armies give to their men a common code of behaviour. Even ones so strange as that of General Anders' Polish Corps, whose odyssey had taken it from Russian concentration camps through Persia and Egypt to the heights of Cassino, make their own conventions. My speculations concerned the futures of the flotsam and jetsam of the war, such as a Russian Turcoman deserter who had reached Rome via a partisan band in Tuscany, and a Dutch priest, one of Monsignore O'Flaherty's most gallant helpers, who had been tortured for two weeks by the Gestapo in Via Tasso before being removed to Germany. Would these two, I wondered, ever revert to their old manner of thinking?

What future lay in store for those countless individuals, the dispossessed of Hitler's Third Reich, who had lost themselves in the concentration camps and underground movements of Europe and who had been forced by circumstance to sever all ties with their families, their countries and their pasts?

For that matter, what would be the fate of the twenty hostages whom the Germans had taken from Nespolo? And of Palmira's husband, Amadeo, who had been captured on the Russian front at the time of the armistice and was known to be in a concentration camp beyond the Urals?

I was awakened from my reverie by the tap of Arturo's hand on my shoulder.

"*Di che cosa stai pensando, Gianni?*"

"I was thinking of Nespolo. It seems so long ago when we were there."

"It's another world," said Arturo. "Do you remember?"

"Of course." I turned to face him. He was leaning back between Rina and Maria with the air of a man who was used to being driven by a chauffeur. Give him a new suit and a cigar, I thought, and he would look like a *pezzo grosso*.

I gazed out of the window. We had crossed the dusty plain which lies between Rome and the southern tip of the Sabine hills. Ahead of us, on the edge of the escarpment, was a small town.

"Is it Tivoli?" I asked.

"Yes," said Maria. "That's where I was machine-gunned when I came to Rome to get the medicine for my South Africans."

We wound our way up the steep hill and came to the outskirts of the town. A heap of rubble surrounded the railway junction and forced us into a long diversion. From Tivoli we crossed a narrow plateau to the foot of another escarpment crowned by a medieval castle. As we climbed upwards round hairpin bends, we could see down beneath us the plain across which we had come and beyond which lay Rome, lost in the haze of summer. The grandeur of the scenery took me by surprise, for neither at Nespolo nor during my blind journey to Rome had I attempted to picture the landscape which linked mountain with plain.

"How beautiful!" I exclaimed.

"*L'Italia è bella,*" said Rina, voicing a parrot-like opinion. Poor Rina, I thought. These miles of countryside were the only landscape which she had ever seen. Or perhaps she was lucky, not to know how ugly places could be.

We passed the castle of Arsoli and drove on eastwards into the Abruzzi, to the outskirts of Carsoli. On my left I could see the railway line which links Rome with Sulmona.

In Carsoli we turned off the highway on to a narrow, dusty road which led up into the high mountains. I could see the twin towers of the church which crowned the village of Coll'Alto, and remembered how they had drawn me towards them on that sunny October morning, till the moment I had spotted the German vehicle parked in the village square. The car ate up in minutes the kilometres which it had taken me hours to complete on foot. On a stretch of road between two corners I fancied that I could recognize the place where I had climbed from the bed of the stream. It was here that the German staff car had passed me, and I recalled the cold eyes of the officer who had sat, with a map on his knees, beside his driver.

We turned right up the stony track which was signposted "*A Nespolo 5 Chilometri*", the car throwing up behind us a cloud of thick, yellow dust. Now Arturo was as excited as I was.

"*Eccoci qui!*" he shouted. "Under that tree! That's where Ida and I were standing when we saw you walking towards us. Do you remember how hard it was raining?"

"I was already so drenched that I was past caring. But tell me again, for I have forgotten. Who did you think I was when you hailed me?"

"I thought you were some *poveretto* who might carry our baggage. But when you asked me whether I was *Fascista* or *Badogliano, madonna mia*, how frightened I was! I thought that you might be trying to catch me out. If you had looked different, fair for instance, I would have feared that you were a *tedesco*."

"That has been a great bit of luck for me all along — that I don't look like a German."

Now we could see Nespolo ahead of us, sprawled on the spur of hill, and climbing towards it, we turned the corner beside which we had met the old man and his donkey, and entered the final approach to the village.

289

Three women, washing their clothes at the roadside well, raised their heads to stare at the unaccustomed sight of a car. My last sight of this well had been when I had walked with the mourners behind the hearse which bore the bodies of the Spitfire's victims. A moment later, we drew up in the little square outside the *dopolavoro*.

It being Sunday, the old men of the village were standing round in little groups, smoking their pipes and gossiping. Now they crowded round the car.

"*E Rina che è arrivata!*" said a toothless *vecchio*, recognizing his niece. "*Rina con Arturo ed altri.*"

"*Ciao, Zio,*" she said. "Get someone to go and fetch Palmira. Tell her that I am here, with Gianni."

All eyes turned on me as I stepped out of the car.

"*E il muto!*" said someone. "*E tornato il muto!*"

"He is an *inglese*! What did I tell you? An ENGLISHMAN!"

"*E tornato l'inglese!* The one who was with Arturo. Do you remember?"

"The one who was arrested in the woods?"

"*Si, si. Il muto.* The one the Germans caught! He is an *inglese*, and he has returned to see us."

Old men threw their arms round me and rubbed their stubbly cheeks against my own. Women kissed me, children fingered my uniform. Berendina hugged me to her bosom and burst into tears. I was near to crying myself. I had not expected that it would be like this, that so many people would know me by sight and greet me as a friend. They must have spent the long winter evenings sitting round the fire and asking each other who the mysterious friend of Arturo's was, the *muto* whom the *tedeschi* had arrested.

Stout Palmira arrived, red-faced and smiling. She led us up the cobbled lane, with half the village on our heels, to the house in which she lived. Outside it stood her donkey, *lu ciucuriedru*, laden with a pannier of firewood. Inside were her many children and her two old uncles. Arturo was beside himself with excitement. These *contadini*, these relations of his wife, were good people, tough and brave. But beneath their hats, their skulls were empty. Only he had had the *furberia* to hide me in the village, to fool the stupid *tedeschi*. This was his day, as much as it was mine.

A jug of wine and a long roll of salami, the traditional symbols of hospitality, were laid before us on the table.

"Eat, *inglese*," said Zio Ettore.

"Drink, *inglese*," said Zio Zompa.

"*Salute!*"

"*Salute!*"

While we drank, Palmira boiled a cauldron of water for our *pasta*. She had sent her young son, Pimpinello, to fetch Italia, and to see if he could find Angelo de'Angelis, who came down to the village every Sunday. I had not seen the old man since the day of my arrest in his vineyard.

It was nearly two o'clock by the time we had all assembled round the table, for, due to the diversion in Tivoli, it had taken us four hours to drive the sixty miles from Rome.

"If I had known that you were all coming, I would have killed a lamb," said Palmira. "Though the *tedeschi* took most of our animals, we managed to hide a few of them away in pits outside the village."

"Tell us about Nespolo," I said. "What happened after we left?"

"All was quiet for a bit. The *tedeschi* never bothered us again about the affair of the 'two'. Paolo and Riccardo managed to cross the Line. They arrived back here yesterday."

"And the twenty hostages?"

"We think they are in a prison in Germany."

Berendina had had a letter from her son Domenico, Palmira told us. But it had been posted three months ago. Her own husband had last been heard of in a camp in a part of Germany which, she thought, had now been overrun by the Russians.

"Then, around Christmas time," Palmira went on, "a few escaped prisoners, *inglesi* and *sud-africani*, arrived in Nespolo. They didn't sleep in the village, but some of us took food up to the shepherds' huts where they were living."

"*Poveretti*," said Maria. "It was the same at Colle Giove."

"It was then that I guessed that you were English," said Palmira, turning to me. "For I said to myself, these men, they speak like Gianni. Then one day the *tedeschi* rounded them all up. They had been told where to look by that *canaglia*, the tart from Trieste. They spread terror in the village. Then they arrested my cousin, the

292

podestà, and took him to Rome, to the Regina Coeli prison. You remember him, Gianni?"

"*Certo, mi ricordo.* After lunch I must go and thank him for saving me. Though I don't think he guessed I was English, he must have known that I was not Arturo's brother."

"You're right, Gianni," said Arturo. "We will go together and thank him."

"But you can't," said Palmira. "I thought you knew. He's dead. They shot him in the Ardeantine Caves."

"*Madonna mia,*" said Rina, and burst into tears.

When we had recovered from our shocked surprise, Palmira continued with her story. Allied troops had swept north through Carsoli on the day after the liberation of Rome. There had been no serious fighting in the area. The Nespolini appreciated their luck in this respect, for they had heard from Paolo and Riccardo of the devastation suffered by the mountain villages closer to the Gustav Line. They had watched from their hill-top the Allied armour roll forward up the valley towards Rieti, but they had yet to see an *anglo-americano* at close quarters.

"And now," said Arturo, when we had finished the second jug of wine, "let us walk round the village and pay a few calls. We will go first to the house in which we lived. Do you remember, Gianni, how you used to peel potatoes with the Signorina Greta?"

Devoid of furniture, for it was now uninhabited, the Platano house looked smaller and darker than ever. It seemed impossible that nine of us had lived together in its three rooms. From there we took the narrow lane which breasted the spur and led us past the church down towards Italia's house in the lower end of the village.

People hailed us as we passed.

"*Ciao* Rina, *ciao* Arturo. Bring in the *inglese* for a glass of wine."

At each port of call, my emotions increased; my speech became more voluble, my feet unsteadier.

"*I* guessed that you were an *inglese*," said an old crone who lived next door to Italia. "I used to watch you from my window when you sat on the balcony reading a child's grammar."

"I didn't," said another. "I thought you were just a poor *muto*."

We finished up in the house of Pina's mother, the *amante* of Paolo. While Rina and Arturo gave her the news of Pina, I talked with Paolo, whom I was meeting for the first time. He had a quiet manner but the fiery eyes of a revolutionary. He told me of the terrible weeks he had spent in the snows trying to cross the Line; and how he had eventually been guided across a high mountain pass by a shepherd.

I already knew that Paolo was a Communist, an extreme rarity at this time in the priest-ridden villages of the Abruzzi. Even so, I was surprised by the strength of his convictions and by his argument. He might have been the model for the hero of Silone's *Pane e Vino*.

"You know," he told me, "when Riccardo and I shot those two Germans, we couldn't guess what we were starting. It was my idea, of course, and I would do the same thing again. But the people of this village, they don't really understand why I had to do it. I am sorry they had to suffer for my action, but we peasants must be prepared to act if we want a better life. In this village everyone is a prisoner of the priests. They have been subjected for so many years to one authority or another, that they have forgotten that they are men. You know that I am a Communist?"

"Yes. Arturo told me. Since when?"

"Oh, for years. I come from this village but I worked in Rome, as a road mender and lorry driver, for two years before the war. Now that *il Fascismo* is dead and buried, I hope to become a politician."

I would have liked to continue our talk and tell him a bit about the bravery of some of Monsignore O'Flaherty's priests, but Arturo and Rina were ready to leave.

"Well, goodbye and good luck," I said to Paolo. "Mind that you don't shoot the first Englishman who comes to Nespolo!"

"But you have already arrived!" said Arturo.

"*Già*. I had forgotten that I counted as an Englishman."

We went back to the *dopolavoro*, where our driver, who had spent the afternoon in Carsoli, was waiting for us. Time was running short if we were to be back in Rome for a late supper with La Nonna, Lucia and Ida.

Maria had decided to stay the night with Palmira and go on next day to Colle Giove. The tears welled up in my eyes as I embraced her, for I was thinking of the time when the German and I had carried her limp body into Angelo's house.

I embraced Palmira, Italia, old Angelo, Zio Zompa and everyone else who had assembled; we set off down the valley, back into the world of the present day.

A wave of contentment surged through me as we drove down the hill towards Carsoli. The welcome given to me by the Nespolini had touched me to the quick and I knew now that they and their village had taken root in the secret places of my heart. I was gloriously drunk — with emotion as well as wine. And, though I had no illusions that the Italian peasant was not sometimes as cruel, avaricious and cowardly as anyone else, I believed that, through the tribulations which I had shared with them, I had caught a glimpse of the classical human spirit as it had persisted ever since La Nonna's forebears had sailed from Greece to Apulia.

For more than anyone else, it was La Nonna who had opened my eyes to two of the outstanding virtues of the Italian people: their talent for snatching the last ounce of enjoyment from the most unlikely circumstances, and their sense of compassion for human frailty.

I felt enriched by the friendships which I had made. I hoped that through them I would have gained a dual perspective on the world: that in the future I would be able to look at it both through the eyes of an English captain and through those of the Italian peasant. The prospect seemed to me to be a step in the right direction.

I had one last thing to do.

"Go slowly and follow the railway," I said to the driver, as we drove west out of Carsoli. And to Arturo, "I want to find the spot where I jumped from the train."

We branched on to a small road which ran just south of the line. I was searching the north side for a grassy hillock topped by a circle of scrub. Beneath it on the other side of the railway, there should be a small house with a garden. It was from the garden that the dog had barked at me and made me decide to retreat across the railway. Where would I be now, I wondered, but for that dog? Already in England? In Germany? Or dead? Certainly not here with Arturo.

About a kilometre from the outskirts of Carsoli I stopped the car, got out, crossed the line and started to walk along the top of the embankment. Arturo came with me.

"Could it be that one?" he asked, pointing to a little hill.

"I think not. There's no scrub on top."

We pressed on, picking our way carefully between the thorn bushes.

"This one here?" he suggested a minute later.

"*Può darsi*. Perhaps. But it doesn't look right. I think there were vines on the lower slopes."

The trouble was that there were so many hillocks, while in my memory there was only one. I felt like a dog which has forgotten where he has buried his bone.

Then I realized that I had never seen my hillock from beneath; it had still been dark when I had scrambled up its face. Another thought struck me. Though I had

297

often visualized myself burying my battle-dress in the scrub at the top and sitting on the slope to survey the distances as they materialized beneath me in the thin light of dawn, it was quite possible that the picture imprinted in my mind's eye bore little relation to reality. I had nursed the idea that I would dig up my battle-dress and present it to Arturo as a *ricordo*. Now I realized the utter impracticability of the scheme. On the way back to the car I told Arturo what I had planned to do.

"It doesn't matter," I concluded. "Probably the worms have already eaten it."

"A pity," said Arturo. "*Era un' idea divertante*."

But throughout the drive back to Rome, my thoughts kept returning to that elusive grassy hill and the symbolic funeral rite which I had enacted on its summit. Had I really buried my old personality beneath the scrub alongside my battle-dress on that October morning?

"*E morto il capitano inglese*," I had said aloud to myself, as I smoothed some leaves over the grave. "The English captain is dead."

I had meant it as a joke, not a prophecy.

Now I knew that it was true.

PART FIVE

Epilogue

I sailed from Naples in a ship carrying many other escaped PoWs, a few of whom I had met before. One of them had fought with a partisan band in Emilia. Another, a chemist in peacetime, had taught the peasants of a Tuscan village to spray their vines with copper sulphate made from the wires of a crashed aeroplane. A third, an old friend of mine, told me how he had discovered that his companion on a farm near Perugia had been my batman in Tobruk. This man had confessed to my friend that he had no intention of reporting his presence when he was liberated. He had fallen in love with the peasant's only daughter, had indeed married her. Such a course of action would have pleased La Nonna, had she but known it. And I like to think of him now, surrounded by children and grandchildren, growing his vines in the fertile Umbrian soil.

Most of us had grown very fond of the Italians, much to the surprise of the journalists who interviewed us when we docked on the Clyde. One of our party, perhaps still dreaming of wine and sunshine, had jumped from the train which was taking us to Glasgow, possibly appalled by the cold mist on the Clyde and the prospect of nothing more cheering than a cup of tea. Or perhaps he was just a compulsive escaper.

My own stay in Britain was brief. I was surprised to find how little was known about the Italian Resistance and wrote indignant letters to the newspapers, pointing out that not all Italians were Fascists. Italy tugged at my heart-strings and, after a few months of soldiering in the south of England, I managed to get posted back there. In March 1945, I joined a Partisan Liaison Unit at Eighth Army HQ, which had spent the winter months near Ravenna preparing for a spring offensive against the Gothic Line.

The final battle of the Italian campaign carried me across the River Po and through the Veneto to Trieste. After the Allies had broken the Gothic Line, the German defence crumbled. The Italian partisans, whose strength lay between the Po and the Alps, had risen in force behind the German lines at the start of the battle, and when advance units of the Eighth Army reached Padua, Vicenza and Venice, these great cities were already in their hands. A week later, the war in Europe ended. After helping to demobilize the partisans in the foothills of the Alps, my unit returned to Venice, where we spent an idyllic summer in a *palazzo* on the Grand Canal, liaising with the Italian Liberation Committees and analysing, for Allied Headquarters, the confused political picture.

Early in the autumn of 1945 I persuaded my commanding officer to send me to Rome for a few days to meet some Italian politicians. As soon as I arrived there I filled up my jeep with as many rations as I could lay hands on and drove round to Via Famagosta. The whole family had assembled to meet me; all, that is, except Iolanda who had gone to Brazil as nurse to a diplomat's family. It was fifteen months since I had seen the Platanos, though Lucia's letters had kept me in touch with their news.

Their lives had changed little. They were not much better off, for Italy was still under military occupation and the Italian economic revival some way ahead. But they were all well and in high spirits. I was delighted to be just Gianni again and not *il capitano*, as I was to my Venetian acquaintances, and to find that La Nonna's tongue had lost none of its liveliness. She was furious with me when I told her that I had taken part in the Eighth Army's last battle.

"*Sei un imbecille!*" she scolded me. "You might have been killed. And then all the risks we ran for you would have been for nothing. Why didn't you come back here? We would have hidden you till the war was over."

I told the family what a big part the partisans had played in the final battle but my accounts were greeted with disbelief. It was an attitude which I kept on meeting during my few days in Rome and it brought home to me that Italy was really two countries, a north and a south. I was at that time caught up in enthusiasm for the new political ideas which had emerged from the predominantly north-Italian Resistance Movement, and which had their cultural counterpart in, for example, the work of the painter, Renato Guttuso, and the film director, Roberto Rossellini, both of whom had fought with the partisans.

Alone of the Platanos, Lucia could sympathize with these enthusiasms. She had just become engaged to a penniless musician and had found a publisher for a collection of her short stories.

Maria was hoping to follow Iolanda to Brazil. Ida was working in a factory. Arturo was still quarrelling with Rina and working in the Banco di Santo Spirito. His hopes all centred on the coffee bar which he planned to build in Monteverde, the suburb in which he lived. I had sent him the money which I had promised to invest in the venture; it appeared to be all the capital he had so far raised. He had already leased a suitable site and obtained from the local authorities the licence to open a café. He had also bought his building bricks. But the building licence had so far eluded him, and he believed, quite erroneously, that in the last resort I could help him obtain it through the agency of the Allied Control Commission.

On my second day in Rome I spent a terrifying half-hour on the pillion of his second-hand motor bicycle — which represented part of my capital investment. We drove at high speed through the narrow streets of Trastevere and twisted between the trams up the road to Monteverde. As we examined the large pile of bricks assembled on the site, Arturo elaborated his plans. In his mind's eye he already saw the simple *espresso* bar as a café with a coloured awning and steel-framed chairs on the pavement outside. He talked of the juke-box he would buy and the meals which his sisters would cook when he had added a wing with a restaurant. Later, perhaps, he would open a branch in the centre of the city.

304

It became clear to me that already he saw himself as the proprietor of a chain of pleasuredomes stretched, like a river of gold, across Italy; he assured me that he had prepared the way with the *municipio* and that he would soon have the *permesso di costruzione* which would bring our bricks to life, but I confess that when I said goodbye to him I was full of misgivings about our joint venture. I consoled myself that Arturo had an extraordinary talent for pulling chestnuts out of the fire. Time and time again he had vindicated his self-confidence. Perhaps he would do so again.

Before leaving Rome, I saw many other old friends. At the Allied Screening Commission Bill Simpson told me how his unit was paying out money and presenting Certificates of Honour, signed by General Alexander, to those Italians who had helped escapers. Bill's staff travelled all over the country checking claims and searching out the many peasants who, through ignorance or modesty, had not come forward. Payment was always made personally, by one of Bill's staff. Many were the stories of the excitement with which the peasants of remote mountain villages had greeted the arrival of someone connected with the dangers which they had endured.

The Platano family had just received 60,000 *lire* from the Screening Commission. This was now worth only about half of the value it had had when I had insisted, fifteen months previously, that they put forward a claim. Although I had cost them much more than this during the eight months when I had lived with them, the money was gratefully received. They placed great sentimental value on their Certificate of Honour, which La Nonna framed and hung above the kitchen table.

The Orso restaurant was now an Allied Officers' Club. I had drinks there with Felix, the barman, and admired the certificate, signed by, among others, Gilbert, Bill and John and displayed on a barrel of beer, which stated that British Officers had often lunched there during the German occupation.

I was able to thank Adrienne Lucidi for her kindness to Lucia during the past year and for giving La Nonna a Christmas present of army rations. Adrienne was still working for the Screening Commission, but after the excitements of her life during the German occupation she was finding difficulty in settling down in the post-war world. In her I found a ready audience for my stories of the northern Resistance, and she gave me an introduction to the Socialist leader, Pietro Nenni, who was one of the Italian politicians whom I had come to Rome to meet.

I was back again in Rome for Christmas, this time in civilian clothes. I was now in the Foreign Service and on my way to Venice, where I was to be in charge of the British Press and Information Office for the next fifteen months.

I went round to Arturo's bank and took him out to lunch. My first question was to ask whether he had got the *permesso di costruzione*.

"Not yet, but it will come."

"But when?"

"Tomorrow, perhaps."

"Always tomorrow! Tomorrow never comes in Italy."

"*Pazienza*, Gianni! It's not like in England. To get a *permesso* needs time. One must work by stealth, like a mole."

"A mole with a nice fat purse!"

"*Sì, sì*, it costs money," he admitted, rubbing his thumb across his fingers. "I have a friend in the *municipio*. He has spoken about our *affari* to a man of importance. A little more time, a few more *soldi*, and we will get our *permesso*. You'll see, Gianni."

But with the long winter nights a new danger threatened. The pile of bricks, lying unguarded on the plot at Monteverde, grew steadily smaller. Each day the vagrant cats, who like to sun themselves on the baked clay, found themselves a few inches nearer to the ground. Arturo's complaints to the police failed to stop the pilfering.

The final blow (and this Arturo could not possibly have foreseen) came early in the new year with the holding of the municipal elections. Against all predictions, the opposition party captured the *sezione* of Monteverde. The new councillors, not having been bribed, saw no reason to grant Arturo his *permesso*. All his cultivation of the old gang represented so much wasted time and money. What remained of the bricks were sold. So was the motor bicycle. The little of my capital which had not been spent was put aside for another day.

At the time I thought that Arturo had taken the blow with philosophical resignation. He seemed to forget about his golden chain of pleasuredomes. At least he had enjoyed his dream while it lasted.

In the spring of 1948, I went to Italy for two weeks to cover the General Election for the magazine *New Statesman*. I was impressed everywhere I went by visible signs of Italy's economic recovery. Production was booming in the industrial north, and in the plains which flank the river Po new villages had risen from the ashes of the old. Beneath the ruins of Cassino, a new city bustled with all the excitement of a middle-west frontier town. It seemed impossible that in the space of three years those stretches of countryside which, in Churchill's words, had known "the red-hot rake of the battle line" could have so soon regained their appearance of a well-kept garden.

The political situation was not so tidy. More than twenty parties were putting forward candidates at the coming election, though the great majority of votes were expected to go to one of the two giants, de Gaspari's Christian Democrats or the Popular Front alliance between Togliatti's Communists and Pietro Nenni's Socialists. All three of these leaders had distinguished themselves in the struggle against Mussolini.

I spent the week leading up to election day in Naples and Rome. Apart from a few adherents to the small monarchist party, which continued to exist even though Crown Prince Umberto had been decisively beaten in the referendum of 1946, most of my Resistance friends were voting for the Popular Front. But the Platano family, according to Arturo, would all be supporting the Christian Democrats.

On polling day I drove from Rome to Nespolo, to see how the new electoral system would work in a mountain village. I stayed the night with Rina's sister, Palmira, and her husband, Amadeo, who had survived his three years in a Russian camp. In the evening we drank wine in the *dopolavoro* with several of my old acquaintances. Among them were old Berendina's son, Domenico, who as one of the twenty hostages, had spent a year and a half in a German concentration camp; and Paolo, the killer of the two Germans from Poggio, who had been the indirect cause of Domenico's imprisonment. True to his intentions, Paolo had taken up politics and was standing for the Popular Front.

Just as he had been about the only man with the guts to shoot the first German who came to Nespolo, Paolo was now the only one with the courage to cross swords with the most powerful man in Nespolo — Don Giuseppe. The village priest, unfortunately, was not the type to eradicate the illiteracy and superstitiousness of his flock. Among the more educated and prosperous peasants of Tuscany and the north, the Popular Front had many supporters. But I was well aware that in the priest-ridden villages of the Abruzzi, victory for the Vatican-sponsored Christian Democrats was a foregone conclusion.

Nevertheless I was surprised, when the results of the poll were declared in the *dopolavoro*, to find that only twenty-three of the three hundred and seventy-nine voting Nespolini had cast their vote for Paolo and the

309

Popular Front. It was a triumph for Don Giuseppe and a slap in the eye for the progressive Left.

Next day I returned to Rome and spent the final evening of my visit dining at Via Famagosta and catching up with the family news. I was unhappy only about Arturo, who was bored with his job and, as usual, in debt. His married life was as tempestuous as ever, and his younger daughter, Marilanda, was in a sanatorium with tuberculosis, a hangover doubtless from undernourishment during the German occupation. I realized that the fiasco of the coffee bar affair had hurt Arturo more than I had at the time imagined.

The following Christmas I had a long letter from Lucia, by then married to her *maestro di musica* and no longer living in Rome. She told me that Babbino had died, that her eldest sister — Maria — had emigrated to Brazil, and that Ida was working in a factory and living with La Nonna in Via Famagosta. Then, for nearly two years, my letters remained unanswered, including one announcing my imminent arrival in Rome in the autumn of 1950, so that even before I telephoned the flat — on an October morning so sunny that even the stones of the Colosseum seemed to sparkle — I had a premonition that something was wrong. Ida answered the telephone. She told me that La Nonna was dead. Then she burst into tears. I said that I would come round immediately.

I found it hard to believe that the little woman in black who opened the door was indeed Ida who, when I had first met her on the road to Nespolo, had reminded me of a plump young partridge. The unforeseen is always shattering, and by the time I had dragged the story from the sobbing Ida, I myself was near to tears. She told me that, a year previously, Arturo had been arrested on a charge of forgery. Under the Italian legal system, a man was held to be guilty until he was proved innocent. Arturo had already spent eight months in prison awaiting trial when, earlier in the year of my visit, a two-years' amnesty had — at the instigation of the Pope — been granted to all prisoners in celebration of the Holy Year. Arturo, who had already served a longer sentence than he would have received had he been found guilty, was released immediately.

That the intervention of her beloved Pope should have spared her son the ordeal of a trial would, had she but known it, have given La Nonna great happiness, but tragically — having been ill for some time — she died a few weeks before the amnesty. Though the official cause of her death was given as food poisoning, Ida told me that she had never recovered from the shock of the arrest of her only son, the adored *maschio*; humiliated by the derision (either real or imagined) of her neighbours and desperately worried about the outcome of the case against Arturo, her zest for life had been shattered. Weakened by the strain of nursing her mother, Ida herself had been very ill.

That same evening, I went to see Arturo at his Monteverde flat, taking with me a bottle of wine which would, I hoped, ease our mutual embarrassment. He was looking older, but fitter than I had ever seen him —

the result, perhaps, of regular prison meals, and of escape from the constant bickerings of his married life.

We began by talking about his old job in the Banco di Santo Spirito. I could readily understand why he had given it up; the day-to-day drudgery gave no scope for his particular talents — his native astuteness, and his flair for improvisation. His pay-packet, too, had been inadequate, and he had been constantly short of money — Rina was by nature extravagant, there were clothes to buy for Stellina's convent education, and doctors' bills for little Marilanda's tuberculosis.

But of the business partnership, which had ended in his imprisonment on a charge of fraud, I could make little sense. It seemed to have been concerned with the collection of bad debts, and after an apparently successful start had gone seriously wrong. What had been the cause of the disaster? An inadequate knowledge of accountancy? Bad luck? Or deliberate fraud on the part of him or his colleagues? I felt reluctant to ask the vital questions — Arturo would have just put on his man-of-the-world expression, shrugged his shoulders, turned out the palms of his hands and muttered, "Non si capisce, Gianni."

Whatever had led to Arturo's arrest, I could sympathize with the frustrations that had probably led to his downfall. He had many admirable qualities and a generous spirit, and flourished in an atmosphere of excitement and intrigue — the very qualities that had saved us both from disaster in Nespolo and had moulded the pattern of our conspiratorial life in Rome. I remembered the nerve with which he had confronted the German *Feldwebel*, the ease with which he had extracted four ration cards for the imaginary "Antonio Maggi" and his non-existent family, and could see how our joint eight-months' adventure had shaped his personality as it had my own. One could argue that he was, like many anti-Fascist Italians, a casualty of the war.

The next day I went with Ida to lay flowers on La Nonna's grave. Ida, it seemed to me, had inherited much of her mother's courage and compassion. As we left the Campo Santo, she took my arm and, smiling up at me, shook it gently and persistently, until I too began to smile.

"*Non ti preoccupi*, Gianni," she said — and it might, I thought, have been her mother who was speaking. "It is life. *Si nasce, si vive, si muore.*"

In 1984 I was invited to Rome for the celebration marking the fortieth anniversary of its liberation; with me were several other escaped PoWs, including Gilbert Smith, Sam Derry and John Furman. I saw many old friends, but sadly none of the Platanos were in Rome, as I already knew from Lucia's letters. Maria was dead, but the other sisters were alive and well in Brazil, where they had emigrated many years previously. Arturo had come to terms with himself and with Rina; he was a traveller for a firm that made Venetian blinds, which I would have backed him to sell to Eskimos. His elder daughter Stellina — who used to infuriate me in Nespolo by talking Italian (when she was a toddler) so much better than I did — was married to an engineer and had a grown-up family; the younger daughter, Marilanda, had died of her tuberculosis when she was eight.

I have left to the last Lucia's own story, an unusual one for the daughter of a railwayman and a peasant. She has become a well-known faith-healer, spiritualist and author, and has been honoured with the title of *Gran Dama dell'Ordine di Malta*. Her career brings to my mind the hungry winter days in Via Famagosta when I would sit opposite her at the table in her room, and watch with fascination the pen in her hand glide over the paper as though it possessed a life of its own. The clue to this phenomenon came several years after the war, when she chanced to take part in a seance and discovered that she had psychic powers. She maintains that — in a state of trance — she received a message that her hands could heal.

She attempted to cure, by the laying-on of hands, the minor ailments of her friends; so successful were her treatments that, before long, patients were coming to her from far and wide in search of therapy for arthritis, ulcers, slipped discs, hernias and other afflictions. Gifts of gratitude flowed in from places as far apart as Copenhagen and Buenos Aires.

After thirty arduous years of curative work in Rome, she retired to her mother's native Apulia, and wrote a book on her spiritual experiences, which was published under the rather formidable title of *Viaggi Spirituali sotto le nubi e al di là delle stelle (Spiritual Voyages Under the Clouds and Beyond the Stars)*; a second book is on its way.

Lucia's gift of healing throws light on a family legend, which I first heard from La Nonna as we sat one night beside a flickering fire in the house at Nespolo. Speaking of her childhood, La Nonna mentioned that her mother had had a reputation for performing miracles. After her mother's death there had even been a suggestion that one day her body should be dug up to see if it showed any of those paranormal symptoms of preservation which are recognized by the Catholic Church as confirmatory signs of sanctity. At the time I had thought this story so implausible that I had wondered whether, with my then limited knowledge of Italian, I had misunderstood it. Now, in the light of Lucia's experiences, it seems possible that her grandmother may have possessed similar talents.

La Nonna had died before Lucia discovered her curative powers; Lucia believes that La Nonna now knows about them — something that I would like to think was true, for nothing would give the old lady more pleasure than the knowledge that her daughter could help the sick.

At the same time I can well imagine the chuckles with which La Nonna, if she was alive to read them, would dismiss the articles about her daughter which have appeared in various parapsychological journals.

"Para — ? What is this para — ? It is the Madonna who does all these cures through the hands of Lucia. *La Madonna sa fa' tutto.*"

And I can see again her wise old smile, and hear again the whoop of laughter with which at Nespolo she always greeted new tales of Berendina and her verminous pet sheep.

Also available in ISIS Large Print:

They Also Serve

Dorothy Baden-Powell

At the Scandinavian Section of the SOE, Dorothy Baden-Powell was engaged in sending saboteurs into occupied Norway and debriefing them on their return to London. After spending a year and a half with the SOE, she was given an assignment in the WRNS to try to break a ring of enemy spies. They were based on HMS Raleigh, a naval training camp at Plymouth and were sending information to Germany about the movements of British warships from nearly every port in the United Kingdom.

She endured the privations of life on the lower deck, the unwelcome scrutiny of a particularly unpleasant WRNS Superintendent, and a trumped-up charge and subsequent court-martial.

Finally, she uncovered an enemy agent trying to be taken on as a sailor, and by a combination of bravery, sheer determination and luck, succeeded in having him captured. With her assignment successfully completed she gladly returned to her job with the SOE.

ISBN 0-7531-9336-1 (hb)
ISBN 0-7531-9337-X (pb)

Undercover Operator

Sydney Hudson

Memoirs of SOE agents have always been rare — so many were either killed in action or executed — and today they are almost unheard of. But Sydney Hudson's story is just about as dramatic and thrilling as any to have ever appeared. After volunteering for guerilla operations should the Germans occupy Britain, he transferred to SOE. He spent most of the Second World War in France, remarkably surviving 15 months captivity and interrogation before making a daring and thrilling escape through the Pyrenees into Spain. Shortly after, he was back in France, again by parachute, to organize resistance operations until the arrival of the US 3rd Army. More secret missions followed behind enemy lines with a female agent. Thereafter he volunteered for further SOE work in the Far East where he served in India and Thailand. He was twice decorated with the Distinguished Service Order for his efforts and also awarded the Croix de Guerre.

ISBN 0-7531-9340-X (hb)
ISBN 0-7531-9341-8 (pb)

Bothy to Big Ben

Ben Coutts

Ben Coutts has packed much more into his 80-plus years than most mortals. Before the war he worked as a ponyman in Perthshire and rural Sussex. Once he had joined up, his wartime experiences were hilarious and tragic by turns. He fought in Africa, was seriously wounded in Tobruk, torpedoed on his trip home in the Laconia, bombed, and when he had made it to the UK, began a long recovery after a series of painful operations. He went on to become a farm-manager in the Highlands, a sheep farmer, a leading stock breeder, show judge and broadcaster, and even a would-be Westminster politician.

ISBN 0-7531-9304-3 **(hb)**
ISBN 0-7531-9305-1 **(pb)**

Battle Tales from Burma

Brigadier John Randle

John Randle served with the greatly respected Baluch Regiment of the former Indian Army right through the fiercely fought Burma Campaign, winning an MC on the way yet, when VJ Day dawned, he was only some 60 miles from where he had started out nearly four years before.

This collection of stories drawn from memory, covers every aspect of a life in the forces from great courage to humour, this presents a personal picture of war at its bitterest.

ISBN 0-7531-9990-4 (hb)
ISBN 0-7531-9991-2 (pb)

Daisy, Daisy

Christian Miller

To pedal from the Atlantic to the Pacific? Surely too big of a challenge to many but the formidable English grandmother, Christian Miller? She had no hesitation in volunteering her small folding bicycle, Daisy, and herself for the challenge.

Daisy, Daisy is the marvellously entertaining story of her meeting with the United States of America and its people. Looking at America with a completely fresh eye, she is able to paint a picture of the countryside, the people and all things strange and wonderful that make up the America she befriended on her long journey. The stories she shares are witty, perceptive — and irresistible.

ISBN 0-7531-9950-5 (hb)
ISBN 0-7531-9951-3 (pb)

ISIS publish a wide range of books in large print, from fiction to biography. Any suggestions for books you would like to see in large print or audio are always welcome. Please send to the Editorial Department at:

ISIS Publishing Limited
7 Centremead
Osney Mead
Oxford OX2 0ES

A full list of titles is available free of charge from:

Ulverscroft Large Print Books Limited

(UK)
The Green
Bradgate Road, Anstey
Leicester LE7 7FU
Tel: (0116) 236 4325

(Australia)
P.O. Box 314
St Leonards
NSW 1590
Tel: (02) 9436 2622

(USA)
P.O. Box 1230
West Seneca
N.Y. 14224-1230
Tel: (716) 674 4270

(Canada)
P.O. Box 80038
Burlington
Ontario L7L 6B1
Tel: (905) 637 8734

(New Zealand)
P.O. Box 456
Feilding
Tel: (06) 323 6828

Details of **ISIS** complete and unabridged audio books are also available from these offices. Alternatively, contact your local library for details of their collection of **ISIS** large print and unabridged audio books.